The Imperiled Presidency

The Imperiled Presidency

Leadership Challenges in the Twenty-First Century

G. Calvin Mackenzie
Colby College

ROWMAN & LITTLEFIELD
Lanham • Boulder • New York • London

Executive Editor: Traci Crowell
Associate Editor: Molly White
Senior Marketing Manager: Karin Cholak
Marketing Manager: Deborah Hudson
Cover Designer: Jen Huppert Design

Credits and acknowledgments borrowed from other sources and reproduced, with permission, in this textbook appear on appropriate pages within the text.

Published by Rowman & Littlefield
A wholly owned subsidiary of The Rowman & Littlefield Publishing Group, Inc.
4501 Forbes Boulevard, Suite 200, Lanham, Maryland 20706
www.rowman.com

Unit A, Whitacre Mews, 26-34 Stannary Street, London SE11 4AB, United Kingdom

British Library Cataloguing in Publication Information Available

Library of Congress Cataloguing-in-Publication Data
Names: Mackenzie, G. Calvin, author.
Title: The imperiled presidency : leadership challenges in the
   twenty-first century / G. Calvin Mackenzie.
Description: Lanham, Maryland : Rowman & Littlefield, 2017. |
   Includes bibliographical references and index.
Identifiers: LCCN 2015051348 (print) | LCCN 2016004012 (ebook) |
   ISBN 9781442260733 (cloth : alk. paper) | ISBN 9781442260740
   (pbk. : alk. paper) | ISBN 9781442260757 (electronic)
Subjects: LCSH: Presidents—United States. | Separation of powers—
   United States. | Political leadership—United States—History—21st century. |
   United States—Politics and government—21st century.
Classification: LCC JK516 .M274 2017 (print) | LCC JK516 (ebook) | DDC
   352.2/360973—dc23 LC record available at http://lccn.loc.gov/2015051348

∞™ The paper used in this publication meets the minimum requirements of American National Standard for Information Sciences—Permanence of Paper for Printed Library Materials, ANSI/NISO Z39.48-1992.

Printed in the United States of America

For
Bill Goldfarb
Patron, Partner, Friend

Contents

Preface

I began teaching and writing about the American presidency in the 1960s. For a young scholar, the presidency was an intensely appealing topic. In the life of the country and the world, presidents mattered—often profoundly. They had deep impacts in setting and accomplishing a national agenda. They spoke for the nation on important matters, both at home and abroad. And while many Americans disagreed with the president on some issues of consequence, most honored the office of the presidency and were respectful in their regard for the incumbent.

A young scholar, starting on this journey today, would begin in a very different place. The institution of the presidency is vastly larger and more complex now than it was then. But the capabilities of presidents and their opportunities to shape the outcomes of American politics and government are substantially more constrained. At home and abroad, American presidents are less consequential, less capable of fulfilling the leadership tasks of a national executive than they were a half century ago.

Casual witnesses to contemporary political discourse may find such a comment strikingly off the mark. Hardly a day goes by when presidents aren't accused of over reaching, of exceeding their constitutional authority, and of threatening the national government's essential checks and balances. While there is some evidence to stoke those accusations, they mask a much greater and more troubling reality. What we observe most often today is not presidents acting despotically, but presidents struggling desperately to lead a country that no longer provides them tools and opportunities adequate to that task. Absent real opportunities to build and lead political coalitions in the country and the Congress, presidents have had little choice but to tug on their much more limited levers of independent authority: executive orders and directives, signing statements, recess appointments, and so on.

The presidency that I described in my early writing and teaching seems antique now. Lyndon Johnson relying on Republican votes to shepherd a civil rights act through the Senate, Ronald Reagan getting a major tax cut through a House of Representatives controlled by Democrats: Did those events really happen? Indeed they did—but in a different time.

This book is the story of how the twenty-first-century presidency came to differ from the one that prevailed for most of the second half of the twentieth century. It relies heavily on contextual explanations. The presidency is different because the context is different: the way we choose presidents, the ways in which they are covered by the communications media, the expectations we impose on them, the nature of the Washington community, the operations of the Congress, and the role of America in the world. Presidential leadership capabilities have diminished not because any wise group of American thinkers consciously sought that outcome. They have diminished because the authority and character of the presidency have not kept pace with the evolving context in which that institution operates.

The argument presented here contravenes much of the contemporary scholarly literature and a common theme in current public discourse: the notion that presidents have come to dominate national politics in ways that undermine a healthy democracy's separation of powers.

This book offers a very different view. America in the twenty-first century faces stern challenges that cannot be met without bold and creative leadership. But the primary source of that leadership, the office of the presidency, has been so weakened by developments in recent decades that it often cannot meet the needs of the American people. The real problem we must recognize and confront is not the improper expansion of presidential power, but the very real contraction and circumscription of presidential leadership capabilities.

Explaining that development, assessing its impacts, and suggesting pathways to a more effective American presidency are the purposes of this book.

Acknowledgments

A scholarly journey like this is never completed alone. For almost forty years, I have been blessed with colleagues at Colby College who have stimulated my thinking and held its products to high standards. Tony Corrado, Sandy Maisel, Dan Shea, and Rob Weisbrot, among many others, have been constant intellectual companions and highly valued friends.

Andy Rudalevige, a masterful presidency scholar and teacher at Bowdoin College, will disagree with some of the arguments presented in this book. But I hope he will know how much his disagreements forced me to focus and tighten those arguments.

The students in my course on the American presidency have never allowed me the comfort of opinion without the burden of careful research, analysis, and explanation. One of those former students, Randi Arsenault, played an important role in encouraging me to write this book and in the early stages of its conception. I had hoped that she might be a fuller partner in this enterprise, but she became too quickly the victim of her own high competence, and her career took off in directions that circumscribed that possibility. Nevertheless, the existence of this book is deeply rooted in her nurturing insistence that it be written.

As the book entered its final stages, Gregory Naigles performed admirable service as fact checker extraordinaire and not infrequent questioner of its conclusions. I am grateful to several reviewers engaged by the publisher who also offered thoughtful and valuable suggestions: James L. Carson, University of Georgia; George C. Edwards III, Texas A&M University; William Howell, University of Chicago; James Pffifner, George Mason University; Jon C. Rogowski, Washington University in St. Louis; Brandon Rottinghaus, University of Houston; and Stephen Wayne, Georgetown University.

My scholarly debts reach far beyond the specific individuals named here. As a student of the American presidency for more than four decades, I have been fortunate to work in a field so heavily populated with creative and resourceful colleagues in the United States and abroad. All that I know and all that I believe have been shaped by their magnificent contributions. These men and women are too numerous to list here, but they are frequently cited throughout the pages that follow.

To all of these people I am deeply grateful.

The book is dedicated to William H. Goldfarb. As my professional career has unfolded, I could not have had a more supportive partner than Bill Goldfarb. His interest in my work, his unfailing encouragement of it, his generosity to me and his college, and the simple pleasure of his company: I count these among the great treasures of my life.

G. Calvin Mackenzie
Waterville, Maine

1

What Kind of Presidency?

In the summer of 2011, the president of the United States was locked in a titanic struggle with the Congress over how to ensure the full faith and credit of the United States, a matter of critical importance to the national economy. The seemingly endless battle was the result, in no small measure, of the previous midterm election that delivered one house of Congress to the president's opposition twenty-one months after he was inaugurated. No government budget had been approved by Congress for more than 800 days. Nearly a quarter of the top positions in the federal executive branch were not inhabited by Senate-confirmed appointees, and there were vacancies in more than 10 percent of the federal district and appeals court judgeships.

Though great national challenges faced them all, cabinet secretaries spent many hours each month in repetitive testimony before the hundreds of committees and subcommittees of Congress. The creation of a program of expanded healthcare protection for millions of Americans that became law in 2010 after decades of failed efforts was under challenge in the courts and the Congress. Reform of the country's tattered immigration laws, plans to revitalize its aging infrastructure, prevention of the looming shortfall in Social Security funding—all central elements of the president's campaign platform—had been left undone in the face of apparent political impossibility. So they would remain for the duration of his two terms in office.

A stranger to contemporary America—a latter-day Tocqueville or Lord Bryce, for example—might easily conclude that the chief executive of the United States is a peripheral figure on the political landscape. A prominent celebrity, to be sure, even a cause for hope and inspiration among some; but in the crucible of practical politics just one actor among many and barely primus inter pares. Any accounting of the record of the modern presidency, the institution that emerged from the great challenges of the twentieth century, would have to reckon that its most common product is failure. A few brief, shining moments are the exception among days and years of programs not passed, opportunities squandered, needs unmet, and promises not kept.

The stranger would also note the harshness of the judgments cast on the country's presidents. Truman and Johnson abandoning the office in the face of almost-certain voter repudiation. Nixon shrinking into humiliating resignation. Clinton impeached. Ford, Carter, and George H. W. Bush defeated when they stood for reelection. With but few exceptions, as the monthly job approval ratings certify, the common pattern has been for new administrations to begin in the glow of optimism and then slide, often quickly and frequently precipitously, into disappointment. What conclusion could our stranger draw but that the American presidency must be an impossible job, one that overwhelms its incumbents? Never has America had greater need for effective and prudent leadership, the stranger might conclude; never has it so consistently failed to get that leadership.

But wait! A rising chorus of voices fills the political landscape calling the president a despot, a dictator, an emperor. In 2012 and again in 2014, for example, the majority leader of the U.S. House issued a report on the Obama administration titled "The Imperial Presidency." It listed dozens of actions in which the president was alleged to have exceeded the constitutional authority of his office. "Our Founders created a series of checks and balances for our democracy to prevent any one of the three branches of government from becoming too powerful," the report concluded. "Today, this system is under threat as the executive branch continues to bypass Congress and use executive action to promote its own agenda."

Such charges fly frequently now across the political landscape. George W. Bush, the Democrats say, authorized warrantless wiretaps, disregarding procedures established in law. He ordered accused terrorists held without trial and subjected them to the judgments of military commissions, all in the absence of legislative authorization, all by presidential fiat. Treaties were abrogated by presidential declaration. Congressional restrictions on the use of torture were deemed not binding in a presidential "signing statement."

And Barack Obama, the Republicans say, ordered American armed forces to support the efforts of a rebel insurgency in Libya without the acquiescence of Congress. And he used executive authority to alter immigration policies, change work requirements for welfare recipients, waive the performance mandates on local school systems, and impose tighter environmental regulations.

If one listened only to the rhetoric that dominates the daily discourse of politics, as our stranger might, it would be easy to conclude that the presidency is an institution run amok. Presidents, it would seem, make policy without law, take actions that directly contravene the wishes of congressional majorities, and pander to their own political constituencies. They routinely end-run the time-honored procedures of public life by issuing executive orders, making recess appointments, and selectively implementing only those elements of law they happen to like.

But the discourse is at odds with the reality. Presidents do those things that are now taken to be signs of executive excess, to be sure. But most of those actions are neither novel nor unusually expansive. Presidents since the earliest days have issued executive orders, made recess appointments, selectively implemented the laws. Such actions occur more frequently now because the traditional modes of presidential leadership are often foreclosed to contemporary incumbents. Those independent actions are more visible now because we live in a time where everything is more visible. They are more widely criticized now because so little else in legislative-executive relations competes for attention.

The deeper reality is that American presidents in the twenty-first century are in a constant struggle for relevance and impact. Their executive actions may suggest to some, especially their political opponents, a kind of inappropriate, even unconstitutional, aggrandizement. But they are more often acts of desperation than of despotism. Contemporary presidents, denied the foundations of real authority and power, have little choice but to tug on the few levers of independent action they possess.

This is not to say that every independent action by a president is inconsequential. Some are—at least within the limited sphere of their focus. Presidential directives to permit the torture of terrorists held prisoner, to waive requirements for schools to meet statutory standards, for the enforcement of immigration laws to be suspended, surely affect the targets of those policies. They also raise the hackles of politicians who disagree with them and of some constitutional scholars who can find no direct warrant for such exercises of presidential authority.

But they do not represent the kinds of policy-making activity that resets the course of public affairs. Decisions by the EPA, directed by the president, to tighten enforcement of power plant carbon emissions is not a national effort to address the full effects of global climate change. Suspension of deportations of some immigrants is not a comprehensive immigration policy and does not begin to resolve the major immigration challenges facing the country. Only law can do those things, and it is hard to find a time in all of American history when it was harder to make new laws effecting comprehensive policy change than it is now.

We should not be surprised that these assertions of independent presidential authority have risen to such prominence. Often they are the only news on the policy front in Washington. With Congress so rarely passing

new laws, most alterations in public policy come from the White House or
the occasional Supreme Court decision. And in the deeply polarized contemporary political environment every independent action by the president
is treated by his opponents as a direct assault, not only on their policy priorities but also on the Constitution and the American people. In a time of
rhetorical hyperbole, mole hills often do become mountains.

Most contemporary incumbents have been what the scholar James David
Barber described as "active-positive presidents." They see power as a means
to achieve beneficial results. They've come to office with agendas and priorities, often with a long list of those. But all soon encounter formidable
forces of resistance.

They've responded in three ways. First, most have sought to plow ahead
with legislative initiatives, especially in the first two years of their administrations. Jimmy Carter flooded and often overwhelmed Congress with
legislative proposals. Ronald Reagan sought the earliest possible enactment
of a broad tax cut. Bill Clinton offered a program for national health insurance. With Congresses at the outset of new administrations most likely to
be politically aligned with new presidents, they have achieved some measure of success.

But then reality sets in. Legislation stalls. A midterm election weakens
the president's party in Congress. The forces of resistance adjust to the
challenges posed by a new administration. This yields a second pattern of
behavior in which presidents shrink their agendas and stay clear of legislative battles they where they are certain or likely to lose. Ronald Reagan back
tracked on his promise to eliminate the departments of energy and education. Bill Clinton accepted as final the defeat of his healthcare proposals in
1994 and presented no subsequent initiative on that issue in the remaining six years of his presidency. George W. Bush retreated from his effort to
privatize a portion of Social Security.

In light of those new realities, presidents turn to a third pattern of behavior. They come to rely on independent forms of executive authority to push
their policy objectives: executive orders and directives, nonenforcement of
laws, signing statements, recess appointments, etc.

As the forces of resistance to presidential leadership have grown, presidents have turned more often to these independent executive authorities
to pursue their policy objectives. This has contributed to a growing sense
that the presidency is unbound, that presidents pay too little attention to
the constitutional limits on their authority and too often act outside the
prescribed policy-making processes.

There is much truth in this assessment. Reliance on independent executive authorities has grown. Sometimes the reliance on those authorities has
resulted in an evasion of Congress. And occasionally, the boundaries of
executive authority, at least as commonly understood, have been trespassed.

The analysis here does not deny that contemporary presidents have sometimes relied too heavily on their independent authority, nor that they have on some occasions acted in ways that jeopardize the restraints the Constitution seems to mandate. In fact, one of the purposes here is to explain the causes of that behavior.

The argument here is that those actions, those uses of independent executive authority, have become more common (and perhaps more threatening) in recent times because the more traditional policy-making avenues have been largely closed to contemporary presidents. They have acted as they have because they've had so few alternatives.

But there is also a second part to the argument offered here. That is, that presidents denied regular access to traditional methods of policy making and thus forced to rely on the back channels of the Constitution simply cannot provide the kind of national leadership that the challenges of the twenty-first century will require.

What cannot be done by law—and in our own time very little can be done by law—must now be done by other means. Presidents have sought those means when possible. They have done so not because these are better ways to govern, not because they are more likely to yield the outcomes that presidents (and often the American people) seek, but simply because they are the only alternatives available to presidents seeking to perform their obligations as national leaders.

The leadership capabilities of the presidency have shrunk for many reasons, but looming largest among those are evolutionary changes in American politics and in the broader public sphere that have had profound and durable effects on that institution. This book seeks to identify those changes, trace their impacts on the presidency, and suggest their consequences for government effectiveness in the years ahead.

This is not a textbook about the presidency nor is it a review or assessment of the overall performance of recent presidents. It draws heavily on contemporary experience and modern scholarship about the presidency to explain the collective impact of a number of developments that have diminished the potential and often real impact of the presidency as a leadership institution in the American political system.

Some elements of this argument directly confront the prevailing conventional wisdom that the American presidency has grown too powerful. That conventional wisdom is by no means wrong in all respects, but it requires us to overlook a good deal of contrary information.

The truth is that no single explanation can possibly capture all the dynamics of an institution as complex as the modern American presidency nor of politics as fluid and unpredictable as those in America. Presidential behavior fits no single mold nor subscribes to any single theory. Common accounts of the modern presidents, in both scholarship and journalism, have focused on the enlargement of presidential power and the overreach of contemporary presidents. That view, as argued here, overlooks some significant evidence suggesting quite the opposite: that the presidents of the United States have grown increasingly constrained in modern times and that the character of leadership that presidents are capable of providing often fails to meet the needs of the American people.

We have in our time a presidency encumbered in multiple and confounding ways. It is a presidency upon which great expectations are imposed but rarely met. It is a presidency, sadly, that fails to provide the American people with the kind of leadership their country requires to meet its critical domestic and economic challenges.

The problems we face are not simple, nor are their solutions. But none will be solved, nor even properly managed, without the guidance of effective national leadership. In recent decades, our political system has not been much of an incubator of effective and durable leaders. Only the presidency seems capable of meeting that need. When there are deficiencies in the leadership capacity of the presidency they ripple deeply and dangerously through our national life.

Few tasks loom as large among our current political challenges as the one we confront here: identifying the deficiencies in the contemporary American presidency, investigating the causes of those, and seeking ways to cure them in time to meet the sobering demands of the twenty-first century.

THE LEGACY OF CONSTITUTIONAL AMBIGUITY

As we are often vexed today by the complexities of maintaining effective leadership in a democratic republic, so were those who first sought to solve this problem. The framers of the American Constitution created an executive office that met two dominant criteria. First, it fit the state of their thinking in 1787 after shedding a monarchy, experimenting with thirteen state constitutions, and enduring a failed first experiment with a national government. Second, it satisfied enough (but by no means all) of the delegates to the Constitutional Convention and their contemporaries in the state-ratifying assemblies.

The framers were neither prophets nor visionaries, despite their hope that they had created a document for the ages. They could not have imagined the scope and character of the country, nor the government that would arise under this Constitution. The first government under its aegis would employ barely a hundred civilians in a country of fewer than 4 million citizens. With few changes in the structural details of the Constitution—and almost none that involve the presidency—that government today employs 2.6 million civilians and serves more than 315 million citizens. We should not be surprised that its strains and stresses are so often apparent.

The daunting task for the framers was to figure out how to create a democratic executive. None had ever existed before in their world, certainly not on the scale that these thoughtful men in Philadelphia were attempting. How, they repeatedly asked themselves, do you have a chief magistrate who is competent and powerful and yet accountable and responsible in the exercise of power? None knew the answer with any certainty though several of them harbored strong opinions. Alexander Hamilton, famously, offered the convention a long philosophical discourse in which he called for the establishment of an hereditary chief executive serving for life. No good executive, he argued, "could be established on Republican principles."[1]

None of the other delegates found comfort in this extreme position, though several of them—notably Gouverneur Morris and James Wilson—shared Hamilton's interest in creating a potent chief executive. But it was an uphill struggle, for America was not then a country ready for a powerful chief executive. Much of the anger that fueled the revolution had simmered in scorn for the colonial governors and the British king. As Edwin Corwin noted in his seminal study of the American presidency,

> The earliest American repository of an executive power at all distinguishable as something other than a mere legislative agency was the governor of the royal province. This functionary, acting independently or with a council, was customarily entrusted with the powers of appointment, military command, expenditure, and—within limitations—pardon, as well as with large powers in connection with the process of lawmaking. . . . The colonial period ended with the belief prevalent that "the executive magistracy" was the natural enemy, the legislative assembly the natural friend of liberty, a sentiment strengthened by the contemporary spectacle of George III's domination of Parliament.[2]

George III, of course, was a special inspiration to those who warned of the dangers of strong executives. In *Common Sense*, the incendiary pamphlet that fanned the flames of revolution, Thomas Paine wrote "monarchy and succession have laid . . . the world in blood and ashes.' Tis a form of government which the word of God bears testimony against, and blood will attend it."[3] Those fears were still very much alive at the Constitutional Convention a decade later.

In the interim, all of the states had written and begun to live under their own constitutions. In all but one of those—New York being the exception—ingenious devices had been created to limit the power of the governor, as political scientist Charles Thach indicated in his study of the creation of the presidency:

> Short terms, strict limitations on reeligibility, and election by the legislature were the outstanding characteristics of the chief magistracy. Nor was the principle of executive unity adopted, for in the exercise of his power the chief executive was controlled by the necessity of acting in accord with the advice of an

executive council chosen, save in Pennsylvania, by the legislature. . . . The chief magistrate was, as Gov. Randolph denominated himself, only "a member of the executive."[4]

Legislative omnipotence was the hallmark of these initial state constitutions. So it was, too, with the first constitution of the national government: the Articles of Confederation. Drafted by the Continental Congress in 1777 but not ratified by the last state until 1781, the articles provided for no executive office whatsoever. The national government was little more than a legislature. Its committees managed the day-to-day business of government, of which there was not very much, since the limited powers of this national government left most civil authority in the hands of the states.

The deficiencies in the articles were soon apparent and yielded widespread discussion of the need for improvement. The delegates who came to Philadelphia in the late spring of 1787 were not of one mind about the need to draft an entirely new constitution, but there was broad consensus among them about the need to centralize more authority in the national government and to provide some sort of institutionalized leadership structure.

But what kind of executive? That was the rub. "Though the delegates agreed that the new Constitution should establish a distinct executive branch," writes the political scientist Richard Ellis, "they had very different ideas about what that branch should look like."[5]

Delegates from two states—Virginia and New Jersey—brought drafts of a new government with them. Both included a national executive. But it was perhaps indicative of the uncertainties of the time that both the New Jersey Plan and the Virginia Plan called for the election of the executive by the Congress. At several points over the summer the convention voted for exactly that kind of a model. But as the debate matured and other pieces fell into place the method of selection was also reconsidered.

The Constitution, ultimately, is less a record of broad consensus among a group of demigods than it is a photograph of the endpoint in a widely careening debate among practical politicians. Had the convention ended in July, the executive would have been radically different from what it became. Some of the delegates, Benjamin Franklin and Roger Sherman among them, found little to admire in the final decisions on the character of the presidency. Yet, they signed the Constitution in spite of their doubts. "The Executive," Franklin predicted fatalistically, "will be always increasing here, as elsewhere, till it ends in a monarchy."[6] George Mason and Edmund Randolph, widely admired delegates from Virginia, could not brook their doubts and declined to sign the final draft.

The debate over the proper character of a "democratic executive" did not end with the convention. It was a centerpiece of the reaction in the press, in letters exchanged among contemporaries, and in the state-ratifying conventions. In the Virginia convention, Patrick Henry declared that this new Constitution had "an awful squinting; it squints toward monarchy. . . . Your President may easily become king. . . . Can he not, at the head of his army, beat down every opposition? Away with your President, we shall have a king. . . . What will then become of you and your rights? Will not absolute despotism ensue?"[7]

"How do you like our new Constitution?" wrote Thomas Jefferson to John Adams after both had examined the draft in late 1787. Jefferson, in Paris, found "things in it which stagger all my dispositions to subscribe to what such an assembly has proposed." The presidency, he wrote, resembled "a bad edition of a Polish King."

> He may be reelected from 4 years to 4 years for life. Reason and experience prove to us that a chief magistrate, so continuable, is an officer for life. . . . Once in office, and possessing the military force of the nation, without either the aid or check of a council, he would not be easily dethroned, even if the people could be induced to withdraw their votes from him. I wish that at the end of the 4 years they had made him forever ineligible a second time.[8]

But Adams had different concerns. If Jefferson was worried that the new president too closely resembled a king, Adams fretted that the powers assigned to this office were too few and those afforded the Senate too many. "You are apprehensive of Monarchy," he responded to Jefferson, "I, of aristocracy."[9]

The months of debate at the convention, the scarcity of detail in Article II, which establishes the executive branch, the broad disagreement in public reaction, and the close votes at most of the state-ratifying conventions, are indicative of the concerns and doubts that prevailed in the founding generation of Americans. The salve for those doubts was caution. And the creation of the American presidency was an exercise in caution. Where power is granted to the president, it is encased in procedural and structural constraints. No opportunity to lead is untethered. The scope of genuine presidential prerogative is narrow and shadowed. Mechanisms of accountability are multiple. The framers hedged all their bets.

It is not an overstatement to suggest that the majority of those engaged in this act of creation saw a chief executive as a necessary evil. Their goal—and it was their accomplishment as well—was to create a president with as little power and as little opportunity for mischief as they could, consistent with the need they all understood for some directing force in the central government. As other democracies later emerged, and other models of democratic executives with them, it became increasingly clear that the legacy of the American Constitution is a chief executive of limited authority and circumscribed opportunities for leadership. Indeed, among the models of democratic executives, it is one of the weakest of all.

THE EMERGENCE OF A MODERN PRESIDENCY

The inherent weaknesses in the structure of the presidency were not imme-diately debilitating to the new country. Government was a tiny enterprise in the early decades and remained at the periphery of life for most Americans until the middle decades of the twentieth century. Whatever constraints the Constitution imposed on the leadership capacities of American presidents were endurable in part because not much was expected of presidents most of the time and because there was sufficient flexibility and ambiguity in the constitutional language to permit presidents to interpret the language in ways that allowed them to meet the demands and needs of their time. As political scientist Thomas Cronin has noted, "in part we have an unwritten constitution whose history is the history of judicial review and of continu-ous reinterpretation by presidents and members of Congress."[10]

In times of dire crisis, like the Civil War, the Constitution was sufficiently flexible to permit necessary deference to presidential leadership. Abraham Lincoln, for example, was not above setting the Constitution aside when he believed it stood in the way of preserving the union. "By general law," he wrote, "life and limb must be protected, yet often a limb must be ampu-tated to save a life; but a life is never wisely given to save a limb."[11]

And occasionally the intersection of pent-up reform demands and a president of forceful personality and significant political skills—an Andrew Jackson or Theodore Roosevelt, for example—could yield a broad but brief period of policy change. But for most of the country's early history, presi-dents competed for influence over public policy, often against forces far stronger and more durable than they.

As a matter of scholarly interest, the presidency was largely an orphan during the first century and a half of the republic. On those infrequent occasions when it became a subject of scholarly inquiry, the assessments were often critical of the kinds of people who became president or of the leadership capabilities of the office defined in the Constitution itself. James Bryce, for example, wrote a much-noticed article entitled "Why Great Men Do Not Become President." Professor Woodrow Wilson's 1885 analysis, *Congressional Government*, found much to bemoan in the structural weak-ness of the presidency and in the kind of people who had filled the office. "The decline in the character of the presidents," he wrote, "is not the cause, but only the accompanying manifestation, of the declining prestige of the presidential office. That high office has fallen from its first estate of dignity because its power has waned; and its power has waned because the power of Congress has become predominant."[12]

Thinking about the role of the president underwent a radical transforma-tion with the Great Depression, the New Deal, and the presidency of Franklin D. Roosevelt. Roosevelt's presidency was many things, of course, but among them was this: it focused the attention of the country on Washington and on the chief executive in ways that were unique and indelible. Americans would never again regard their president as a peripheral character in their lives. And students of government would never again regard the presidency as a side-show. Roosevelt changed all of that because he was president for so long at a time of such deeply felt challenges and because his presidency coincided with the emergence of entirely new forms of public communication.

The significance of Roosevelt's presidency in revising the scholarly study of government was abetted by another characteristic. Roosevelt's administration was a magnet for many of the leading intellectuals of the time. Some of them—no small number—took positions in the government. Others benefited in important ways from the income-supplementing programs of the New Deal like the WPA. And others, though not working in government nor pocketing money from it, were in thrall of Roosevelt's intellectual respectability. So it is no surprise that the Roosevelt presidency—a powerful, active president steering the country through crisis, in the common conceptualization—came to dominate subsequent scholarship.

The historian William Leuchtenberg wrote, for example,

> Roosevelt left his mark on his successors in a great many ways. . . . No one before Roosevelt had so dominated the political culture of his day, if for no other reason than no one before him had been in the White House for so long, and in the process he created the expectation that the chief executive would be the primary shaper of his times—an expectation with which each of his successors has had to deal.[13]

The heroic presidency model soon became normative: there *should* be a powerful, active presidency at the center of the government. The mid-century textbooks on the presidency took this as an article of faith. The most widely adopted of those, Clinton Rossiter's *The American Presidency*, called the office "one of the few truly successful institutions created by men in the endless quest for the blessings of free government. . . . I would be less than candid were I not to make clear . . . my own feeling of veneration, if not exactly reverence, for the authority and dignity of the Presidency."[14]

Writing in *Encounter* magazine on the eve of the Kennedy administration he would soon join, Arthur M. Schlesinger Jr. affirmed this positive view of an activist presidency: "The heroic leader has the Promethean responsibility to affirm human freedom against the supposed inevitabilities of history. As he does this, he combats the infection of fatalism which might otherwise paralyze mass democracy. Without heroic leaders, a society would tend to acquiesce in the drift of history."[15]

James David Barber, one of the most prominent students of the presidency in the latter decades of the twentieth century, wrote, "No President since Roosevelt has come close to his achievements in domestic and foreign policy. We would do well to find and advance to the Presidency another Roosevelt, another President who combines his vigor, his values, and his political competence."[16]

In the spring of 1960, a young political scientist and veteran of the Truman White House published what became the leading text on the presidency in the second half of the twentieth century. His name was Richard Neustadt and the book was titled *Presidential Power*.[17] John Kennedy had encountered Neustadt's book during his run for the presidency and after winning election he invited Neustadt to prepare a memo with guidance for a new president.[18]

In both the memo and the book, Neustadt's preoccupation was with how presidents could obtain power and use it to their benefit. The assumption prevailed in both—as it did widely in the scholarship of the time—that presidential power was desirable, perhaps even essential, for successful governance. Questions that had once prevailed about the proper balance between legislative and executive power were set aside. The desirability of expansive presidential power was increasingly assumed and the question became how to accomplish that objective.

This transformation in thinking occurred simultaneously with the ascension of the Democratic Party in national politics. Roosevelt and Truman held the White House for twenty years. Eisenhower, though a Republican, had no intention of reverting back to a Taft or Coolidge presidency and largely accepted the responsibilities of active leadership that he had inherited from his two predecessors. Kennedy and Johnson both had deep ties to the earlier Democratic administrations and assumed, with little reflection, the propriety of activist presidential leadership.

Most of the leading scholars of the time, especially historians and political scientists, applauded what they were seeing in Washington. James McGregor Burns, a Pulitzer prize-winning historian and coauthor of the leading American government textbook of his time, called this

> the most splendid era of American political leadership since the Founding. From the 1930s to the 1960s, it was the era not only of great Democratic presidents, but of brilliant *collective* leadership. Generations of committed, creative reformers reached from the West Wing of the White House through the departments and agencies down to the grassroots, to the well of that great leadership, the tens of millions of citizens who put them into office and kept them there.[19]

The scholarship on the presidency during and immediately after this period was remarkably consistent, almost formulaic. The empirical and the normative overlapped and intersected: what was observed was what was desired. Thomas Cronin captured the consistent character of the scholarship in an insightful article about the "textbook presidency":

Textbooks summarize current thinking and guide the work of contemporary researchers. For more than twenty years after the Franklin D. Roosevelt presidency, most textbook treatments of the presidency seriously inflated presidential competence and beneficence. . . . What resulted very often was a storybook view that whatever was good for our president must be the right thing.[20]

The liberal view of government at the time—that there ought to be an expansive government led by an activist president—was reflected in the scholarship of the time because so many of the authors of that scholarship were personally sympathetic to those liberal views. Conservative disagreement was barely visible on the academic fringes and in small-circulation magazines like the *National Review*. In those places, one could hear a few voices that questioned the desirability of an activist presidency, especially a president who could dominate the legislature.

Conservatives worried that an activist presidency was just the point of the lance for government expansion. Liberals, they believed, wanted more power in the presidency to energize the enlargement of government's role in American society. Some of the conservative resistance to government expansionism came to be expressed as a reaction to what they called the "aggrandizement" and "usurpation" of presidential power. Barry Goldwater, the conservative Republican candidate for president in 1964, often criticized his opponent for what he called "political Daddyism."[21] In a campaign manifesto, he wrote:

Only recently, a colleague of mine in the United States Senate flatly described the legislatures of America—all of them, state, local, national—as the major stumbling block in the democratic process. The charge is fantastic. What it says is that representative government—which is the essence of freedom itself—is the enemy of freedom. And the solution which my colleague offered was as fantastic. He said that an increase in executive power would be the answer—an increase in the very centralization of power which always has been contrary to broadly based democratic processes. The whole history of freedom has been simply the history of resistance to the concentration of power in government.[22]

Through the 1960s and into the 1970s, the opposing sides in this debate crystallized. Liberals were presidentialists, applauding the expansion of presidential power as a way to overcome the resistance of backwater legislators to progressive goals, especially in civil rights. Conservatives formed their lines around the Congress and states' rights. Here, they found the "true voice of the people" that they believed liberals too often disrespected and presidents too often disregarded. Constraining the expansion of presidential power became an important part of the conservative strategy for diminishing the role of the federal government.

But then Americans found themselves in what appeared to be an enduring era of divided government. In 1969, Richard Nixon was the first president in more than a century to start an administration with both houses of Congress in the hands of the opposition party. To observers at the time that seemed merely an aberration. But over the years that followed, it became increasingly clear that divided government was the new normal. It appeared that the country was entering a period when Republicans would dominate the White House and Democrats the Congress. In the House of Representatives, for example, there had been no break in Democratic majorities since 1955.

By the time Ronald Reagan became president in 1981, with Democrats still in control of the House of Representatives, a major shift in ideological conceptualizations of the presidency had begun to take root. Liberal scholars who had long been cheerleaders for the model of an activist presidency were suddenly filled with doubts. Arthur Schlesinger Jr., for example, the faithful historian of the New Deal and a prominent member of John Kennedy's White House staff, led the retreat in a book called *The Imperial Presidency*.

On the other end of the ideological spectrum, conservatives were taking note that the base of their political power was now in the White House. Many of them began to find reasons to admire the model of an activist president—so long as the president was one of them. A key figure in this transition was Dick Cheney. Cheney had been trained as a political scientist at the University of Wisconsin, but his academic career never got started. A fellowship in Washington while a graduate student soon turned into a series of high-level mentorships that landed him as chief of staff to President Ford when he was thirty-four years old. In that position, in the aftermath of Watergate and with a Congress dominated by Democrats, Cheney came to rue the constraints on presidential power. Two years after Ford was defeated, Cheney won a seat in Congress from his home state of Wyoming, but even in the House of Representatives he remained an advocate for expansions of presidential power.

When Ronald Reagan was elected in 1980, his soon-to-be chief of staff, James Baker, visited Cheney and solicited his advice. Baker's cryptic notes from that meeting survive and they read, in part: "Pres. seriously weakened in recent yrs. Restore power & auth to Exec Branch—Need strong ldr'ship. Get rid of War Powers Act—restore independent rights."[23] In a speech in 1996, Cheney repeated this theme: "I think there have been times in the past, oftentimes in response to events such as Watergate or the war in Vietnam, where Congress has begun to encroach upon the powers and responsibilities of the president; that it was important to go back and try to restore that balance."[24]

In the years that followed the defeat of Barry Goldwater in 1964, conservatives had begun to construct an intellectual infrastructure designed, in part, to counter the think tanks and advocacy organizations that sided with liberals. Prominent among these were the Heritage Foundation that sponsored studies of government and policy that supported conservative positions and the Federalist Society that sought to encourage more challenges to liberal domination of law school faculties and to breed a stable of suitably conservative lawyers whom Republican presidents could appoint to federal judgeships.

Conservatives stopped being conservative about executive power. In the journals and other discourses of these organizations enthusiasm began to coalesce for a doctrine called the "unitary executive theory." In rudimentary terms, the unitary executive theory held that the language of Article II of the Constitution should be interpreted in its broadest form. Once the Congress has passed a law, its duties are done and its opportunities to affect public policy foreclosed. Everything that happens thereafter is under the control of the president and Congress should not meddle—nor should judges—in the implementation of public policy.

The unitary executive theory goes even further on matters of foreign and national security policy, holding that these are uniquely and nearly totally presidential responsibilities. As commander-in-chief, for example, presidents may deploy American forces in any way they deem essential for national security. They need not secure the approval nor even the acquiescence of Congress in these deployments, and Congress should exercise no subsequent control over them.

Central to the unitary executive theory that became increasingly attractive to conservatives was the conception of the legislature as an intrusion, almost a distraction, in the day-to-day business of running the government. Even so nonideological a conservative as George H. W. Bush echoed this theme. In a speech at Princeton University in the spring of 1991, Bush said:

> The most common challenge to Presidential powers comes from a predictable source . . . the United States Congress. . . . Six times in my Presidency, I have vetoed bills that would have weakened Presidential powers. . . . Elsewhere, Congress has also taken aggressive action against specific Presidential powers, including the power to appoint or remove employees who serve at the President's pleasure. It sometimes tries to manage the executive branch—micromanage the executive branch—by writing too-specific directions for carrying out a particular law. And when this happens, the President has a constitutional obligation to protect his Office and to veto the legislation. . . . Presidents define themselves through their exercise of Presidential power.[25]

There was, of course, a liberal reaction to this new-found conservative affection for presidential power. Schlesinger's book on the imperial presidency, first published in the midst of the Watergate scandal, went through several editions. It inspired a stream of scholarship critical of abuses of presidential authority. Liberal writers began to seek a proper balance between the still-admired possibilities of an activist presidency and the concomitant risks of executive extremism—especially in foreign and national security policies.

By the beginning of the twenty-first century, a new spark began to fire liberal concerns about presidential power. This was the war on terror that unfolded during the administration of George W. Bush. The Bush administration relied heavily on the unitary executive theory in justifying the design and implementation of its war on terror. Soon that theory itself became a prominent target of critics of the war that Bush initiated.

The most prominent and negative assessment of the unitary executive theory, *Takeover: The Return of the Imperial Presidency and the Subversion of American Democracy*, was written by a journalist, Charlie Savage. The earlier reporting that was the basis for the book won a Pulitzer Prize in 2007. Savage wrote:

> The Bush-Cheney administration took vigorous steps to impose greater discipline and control on the permanent government, seeking to stamp out pockets of independence inside the executive branch. The administration tried systematically to subjugate and circumvent career officials who raised objections to their policies, and it tried to game the system to make sure that any advice the professionals provided would support the president's preexisting policy preferences. This was the Unitary Executive Theory in action—enforcing the notion that every official inside the executive branch is nothing more than an appendage of the president and should take no action and offer no opinion opposed by the White House.[26]

The debate about the Bush administration's response to the terrorist attack on the United States was more than just a question of tactics or even strategies. It was also a very public disagreement about the role and authority of the president of the United States. President Bush and Vice President Cheney argued for a presidency of few constraints, and they acted—often forcefully and fearlessly—on that belief. The administration's opponents took a much narrower view of presidential power, arguing that the Bush-Cheney approach clearly exceeded the warrants of the Constitution.

One thing is clear from this brief history of conceptions and counter-conceptions of presidential power: those who agree with the substantive purposes for which presidential power is being used tend to be advocates of a more activist presidency, and vice versa. When liberals dominated in the White House, liberal scholars and politicians found much to like in the activist model of the presidency. When conservatives came to dominate the White House, liberals retreated from that view as conservatives were drawn to it. The old rule of politics prevails here as in so many other places: where you stand depends upon where you sit.

CONTEMPORARY PERSPECTIVES ON THE PRESIDENCY

Scholars of the presidency have long sought to look beyond the politics of the moment in their analyses of presidential power. But their work has yielded little consensus. Even after more than 200 years of experience and reams of analysis, debate persists about the role of the presidency in American government and American life. The presidency, like a finely cut gem, has many facets. Each jeweler can set the stone to catch the one that gleams brightest. So it is with analysts of the presidency. Some think the office has grown much too powerful. Some find it too weak. To others, its role is just about right and requires little or no change.

The community of those who think the presidency has grown too powerful and outgrown its constitutional constraints is well populated. Edward Corwin, one of the leading writers on the presidency in the middle decades of the twentieth century, produced five editions of his classic work *The Presidency: Office and Powers*. His concerns about the expansion of presidential power seemed to grow with each edition. In the last of those that appeared in his lifetime, Corwin cited several hundred judicial decisions in most of which expansions of presidential power were approved by the courts. He worried that the Constitution was increasingly failing to constrain the executive power within the broader framework of government. The "personalization" of the presidency, he fretted, invited "two dangers: the slowing down of the legislative process to an extent that unfits it for a crisis-ridden world in which time is often of the essence, and—in consequence—autocracy."[27]

Arthur M. Schlesinger Jr. created a mini-industry with the publication of his book *The Imperial Presidency* in 1973. Long a supporter of liberal, activist presidents, Schlesinger had become alarmed at the excesses he observed in the Nixon administration and confessed in this book that the powerful presidency was a two-edged sword. He noted especially how the growing role of the presidency in foreign affairs had broadened the base of presidential power, and how difficult it had become to confine that power solely to one area of presidential operations.

> The perennial threat to the constitutional balance . . . arises in the field of foreign affairs. . . . Confronted by presidential initiatives in foreign affairs, Congress and the courts, along with the press and the citizenry, often lack confidence in their own information and judgment and are likely to be intimidated by executive authority. The inclination in foreign policy is to let the president have the responsibility and the power—a renunciation that results from congressional pusillanimity as well as from presidential rapacity. The more acute the crisis, the more power flows to the president.[28]

In later years, the difficulties confronted by Presidents Ford and Carter and later the first President Bush and President Clinton forced Schlesinger to reconsider his earlier alarms about expansive presidential power. In a *New York Times* article in 1998, "So Much for the Imperial Presidency," he suggested that presidential power, like the tide, ebbed and flowed. But then the Bush administration revived his concerns. The 2004 edition of *The Imperial Presidency* returned to full force the fears expressed in 1973. "The impact of 9/11 and of the ever-changing terrorist threat," he wrote, "gives more power to the imperial presidency and places the separation of powers ordained by the Constitution under unprecedented and at times unbearable strain."[29]

The historian Garry Wills weighed in on this debate in 2010 with a book entitled *Bomb Power*. Wills offered the unique theory that the broad expansion of presidential power in recent decades—"far from the design of the framers of the Constitution"—could be attributed in large measure to the development of the atomic bomb.[30] So much deference had accrued to the president as a consequence of his control over nuclear weapons, argued Wills, that resistance to him in any policy field had become much more difficult. "Executive power," he wrote, "has basically been, since World War II, Bomb Power."[31]

The cult of personality that grew up around the presidency after World War II, largely enabled by the communications revolution of that period, worried other students of the presidency. Bruce Ackerman, a Yale University law professor, wrote in the *Harvard Law Review*, of his concern about "the way a personalistic presidency undermines bedrock democratic ideals. Whether it takes the form of obsessive fixation on the pecadillos [*sic*] of Warren Harding or Bill Clinton, or the adulatory worship of heroes like Franklin Roosevelt or Ronald Reagan, the cult of presidential personality goes against the grain of republican self-government. It is downright embarrassing for a constitution to ask free and equal citizens to place so much trust in the personal integrity and ideals of a single human being."[32]

Other legal scholars have watched with dread what they regarded as the twisting of the law by recent presidential administrations to provide justifications for their questionable actions. William P. Marshall, for example, wrote in the *Yale Law Journal*,

> the President has at his command resources unimaginable at the time of the Founding. In addition to the enormous military power that the President is able to unleash without any significant *ex ante* check, the President has at his disposal agencies such as the CIA and the FBI, which provide the President with ample opportunity to use their enormous capabilities for mischief, including the invasion of individual rights through investigation, surveillance, and detention. At the same time, because their activities are inherently secretive, these agencies are not meaningfully subject to effective oversight by the other branches or by the media.

> The result of this is that Congress and the courts seem increasingly unable to check and balance presidential power in particularly critical areas. . . . Too much presidential power now lies unchecked.[33]

Jenny S. Martinez, a specialist in international law, compared the constraints on the American presidency with those imposed on chief executives in other countries. She was especially interested in determining whether there was international support for the unitary executive theory. Her findings, she writes, are "a counterweight to recent arguments that executive power, by its very nature, requires unchecked authority to act independently based on invocation of inherent power. Other contemporary democracies generally recognize legal or constitutional limits on executive power. Those limits preserve a balance of political power with the legislature and the courts that protects liberty; this balance is maintained even in matters touching on war, foreign affairs, and national security."[34]

To Matthew Crenson and Benjamin Ginsberg, political scientists whose book *Presidential Power: Unchecked and Unbalanced* is a strongly worded indictment of efforts to enlarge presidential power, the fault lies less with presidents themselves than with the citizens they govern. "The expansion of presidential power is both a symptom and source of an ongoing decay in America's democratic processes," they write.[35] Presidential power grew, they argue, because congressional power declined. And that decline occurred because of a decrease in citizen engagement. Congress relies

> on its authority as the voice of a large and vigilant electorate to bend the executive to its purposes. But its commands lost their efficacy as the electorate diminished and the citizens who composed it were converted into mere customers in the marketplace of public services. And, while the decline of party liberated presidents from a political encumbrance, it damaged the chief mechanism through which Congress called itself to order. Congress could no longer act as a coherent body able to stand up to the single-mindedness of a vigorous chief executive.[36]

Crenson and Ginsberg go on to argue that the courts have been complicit in the steady enlargement of the chief executive, having taken "extraordinary claims for presidential power made for limited purposes and rationalized them so that presidents could employ them more generally and routinely."[37]

Among the critics of the post-World War II growth in the role of the American president in government, few have been more persistent than Louis Fisher. Long an employee of the Congressional Research Service, a support agency for the Congress, Fisher has produced a series of independent monographs analyzing all of the most important separation of powers controversies. In each of these, he has identified the constitutional principles that kept presidents in check for the first century and a half of the American experience but which have withered in the most recent half century.

In Fisher's view, both Republican and Democratic presidents have taken advantage—improper advantage—of secrecy and deception on the one hand and legislative incompetence on the other to steadily shift the balance of governmental power in their favor. "The general drift of authority and responsibility toward the President is unmistakable," he writes. "More threatening is executive activity cut loose from legislative moorings and constitutional restrictions. The record of recent decades is disturbing to those who fear unchecked executive power."[38]

But the landscape of presidential analysis is not solely inhabited by those who observe and fear an expansion of executive authority. Less well populated but equally long in historical lineage is a chorus—well, maybe a quartet—of presidential analysts who take the position that the presidency is too weak an institution. The intellectual godfather of this group is Alexander Hamilton. At the Constitutional Convention, Hamilton was a constant advocate of significant executive power. And in several of the *Federalist* papers that he wrote, he defended the presidency that the new Constitution created. In a famous passage in *Federalist 70*, he argued, "Energy in the executive is the leading character in the definition of good government. A feeble Executive implies a feeble execution of the government. A feeble execution is but another phrase for a bad execution; and a government ill executed, whatever it may be in theory, must be, in practice, a bad government."

Long before he was elected to the presidency, Woodrow Wilson was the leading public and scholarly critic of the Constitution's separation of powers. "As a matter of fact and experience," Wilson wrote in *Congressional Government* in 1885, "the more power is divided the more irresponsible it becomes."[39] Had they the chance to review the first century of the government they created, he believed, the framers of the Constitution "would be the first to admit that the only fruit of dividing power had been to make it irresponsible."[40] He added:

> If there be one principle clearer than another, it is this: that in any business, whether of government or of mere merchandising, *somebody must be trusted*, in order that when things go wrong it may be quite plain who should be punished. . . . *Power and strict accountability for its use* are the essential constituents of good government.[41]

The fatal defect that Wilson observed in the Constitution's separation of powers was the consequent absence of effective leadership. "There can be no successful government without leadership or without the intimate, almost instinctive, coordination of the organs of life and action," he wrote in *Constitutional Government* in 1908.[42]

Wilson was, of course, unique among scholars of the presidency in that he became president. And like his predecessor once removed, Teddy Roosevelt, he sought to implement a conception of presidential power and responsibility far broader than other presidents of the late nineteenth and early twentieth centuries. Roosevelt, hyperkinetic and often frustrated by the slow pace of legislative action, mused, "If only I could be president and Congress for ten minutes."[43]

Wilson, no doubt, would have shared this fantasy. "The president is at liberty both in law and conscience," he wrote, "to be as big a man as he can be. His capacity will set the limit; and if Congress be overborne by him, it will be no fault of the makers of the Constitution, it will be from no lack of constitutional powers on his part, but only because the President has the nation behind him, and Congress has not."[44]

As noted earlier, much of the liberal scholarship of the middle decades of the twentieth century reflected these earlier criticisms of the constitutional constraints on the president's ability to advocate the national interest as against the parochial and regional—and later special—interests that guided many members of Congress. In *The Deadlock of Democracy*, a widely noted book published in 1963, James MacGregor Burns argued that "To act, American leaders have had to gain the concurrence not simply of a majority of the voters, but of majorities of different sets of voters organized around leaders in mutually checking and foot-dragging sectors of government. . . . We can choose bold and creative national leaders without giving them the means to make their leadership effective. Hence we diminish a democracy's most essential and priceless commodity—the leadership of men who are willing to move ahead to meet emerging problems."[45]

More than forty years later, he was making the same arguments:

> Under a system that meticulously divides and fragments power and responsibility, transforming leadership has been extraordinarily difficult, except in crises such as war or economic calamity. And while the institutional stalemates remain the same, the demands facing government have accelerated. The incremental changes presidents and legislators make through transactional leadership are inadequate to the ever-rising flood of dire problems.[46]

To Richard Neustadt, the Constitution was not the primary constraint on presidential power. "The things he personally has to do," wrote Neustadt of presidents, "are no respecters of the lines between 'civil' and 'military,' or 'foreign' and 'domestic,' or 'legislative' and 'executive' or 'administrative' and 'political.' At his desk—and there alone—distinctions of these sorts lose their last shred of meaning."[47] Power, in Neustadt's view, was a product of presidents' skills and the strategies they employ, not of any specific constitutional language. To be a powerful president, one needs to take full advantage of the opportunities the office and the times present.

But for all the respect Neustadt's analysis earned, he has never lacked critics. Stephen Skowronek, like Neustadt a supporter of the notion that effective presidential leadership is a critical ingredient in successful government performance, wrote in *Presidential Leadership in Political Time* that national politics is marked by recurrent cycles of reconstruction, disjunction, articulation, and preemption. All presidents come to office at a particular point in political time and their opportunities are shaped by the roles and actions of their immediate predecessors.

"The perspective of political time refers us back to the politics of leadership in earlier periods," Skowronek writes, "to prior sequences of change in which presidents took on similar political challenges in leadership and wrestled with them to similar political effect. The recurrent patterns revealed in this way indicate the range of political possibilities for presidential leadership in the American system."[48]

Another Neustadt critic, political scientist Matthew N. Beckmann, looked at more recent studies of presidents and found that they "refuted the thesis that presidential power is personally derived. We now know that if presidents' personal 'skill' plays a part in their legislative influence, it is far from the central part. Again, constitutional edicts and political context delimit what a president can achieve—occasionally for better, often for worse."[49]

A leading presidential scholar, George C. Edwards III, has written several books refuting Neustadt's notion that presidential power is the power to persuade. "Presidential power is *not* the power to persuade," he argues. "Presidents cannot reshape the contours of the political landscape to pave the way for change by establishing an agenda and persuading the public, Congress, and others to support their policies . . . the political system is too complicated, power too decentralized, and interests too diverse for one person, no matter how extraordinary to dominate."[50]

Beyond the academic voices of concern over the limits of presidential authority, there has developed as well a school of politicians and public officials who make the case that contemporary presidents are confined in their leadership efforts by an outmoded constitution, a dysfunctional Congress, and a politics that makes the production of governing coalitions harder than it has ever been. This is a view, as noted earlier, that gained particular credence among conservatives during recent Republican administrations. John Yoo, a law professor and controversial member of the staff of the Office of Legal Counsel during the presidency of George W. Bush, later wrote of the high price the country pays for its pursuit of a "risk-free presidency":

> The restraints necessary for a risk-free presidency may sap the executive of those unique qualities that allow it to act decisively when the nation's security is at stake. A system that could abort another Nixon could also hamstring another

Lincoln or FDR. . . . If allowing presidents to exercise their constitutional powers risks executive abuse, it also brings with it the promise of flexibility and
energy to meet the challenges of war.[51]

The American people also have a voice on this subject. Increasingly in
recent years, surveys have revealed a popular frustration—one might even
say dismay—with the quality of leadership throughout American society,
but especially among its politicians. A 2007 study by the Center for Public
Leadership at the John F. Kennedy School of Government found that more
than three quarters of Americans surveyed "now believe there is a leadership crisis in this country. . . . Fully half of all Americans, when asked how
much confidence they have in their leaders, answer 'not much' or 'none at
all.'" When asked if we have better or worse leaders today than twenty years
ago, 63 percent said "worse."[52]

Between the too weak and too powerful schools of presidential analysis
lies another group who are less troubled by the condition of the contemporary presidency. We might call this the "just right" school or the "don't
worry, we always muddle through" school. Consistent among the arguments of these defenders of the contemporary presidency are two notions.
One is that we have a long history and somehow we've always managed
to survive and prosper; presidents always seem to find a way to make the
system work, even when our backs are to the wall. The other consistent
thread in this argument is that all the alternatives to the current structure of
the American presidency might either be worse or are impossible to accomplish. That is to say, we're pretty much stuck with what we have.

Thomas Cronin, who's been writing insightfully about presidents for
more than four decades, raised grave questions about the actions of the
post-9/11 Bush administration and then posed the summary question in
his most recent book: "Is an eighteenth-century constitutional framework
adequate or well-suited to serve twenty-first-century needs?" His answer?
"I shall argue here that it is and that the Bush administration heralds an
unwelcome aberration from our cherished, yet still viable, tradition."[53]

In 2005, political scientist Andrew Rudalevige explored, yet again, the
possibility that we were confronting an "imperial president." Like Cronin,
he found much in the actions of the Bush administration that suggested
a presidency that had outgrown its constitutional boundaries. But instead
of ringing a fire bell in the night, he sought to put this recent presidential
behavior in historical perspective. "The presidency," he wrote, "is contin-
gently, not inherently, imperial."[54] The relationships among the branches of
government change constantly, he argued, and "If power in government is
defined as effective influence over governmental outcomes, then the relative
power of the legislative, judicial, and executive branches has always ebbed
and flowed over time. Across the sweep of American history, each branch

continually pushes the boundaries of its power and is met, or not, by resistance from the others. The players change, but the dance goes on."[55] No great cause for alarm here; if you're unhappy with the role of the presidency, just wait until the tide changes.

Two law professors, Eric Posner and Adrian Vermeule, take a different approach to reach the conclusion that we should stay with what we have. They examine executive institutions in a number of countries including the United States and argue that "We live in a regime of executive-centered government, in an age after the separation of powers, and the legally constrained executive is now a historical curiosity."[56] To them, it would be foolish to try to prevent presidents—or executives in any form of democratic government—from providing the kinds of essential leadership that modern governments and modern societies require. The ancient ideals of separation of powers and legislative control of executives, which they call "liberal legalism," are not only out of date but also unnecessary.

They point out that recent trends in the United States have yielded a lessening of the legal constraints on presidents, but that simultaneously there has occurred a strengthening of their political constraints. "As the bonds of law have loosened," they argue, "the bonds of politics have tightened their grip. The executive, 'unbound' from the standpoint of liberal legalism, is in some ways more constrained than ever before."[57]

What is their solution? Nothing. They suggest in the firmest tone: "executive-centered government in the administrative state is inevitable, and . . . law cannot hope to constrain the modern executive. If our claim that the administrative state also tends to produce political constraints on the executive is correct, however, liberal legalism's fears of executive tyranny are overblown."[58]

Their message to those who fear the expansion of executive power—their term is "tryrannophobia"—is don't worry. What the Constitution and the laws no longer hold in check politics now does. "There are real constraints on executive government," they conclude, "but formal constitutional procedures are not their source."[59]

What one finds in this brief review of analyses of the presidency is anything one wishes to find. Those who believe the president is too powerful and that presidential power has expanded dangerously can find arguments to that effect. So, too, can those who believe the opposite. And those who are satisfied with things as they are or who see no feasible way to make significant changes can find arguments that support the status quo.

And, of course, this is not a static literature. Each new president—in some ways, each new year—brings new evidence and new causes for concern or satisfaction. Our experience teaches us what many of the framers of the Constitution already knew: that the creation of an executive in a democracy is an enterprise that is always complicated and sometimes dangerous.

On the one hand, Americans want an executive who is competent and effective. On the other, they want an executive who will behave within proper constitutional bounds.

But between these two poles of competence and constitutional piety is the vast territory in which presidents must operate every day. Inevitably some of their actions will strike some American citizens as being out-of-bounds—and strike others as merely inadequate. And, as we have seen, such reflections often yield criticisms of the institution of the presidency and calls for reform. This is the constant energy source that fuels the steady flow of presidential analysis.

THE GOALS OF THIS BOOK

The argument here is that the contemporary presidency is a deeply flawed institution in an increasingly incompetent system of government. The presidency has become much too weak a force in domestic and economic policy and thus fails to provide the kind of leadership the country needs to meet the complex and growing demands of a changing world. The modern legislative process too often becomes a graveyard for presidential initiatives and campaign promises. Presidents are severely handicapped in their ability to direct the executive branch. The efficiency of presidential efforts to implement public policy is often undermined by congressional and judicial meddling. Endless election cycles are a constant distraction to effective leadership of the national government. The result of all these developments is a presidency that cannot provide its incumbents with the tools of competent national leadership in domestic and economic policy.

The conventional focus of analysis in studies of the American presidency is "presidential power." Richard Neustadt's seminal book bearing that name dominated much of presidential scholarship in the second half of the twentieth century. Presidential power is the focus here as well, but for our purposes that term requires a more precise definition.

Here, we will examine the current state of presidential leadership capabilities. To lead effectively, presidents require certain capacities. Those include significant abilities as both a directing and a driving force to guide the development of public policies. Presidents should be able to play a central role in shaping the national political agenda, in recommending the laws necessary to implement that agenda, and in forging the political and legislative coalitions needed to enact those laws.

To do that, presidential leadership capability has two other important components. One is the ability to construct an administration staffed by competent, creative, loyal, and energetic public officials who take their places quickly and stay in them for sustained periods. The second is the ability—essential to the development of support for presidential initiatives—to communicate with the American people in ways that are clear, inspiring, persuasive, and, when necessary, comforting.

Presidential leadership capabilities are the dependent variable in this analysis. The argument offered here will be that many of the independent variables in the American political universe—the ambiguities of the Constitution, evolution of the electoral process, decline of political parties and rise of special interest groups, alterations in the communications media, to name a few—have now accumulated in ways that deeply diminish the leadership capacities of contemporary presidents.

This shrunken role of the presidency has very significant and dangerous consequences for America in our time and in the decades that lie ahead. Only significant reform can prevent those consequences from enduring. As this analysis unfolds, it will offer a menu of options for modernizing the American presidency to fit the needs and challenges the American people now confront.

At the heart of this book is a simple notion. Leadership matters. Societies make progress when they're well governed. And government can produce that progress when it's well led. But the opposite is also true. Societies regress, sometimes even wither, when they are poorly governed. And weak leadership is the primary cause of that.

The consequences of continuing to endure the deficiencies in the American presidency are great and grave. The high hope here is that this book contributes to an understanding of those deficiencies and to a discussion that will encourage corrective efforts.

NOTES

1. James Madison, *Notes on the Debates in the Federal Convention of 1787* (New York: W.W. Norton, 1966), 135.

2. Edward S. Corwin, *The President: Office and Powers*, 4th ed. (New York: New York University Press, 1957), 5–6.

3. Thomas Paine, *Common Sense*, accessed October 3, 2015, http://www.ushistory.org/paine/commonsense/sense3.htm.

4. Charles C. Thach, "Creation of the Presidency," *Classics of the American Presidency*, edited by Harry A. Bailey, Jr. (Oak Park, IL: Moore Publishing Company, 1980), 4.

5. Richard J. Ellis, Introduction to *Founding the American Presidency*, edited by Ellis (Lanham, MD: Rowman and Littlefield, 1999), 5.

6. Ellis, *Founding the American Presidency*, 9.

7. Patrick Henry's speech to the Virginia ratifying convention, June 5, 1788, accessed October 3, 2015, http://www.constitution.org/rc/rat_va_04.htm.

8. Julian P. Boyd, ed., *The Papers of Thomas Jefferson* (Princeton, NJ: Princeton University Press, 1950–), vol. 12, 350–51.

9. Boyd, ed., *The Papers of Thomas Jefferson*, vol. 12, 396.

10. Thomas E. Cronin, Introduction to *Inventing the American Presidency*, edited by Cronin (Lawrence, KS: University of Kansas Press, 1989), xi–xii.

11. *The Writings of Abraham Lincoln*, accessed October 3, 2015, http://www.classic-literature.co.uk/american-authors/19th-century/abraham-lincoln/the-writings-of-abraham-lincoln-01/ebook-page-42.asp.

12. Woodrow Wilson, *Congressional Government: A Study in American Politics* (Boston: Houghton Mifflin, 1885), 43.

13. William E. Leuchtenberg, *In the Shadow of FDR: From Harry Truman to Barack Obama*, 4th ed. (Ithaca: Cornell University Press, 2009), ix.

14. Clinton Rossiter, *The American Presidency*, 2nd ed. (New York: New American Library, 1960), 13–14.

15. Arthur M. Schlesinger, Jr., "On Heroic Leadership and the Dilemma of Strong Men and Weak Peoples," *Encounter* 15/6 (1960): 3.

16. James David Barber, "How to Fill the Gaps in Political Biography," manuscript essay, p. 4 (Quoted by William E. Leuchtenberg, *In the Shadow of FDR*, 253).

17. Richard E. Neustadt, *Presidential Power and the Modern Presidents: The Politics of Leadership from Roosevelt to Reagan* (New York: The Free Press, 1991) was the final edition of this book.

18. Neustadt, "Memo on Presidential Transitions," *American Prospect* 3 (1992), accessed October 3, 2015, http://prospect.org/cs/articles?article=memo_on_presidential_transition.

19. James MacGregor Burns, *Running Alone: Presidential Leadership JFK to Bush II: Why It Has Failed And How We Can Fix It* (New York: Basic Books, 2006), 178.

20. Cronin, "The Textbook and Prime-Time Presidency," in *The State of the Presidency*, edited by Cronin, 2nd ed. (Boston: Little Brown, 1980), 76.

21. Quoted in "The Underdog Underdog" in *Time* (November 6, 1964).

22. Barry Goldwater, *Where I Stand* (New York: McGraw-Hill, 1964), 90.

23. Charlie Savage, *Takeover: The Return of the Imperial Presidency and the Subversion of American Democracy* (New York: Little Brown, 2007), 43.

24. Savage, *Takeover*, 9.

25. George H. W. Bush, "Remarks at Dedication Ceremony of the Social Sciences Complex at Princeton University in Princeton, New Jersey," May 10, 1991, accessed October 3, 2015, http://www.presidency.ucsb.edu/ws/index.php?pid=19573&st=&st1=#axzz1V0xdEujf.

26. Savage, *Takeover*, 282.

27. Corwin, *The President: Office and Powers*, 299.

28. Schlesinger, *The Imperial Presidency* (New York: Houghton Mifflin, 2004 ed.), ix–x.

29. Schlesinger, *The Imperial Presidency*, xxiv.

30. Garry Wills, *Bomb Power: The Modern Presidency and the National Security State* (New York: Penguin Press, 2010), 222.

31. Wills, *Bomb Power: The Modern Presidency and the National Security State*, 4.

32. Bruce Ackerman, "The New Separation of Powers," *Harvard Law Review* 113 (2000): 663.

33. William P. Marshall, "Break Up The Presidency? Governors, State Attorneys General, and Lessons From Divided Executives," *Yale Law Journal* 115 (2006): 2470.

34. Jenny S. Martinez, "Inherent Executive Power: A Comparative Perspective," *Yale Law Journal* 115 (2006): 2510–11.

35. Matthew Crenson and Benjamin Ginsberg, *Presidential Power: Unchecked and Unbalanced* (New York: W. W. Norton, 2007), 367.

36. Crenson and Ginsberg, *Presidential Power: Unchecked and Unbalanced*, 12.

37. Crenson and Ginsberg, *Presidential Power: Unchecked and Unbalanced*, 306.

38. Louis Fisher, *Constitutional Conflicts Between Congress and the President*, 5th ed. (Lawrence, KS: University of Kansas Press, 2007), 287.

39. Wilson, *Congressional Government*, 93.

40. Wilson, *Congressional Government*, 285.

41. Wilson, *Congressional Government*, 283.

42. Wilson, *Constitutional Government in the United States* (New Brunswick, NJ: Transaction Publishers, 2007), 56–57.

43. Quoted in John Milton Cooper, *Woodrow Wilson: A Biography* (New York: Alfred A. Knopf, 2009), 10.

44. Wilson, *Constitutional Government in the United States*, 70.

45. Burns, *The Deadlock of Democracy: Four-Party Politics in America* (Englewood Cliffs, New Jersey: Prentice-Hall, 1963), 324–25.

46. Burns, *Running Alone: Presidential Leadership JFK to Bush II: Why It Has Failed And How We Can Fix It*, 189–90.

47. Neustadt, *Presidential Power and the Modern Presidents*, 154.

48. Stephen Skowronek, *Presidential Leadership in Political Time* (Lawrence, KS: University of Kansas Press, 2008), xi.

49. Matthew N. Beckmann, *Pushing the Agenda: Presidential Leadership in U.S. Lawmaking, 1953–2004* (New York: Cambridge University Press, 2010), 15.

50. George C. Edwards III, *The Strategic President: Persuasion and Opportunity in Presidential Leadership* (Princeton, NJ: Princeton University Press, 2009), 188.

51. John Yoo, "Fighting The War On Terrorism Requires Relaxing Checks On Presidential Power," in *Debating the Presidency: Conflicting Perspectives on the American Executive*, edited by Richard J. Ellis and Michael Nelson (Washington, DC: CQ Press, 2010), 129.

52. Center for Public Leadership, *National Leadership Index 2007: A National Study of Confidence in Leadership* (Cambridge, MA: Center for Public Leadership, John F. Kennedy School of Government, Harvard University, 2007), 1, 20.

53. Cronin, *On The Presidency: Teacher, Soldier, Shaman, Pol* (Boulder, CO: Paradigm Publishers, 2009), 120.

54. Andrew Rudalevige, *The New Imperial Presidency* (Ann Arbor, MI: University of Michigan Press, 2005), 262.

55. Rudalevige, *The New Imperial Presidency*, 14.

56. Eric A. Posner and Adrian Vermeule, *The Executive Unbound: After the Madisonian Republic* (New York: Oxford University Press, 2010), 4.

57. Posner and Vermeule, *The Executive Unbound*, 5.

58. Posner and Vermeule, *The Executive Unbound*, 14.

59. Posner and Vermeule, *The Executive Unbound*, 61.

2

Why Presidents Disappoint

A profound discovery strikes anyone who studies the changes in the American presidency over the past century: the expectations Americans impose on their presidents frequently exceed the capacity of presidents to meet them. The American presidency at the beginning of the twenty-first century is many multiples larger and more competent than the office inhabited by Theodore Roosevelt or Woodrow Wilson. But in many ways, the duties of a president—both actual and presumed—have expanded much faster than the real authority of the presidency. The consequence is a persistent gap between expectations and reality, between goals and accomplishments. Presidents fall short of public expectations and are usually diminished in stature and power as a result. The typical contemporary presidency ends in disappointment.

This chapter explores this phenomenon by reviewing the twentieth-century expansion of the federal government and its impact on the presidency. We examine the growth in resources and capacity of the presidential office that was an inevitable consequence of the expansion of the federal role. We look, too, at the evolution of American citizens' perceptions and expectations of the president. We conclude with an examination of the gap between expectations and performance and its consequences for government in the twenty-first century.

THE FEDERAL COLOSSUS

Most popular histories trace the beginnings of big government in America to the 1930s. But the seeds were planted much earlier. By the time Herbert

Croly had published his Progressive manifesto, *The Promise of American Life*, in 1909, Theodore Roosevelt, Robert LaFollette Sr., and others of similar mind had already laid the foundation for an expanded federal establishment.

Croly offered a set of intellectual arguments for a political movement that was already at flank speed. "American government demands more rather than less centralization merely and precisely because of the growing centralization of American activity," he wrote. "The American democracy can . . . safely trust its genuine interests to the keeping of those who represent the national interest. It both can do so, and it must do so."[1]

The Progressive era was short lived. Woodrow Wilson's second term and World War I mark its political terminus. But during the decade and a half that began the twentieth century, the federal government moved steadily into the private economy and began to establish its role as a protector of those who were vulnerable to the excesses of corporate America. By 1917, the United States had a central bank and an income tax. The federal government regulated the marketing of food and drugs, meat, the railroads, and mergers among corporations.

While World War I may have marked the end of the Progressive era in domestic policy making, it continued the momentum of federal expansion. The war brought wage and price controls, federal contracting on an unprecedented scale, industrial standardization, debt financing, and widespread exercise of the most invasive act of sovereignty: conscription. It also encouraged significant and in many cases permanent enlargement of the capacity of the national government. "World War I had several distinct effects on the structure of the state": wrote political scientist Marc Eisner, "it resulted in greater centralization of authority; it required rapid bureaucratic professionalization; and it forced a search for new patterns of interest intermediation."[2]

The government that Woodrow Wilson turned over to Warren G. Harding in 1921 had much broader responsibilities and spent a good deal more money ($5.1 billion in expenditures) than the one that Theodore Roosevelt had inherited twenty years earlier ($524 million in expenditures).[3]

The pace of expansion slowed during the 1920s, but there was very little backtracking. Most of the policy initiatives of the Progressive era remained in effect and became part of the bedrock of federal activity. When the Depression forced Herbert Hoover from office and cleared the way for Franklin Roosevelt, he and his supporters in Congress built much of the New Deal on the ideas and initiatives they had learned as young Progressives. But the suffering caused by the economic catastrophe afforded them nearly unlimited opportunities to expand the federal government into areas that had been well beyond its boundaries in the past. From 1933 to 1939, federal spending more than doubled and there was a 60 percent increase in the number of civilians working for the federal government. Yet the overall numbers remained relatively small. At the end of the decade, barely a million civilians in a population of 132 million worked in the federal bureaucracy and federal spending for fiscal year 1939 was less than $9 billion.[4]

But then came the greatest war in the history of the world. And with it came mobilization on a massive scale. Federal expenditures grew to more than $100 billion by the last year of the war.[5] Millions of citizens were drafted and more than fifteen million served in uniform. Purchases of consumer goods, gasoline, meat, and many other commodities were subjected to federal rationing. Labor contracts and prices charged for goods came under the watchful eye of federal bureaucrats. Contracts for war materiel superheated the dormant economy. Federal civilian employment rose to 3.5 million. And the number of Americans paying federal income taxes grew from fewer than 4 million in 1939 to over 42 million by the end of the war, a process facilitated by the initiation of "temporary" tax withholding in 1943.[6]

Some of this was exceptional, an artifact of the war. But big government—that is, a much more pervasive and powerful federal government—was here to stay. The immediate postwar years brought several new challenges, but two loomed especially large. One was the reintegration of millions of veterans into the civilian economy. How could an economy, so recently near the brink of disaster, accommodate more than ten million jobseekers? Many of those veterans and millions of citizens looked to the federal government for answers. And answers they got: a Veterans Administration that would tend to the direct needs of individual veterans, the G.I. Bill of Rights that would provide housing and educational subsidies for veterans, and an Employment Act in 1946 in which the Congress declared "that it is the continuing policy and responsibility of the Federal Government . . . to promote maximum employment, production, and purchasing power."[7]

The other major challenge was foreign: the looming threat of the Soviet Union. The Soviets had been America's ally in the war and had suffered grievously. But they emerged from the war with a large and powerful army and an extraordinary sense of national pride and confidence. To them, the outcome of the war was an emblem of the triumph of communism and a potent incentive to seek its spread throughout the world and especially to those countries most devastated by the war itself. It was soon clear to American policy makers and strategists that the practice of military demobilization that had been followed after all previous American wars would not be prudent after this one.

So in the half decade that followed the end of World War II, the United States broadly reorganized its defense establishment, maintained a large standing army and naval presence all over the world, and developed a

national security policy called "Containment" that would guide its international activities for much of the next half century.

The broad reach of the federal government, which most Americans take
for granted now, did not occur in an instant or an hour. It was the product
of more than a century of experience, and it was driven by a multitude of
causes. In part, the growth of the federal government was a response to
changes in American society and the American economy. As the economy
nationalized and local producers gave way to large corporations, states
were overwhelmed in their efforts to prevent market excesses and to protect workers and consumers. Only the federal government had sufficient
scope to accomplish that. New technologies like electricity, airplanes, and
radio often yielded a demand for federal subsidies or federal regulation to
smooth the development of commercial implementation.

The Depression escalated the call for and weakened the opposition to a
federal pension system, federally subsidized employment, and welfare payments to children and vulnerable families. World War II and its aftermath
and the invention of the atomic bomb and its acquisition by American
adversaries created and institutionalized the national security state.

And then there was the ratcheting effect that came with all of this. As one
important study of federal expansion has noted, "the federal government
increased in size because it increased in scope."[8] Once a particular function
came under the jurisdiction of the federal government, once the political
decision had been made that something was an appropriate federal activity, then the question for the future was less likely to be whether the federal
government should be doing something but rather how much—most often,
how much more—it should be doing. For example, in 1937, the Social
Security Act was amended to create the National Institutes of Health—a
federal agency largely engaged in health-related research. Once the decision
had been made that basic medical research was an appropriate federal activity then the questions followed: What kinds of research and how much?
The answers steadily expanded the scope of federal activity: Mental Health
(1946); Allergy and Infectious Disease (1948); Dental Health (1948);
Heart, Lung, and Blood (1948); Arthritis, Metabolism, and Digestive Diseases (1950); Child Health and Human Development (1962); General
Medical Sciences, to cover diseases that did not have their own institutes
(1963); Alcohol Prevention and Drug Abuse (1966); Environmental Health
Science (1966); Eye Institute (1968); Aging (1974); and Neurological and
Communicative Disorders (1976).[9]

As the prominent political scientist James Q. Wilson noted in his analysis
of the fundamental changes affecting American politics:

> Until rather recently, the chief issue in any congressional argument over
> new policies was whether it was legitimate for the federal government to do

something at all. . . . Once the legitimacy barrier has fallen, political conflict takes a very different form. New programs need not await the advent of a crisis or an extraordinary majority, because no program is any longer "new"—it is seen, rather, as an extension, modification, or an enlargement of something the government is already doing. Congressmen will argue about "how much," or "where," or "what kind," but not about "whether." . . . Since there is virtually nothing the government has not tried to do, there is little it cannot be asked to do.[10]

The establishment of a large federal presence in the economy, the steady expansion of responsibilities and problems deemed legitimate areas of federal jurisdiction, the inevitability of international obligation for a military superpower in a nuclear age: all of these have yielded a federal government role vastly different from the one imagined by the country's founders. Each stage in this expansion has put new stresses on the institutions and processes of government, even on the Constitution itself. A government designed for a country of 3 million citizens before industrialization and urbanization, in a world of rare external threat, has often been severely challenged by the new trials it has encountered over time.

Inevitably, the expansion of the federal government deeply altered the role of its leader, the American president. When activities in Washington were little more than a peripheral presence in the lives of most Americans, the president had little to do and was rarely seen or heard. But more and more, as Americans looked to the national government to help them solve their problems, the president became the focus of their demands and expectations. And the president, standing largely alone as the government around him ballooned, was forced to find new and better ways to respond.

THE PRESIDENT NEEDS HELP

When spring rounded into summer each year in the first decade of the twentieth century, Washington became a ghost town. Congress adjourned, often for the year. Its members returned to their "real jobs" back home. The bureaucracy, such as it was, slowed to a near standstill, performing only those functions that could not be deferred until fall. And Theodore Roosevelt headed to Sagamore Hill, the family estate at Oyster Bay on Long Island. He spent his days and nights there largely in the company of his rambunctious children. The government made only small claim on his attention, as his biographer Edmund Morris describes:

No matter where Roosevelt spent the night, his presence was required in the library at Sagamore Hill every weekday at 8:30 A.M. Secretary Cortelyou, oily and purposeful as an otter, would come up the drive with a leather bag full of mail, and for the next few hours "typing machines" would click, and a Morse transmitter rattle, as he and the President dispatched affairs of state. Since the government was in recess, their business was neither copious nor demanding. Cortelyou was usually on his way by noon, and Roosevelt, looking like a large plump urchin in negligee shirt, linen knickers, and canvas shoes would play a set of tennis before lunch.[11]

Two decades later, not much had changed. Washington still emptied out in the summer. Calvin Coolidge made long visits to the family farm in Vermont and took lengthy vacations at other spots around the country. In 1927, he enjoyed the Black Hills of South Dakota so much that he stayed three months instead of the planned three weeks. He managed the business of the country from a small summer office in the high school at Rapid City, where he announced his decision not to seek reelection in 1928 by posting a handwritten note on the door.

Even in cooler months in these years before air conditioning, the pace of life in Washington imposed few burdens on presidents. Peacetime federal expenditures stayed below $4 billion through the 1920s. There were few lobbyists or reporters in the nation's capital. Foreign affairs consumed little of a president's attention or time. Foreign leaders rarely came to visit and presidents did not travel outside the country. The White House was essentially that: a house. Presidents worked downstairs, but few others worked there with them. Most of those who did were clerks or secretaries. The entire budget for the president's staff and office expenses under Calvin Coolidge was about $80,000 a year.[12]

That's not to say there weren't issues that caused some concerns about how the government was led and managed. William Howard Taft believed the primary responsibility of the president was to assure the efficient and economical management of the policies enacted by Congress. But he worried that presidents were not adequately equipped for that task and he appointed a commission to study the management of the federal government. This was the first of many such commissions that would appear over the decades that followed.

This Commission on Economy and Efficiency—often called the Taft Commission—considered a number of what today would be labeled management issues, but focused its heaviest attention on the absence of a national budget. Indeed, its report was titled *The Need for a National Budget*. For all of our history up to that time, the president had largely been a bystander in the annual budgeting process. Presidents could recommend certain expenditures or revenue measures to the Congress, but there was no annual process of rounding up the expenditure estimates from the departments and subjecting them to a central review or discipline before sending them to Congress. In most cases, the departments dealt directly with their counterparts in Congress and the president was on the sidelines.

The Taft Commission recommended the establishment of an annual budgeting process in which the departments would send their estimates to the president who would review and, if desired, make changes in them before submitting an annual executive budget recommendation for the entire government to Congress. Since this would be a larger task than presidents had ever before been expected to perform, the Commission recommended the creation of an executive agency, a bureau of the budget, to assist the president.[13]

The political context is noteworthy here. Though not the policy activist that Theodore Roosevelt had been, Taft was a genuine Progressive. And he shared the Progressive view that the president was, as the Commission stated, "the one officer of Government who represents the people as a whole."[14] In a time when politics was often little more than conflict among factions, the Progressives offered the then novel view that the presidency was a representative institution, and its constituency was the entire country. It was therefore essential in their view that the president have the opportunity and authority to represent the national interest in the most important of all government functions: the getting and spending of the people's money.

But not everyone agreed. The Commission offered its recommendation just as Taft was losing his bid for reelection. Woodrow Wilson, who succeeded him, supported the concept of a national budget, but Congress was less enthusiastic. The Congress was going through a major transition in the second decade of the twentieth century, having replaced one organization of power in which the Speaker dominated with another in which standing committees and their chairs became the major beneficiaries. Those newly empowered committee chairs were not eager to surrender any of their control over federal expenditures to an untried but potentially risky new budget process, nor were they ready to breach their long-standing direct relationships with the departments. "The idea of the budget was something new," notes historian Jonathan Kahn, "and the need for it was not self-evident."[15]

So the Taft Commission proposal lingered on the back burner of national politics for almost a decade. But the growth of the federal government during Woodrow Wilson's first term and the exigencies of mobilizing for World War I in his second forcefully demonstrated the need for a better system of managing national finances. Finally, in 1921, the Congress acted. The Budget and Accounting Act of 1921 created the first national budget process and provided a significant role for the president.

This was an executive-centered budget process, but it was not executive controlled. The act established the Bureau of the Budget to assist the president in reviewing departmental estimates and preparing the annual submission to Congress. But there was no formal presidential office at the time, so the Bureau of the Budget was located in the Treasury Department.

The Congress was quite clear in noting that the bureau's functions would be managerial not political, that its staff would not be subject to the ebb and flow of elections but would instead be composed of people chosen for their "neutral competence." Its mission, noted political scientists Roderick Kiewit and Matthew D. McCubbins, was to provide "impartial policy analysis and independent judgment."[16]

The Congress further hedged its bets by moving the Treasury's auditing functions into a new agency, the General Accounting Office, in the legislative branch. And, of course, the Congress retained ultimate control over all revenues and expenditures by underscoring the requirement that all must be enacted in law. The president could now propose, but only the Congress could dispose.

Nevertheless, the Budget and Accounting Act of 1921 signaled the beginning of a new phase in the development of the American presidency. The president's role in national affairs had expanded. As the federal government began to grow, the responsibilities of the presidency grew as well. The Budget Act created new resources to assist the president in performing this expanded role. And, at least to those of Progressive bent, the president's unique representational obligation to speak for all the people in the factional debates of politics was certified.

If the effects of this evolution were not immediately apparent in the somnolent governance of the 1920s, they would be soon. Three great forces coalesced in the middle decades of the twentieth century to impel the establishment of what has come to be called the modern presidency. Two of these were clearly emergent in the 1930s, the third would arrive a decade later.

One, of course, was the rapid and broad expansion of the federal government's domestic policy agenda that occurred with the response to the Depression. The early years of the New Deal were a time of frenetic government building. Much of this was characterized as the "response to an emergency" and "temporary." Some of it was. The Works Progress Administration, Civilian Conservation Corps, National Industrial Recovery Act and others came quickly and were gone by the end of the decade. But much was not temporary. New Deal inventions like agricultural subsidies, Social Security, bank and securities regulation, collective bargaining rights, and many other products of that decade remain at the core of government functions today.

Irrespective of the fates of individual programs, the concept of an essential federal role in the national economy was deeply and permanently embedded during this time. There would be no turning back from that. Franklin Roosevelt spoke of the "changed concept of the duty and responsibility of government toward economic life."[17] The historian Eric Foner pointed out that the Depression "transformed expectations of government,

reinvigorating the Progressive conviction that the national state must protect Americans from the vicissitudes of the marketplace . . . the New Deal
recast the idea of freedom by linking it to the expanding power of the
national state."[18]

A second prop for the modern presidency was the invention of new
forms of mass communication technology. It is well to remember that
the president who coined the term "bully pulpit" never really had one.
Theodore Roosevelt never spoke into a microphone that amplified his voice
and was never heard on commercial radio. No American president could
speak to an audience beyond those in his immediate presence before 1920
when the first commercial radio station, KDKA in Pittsburgh, went on the
air. The early days of radio were of little value to presidents of the 1920s.
There were few broadcast stations and few homes had receiving sets. Neither Harding nor Coolidge found radio of much value. Hoover began to
speak on radio more often, but some of his associates thought it a platform
unworthy of a president.[19] No real plan emerged for strategic use of the new
medium, despite the initial appearance of national networks and the growing popularity of radio sets in American homes.

For Franklin Roosevelt, however, radio was a godsend. By the time of
his inauguration, radio stations were springing up all over the country, the
radio networks had captured the national imagination and begun to take
hold of the popular culture, and a radio set had become an essential device
in more than two-thirds of American homes. More Americans had a radio
in their home than a telephone.[20]

Franklin Roosevelt saw his opportunities and he took them. He used the
radio in several ways, but most famously for "fireside chats" with the American people. There weren't many of these—one every five months on average
over his more than twelve years in office—but they were timed strategically
to permit him to calm national fears and to explain his policy initiatives in
response to the Depression and later in the war against Germany and Japan.

This began an important and enduring element of the modern presidency: what political scientist Samuel Kernell has called "going public."
Presidents after Roosevelt could not disregard the powerful instruments of
mass communication that were now theirs to use. By the 1950s television
had become the dominant mode of presidential communication. Later in
this book, we will explore in more depth the significant impact of these
technologies, first as a source of significant opportunity for presidents and
later—as the communications media evolved—as a burden for presidents
to bear. But since Roosevelt's time, every administration has had to include
communication strategies as a central part of its efforts to lead the country.

When Roosevelt sought to focus America's attention on the growing threat
arising in Japan and Germany, he confronted—and was often tightly constrained by—a deep-seated American devotion to isolationism. In August

1941, for example, Roosevelt asked Congress to extend the military draft it had initially approved in the previous year. This came at a time when Japanese military power was spreading rapidly through Asia; and Germany, having conquered most of the nations of Western Europe, had carried out a devastating aerial blitz of London. Yet so strong were America's isolationist impulses, that Roosevelt's request passed the House by only a single vote.

But isolationism could not survive the attack on Pearl Harbor. And when World War II ended, everything had changed. Two superpowers, with competing philosophies and each soon possessing unprecedented weapons of destruction, loomed over the postwar world. In an age of long-distance bombers and intercontinental ballistic missiles, America's geographical protections no longer mattered very much. America was a major player on the international stage, and American presidents could not avoid the responsibilities and burdens that came with that new reality.

All of this—the expanding domestic agenda, the opportunities provided by new communications media, and the pressures of the Cold War—changed the American presidency very deeply. Early in that evolution it became clear the presidents were ill equipped for this steady increase in burdens and responsibilities. At the end of his first term, Franklin Roosevelt appointed a Committee on Administrative Management to study the evolving role of the president and to recommend improvements in the president's capacity to manage the federal government. The Brownlow Committee (as it came to be called after its chair Louis Brownlow) issued a report in 1937 that assessed the growing burdens on the presidency and stated simply, "The president needs help."[21]

The Congress initially resisted most of the recommendations of the Brownlow Committee, but in 1939 it passed an Administrative Reorganization Act that authorized the employment of six staff assistants and gave the president the authority to recommend future government reorganization plans to Congress. Roosevelt used that authority in 1939 to establish an Executive Office of the President (EOP). He subsequently issued Executive Order 8248 to define the components of the new Executive Office—creating a White House Office within the EOP and transferring the Bureau of the Budget there from the Treasury Department.[22]

While presidents had found ways to procure staff assistance in the past, this marked the first formal recognition that the presidency was an institution not simply a person. And it also signified a new understanding that the responsibilities of presidents had expanded to the point where no single individual could be expected to manage them alone or with merely ad hoc support. Presidents would always need help.

In the years that followed, the EOP grew to include a diversity of functions, most of them established by statute. And as the array of functions under the president's purview expanded, the number of people working in the EOP and the annual cost of that enterprise expanded as well. By Fiscal Year 2010, $830 million was appropriated for the EOP.[23] This doesn't cover all the costs of that office. Some—the cost of operating Air Force One, for example—are included in other budgets, and some are classified. According to a detailed study by Bradley Patterson of the Brookings Institution, the staffing levels in 2007 for the 135 units that compose the EOP totaled 6,574.[24]

By the end of the Nixon administration, the formal structure of the Executive Office had stabilized, and the contemporary structure is similar to what it was then. The presidency, in the terminology preferred by political scientists, had become "institutionalized." While newly elected presidents retain substantial latitude in choosing the people who serve in the Executive Office, especially in its core element the White House Office, the formal structure of that office changes little from one administration to the next.

But what do these hundreds of people do, these people who compose what we think of as the White House staff? They do many things. They recruit personnel to fill out the thousands of executive appointments a president must make. They schedule and manage the logistics of the president's extensive travels in the United States and abroad. They write the president's speeches. They oversee social events at the White House and presidential interactions with the steady stream of foreign leaders who visit there. They monitor national security matters, oversee all new rules and regulations issued by the departments, coordinate the preparation of the national budget and the president's annual economic report.

But more than anything else, the people who work for the president help him to cope with the intricate and incessant political relationships that have become the primary characteristic of modern presidential leadership. The administrative burdens of the presidency are large and constant, and they explain a significant portion of the growth of the institutionalized presidency. But an equally powerful explanation is the expansion in the complexity and difficulty of the politics and political relationships a president must manage to have any hope of accomplishing policy objectives or retaining public support. Scores of White House aides spend their days speaking with and for special interests, responding to the queries of journalists and seeking to shape their reporting, roaming Capitol Hill in pursuit of support for presidential initiatives, and planning and implementing the president's travel and outreach strategies.

"We find that presidential staff growth is driven primarily by changes in presidents' bargaining relations with Congress, the media, and the public, and only secondarily by a general growth in government's responsibilities," conclude political scientists Matthew Dickinson and Matthew Lebo in one of the most careful recent studies of the institutionalization in the presidency. "The White House Office," they conclude, "is predominantly a political office; its members assist the president primarily by providing information and advice pertaining to his political interests."[25]

In many ways, it would appear that the evolution of the presidency from the limited model envisioned in the Brownlow Committee report to its contemporary size and reach would substantially increase the power of the president to shape policies and events. Modern presidents are temporary employees. They enter the slipstream of history and must function in a permanent government of structures, protocols, and relationships that precede their arrival and will survive their departure. Presidents benefit from the increased competence at the top of the branch of government they lead. With the support they now possess, contemporary presidents can travel broadly, speak often, consult widely, maintain dizzying daily schedules, and relax when necessary at Camp David or other comfortable places of their choosing.

But as political scientist John P. Burke noted in his study of White House enlargement, staff growth "has proven to be a double-edged sword. Presidents have fared better and worse with staff assistance. Some have understood the challenge that a large-scale staff presents. . . . Other presidents have been less successful, failing to devise strategies and tactics of management for making the White House staff work effectively."[26]

To Richard Neustadt, concerns over unity of purpose in the White House staff grew larger as the staff expanded. "Only those who see the President repeatedly can grasp what he is driving at and help him or dispute him," Neustadt wrote. "Everybody else there is a menace to him. Not understanding, they spread wrong impressions. Keeping busy, they take their concerns for his."[27]

With every expansion in the presidency has grown a tendency for it to become a magnet for thorny issues and difficult decisions. Much of what used to get done in the agencies and departments now floats to the top and ends up on the White House agenda. Matters great and small command the president's attention and clog the decision-making channels. In 2001, for example, weeks of White House staff time and many hours on the schedule of President George W. Bush—"months of listening and reflecting," he called it—were filled with intense internal deliberations over the issue of fetal stem cell research.[28] In the past, one can readily imagine, this would have been a matter resolved in the Department of Health and Human Services. But like nearly all issues these days, this one had a political valence. And that drove it to the White House.

In addition, it's important to note that the institutionalization of the presidency has created a new bureaucracy—or, one might argue, a counter-bureaucracy. Much of what goes on in the executive office is an effort to oversee, direct, and often countermand the actions of bureaucrats and even presidential appointees in the agencies and departments. And the presidential bureaucracy is subject to many of the pathologies common to all bureaucracies: over specialization, confused lines of authority and accountability, turf battles, and constant self-aggrandizement.

These are perennial problems that afflict every president. "Throughout my political career," wrote Gerald Ford in his memoirs, "nothing upset me more than bickering among members of my staff. It was time-consuming, terribly distracting and unnecessary. I had told my aides I wouldn't tolerate it. But it continued, even accelerated, when I entered the White House and—given the ambitions and personalities of the people involved—there didn't seem to be any way to put an immediate stop to it."[29]

We have seen, too, the opportunities for scandal and embarrassment to the president that can occur in a larger, more bureaucratized White House. When the scale of White House operations makes it impossible for presidents to maintain close personal relationships with many of their aides, sometimes those aides go off on their own. Senators William Cohen and George Mitchell described such White House staff activities in their book about the Iran-Contra scandal:

> Burning with patriotic zeal, intoxicated by the power and trappings of high public office, convinced beyond any doubt of the rightness of their cause, bristling with contempt for those who lacked their power and certainty, especially those in the Congress, a handful of men tried to use the powerful machinery of the United States government to achieve their mission.[30]

The irony, then, is that while the growth in presidential capacity may have served recent presidents well in some ways, it has complicated their job in others. A larger presidential establishment inevitably draws more issues to the White House and forces more decisions to the top. The president may have more help in doing his work, but there is much more work to do. More, and more independent, staff members increase the opportunities for self-indulgence and self-dealing, not infrequently to the president's detriment.

And with the expansion of the presidency has come an even greater expansion of demands upon the president and a heightening of expectations for presidential performance. This has created a gap, an enduring gap between what is expected of presidents and what they can actually deliver in response.

SUPERHERO

Jimmy Carter entered the White House with the promise that he would take the presidency to the people. And, for a while at least, he sought to do that. Less than two months after his inauguration, he journeyed to Clinton,

Massachusetts, to hold the first of several "town meetings." The questions he was asked that night suggest the range of issues for which the American people now hold their presidents responsible: peace in the Middle East, the effect of oil spills on fisheries, regulation of trucking, closure of a local army base, veterans' benefits, abortions, college tuitions, health insurance, judicial appointments, protection of small businesses, and the minimum wage. But the president was also asked about paving problems on a local road and the revitalization of Clinton's downtown.[31] The citizens who were present that night expected the president to speak knowledgeably on all these issues and to have plans in place to deal with all of them as well.

Most Americans bear these same expectations: that the president will have an opinion and a policy on every issue that affects their lives. The president has become the focal point of American public life, the surrogate in many citizens' minds for "the government." Presidents are expected to oversee a healthy economy and fix a sick one, to ensure the freedom of the marketplace but to protect against its excesses, to keep the country and its people safe from external threat. Even two decades after the end of the Cold War, it was possible for one candidate in the 2008 election to cast doubt on her opponent by asking in a televised ad "It's 3:00 AM, your children are safe and asleep, but there's a phone in the White House and it's ringing. Who do you want answering the phone?"[32]

"The chief executive of the United States is no longer a mere constitutional officer charged with faithful execution of the laws," writes Gene Healy of the Cato Institute. "He is a soul nourisher, a hope giver, a living American talisman against hurricanes, terrorism, economic downturns, and spiritual malaise. He—or she—is the one who answers the phone at 3 a.m. to keep our children safe from harm. The modern president is America's shrink, a social worker, our very own national talk show host. He's also the Supreme Warlord of the Earth."[33]

Political scientist Stanley Renshon suggests that as the role of the federal government expanded, "this trend was accompanied by the belief that we must look to the president as the 'engine of progress,' the savior of the political system, the fulcrum of the entire governmental system."[34]

Where do these expectations come from?

One answer is that they come from presidents themselves, when they are candidates for that office. Campaign rhetoric in America has always soared beyond the reasonable boundaries of presidential capacity. Candidates do not win elections by describing the limits on what presidents can accomplish but rather by suggesting the absence of such limits. Americans want their presidents to be superheroes and are willing to suspend disbelief when candidates for that office don their rhetorical capes. In 1964, Lyndon Johnson repeatedly minimized the conflict in Vietnam by saying: "Some others are eager to enlarge the conflict. They call upon the U.S. to supply

American boys to do the job that Asian boys should do. We are not about to send American boys nine or ten thousand miles away from home to do what Asian boys ought to be doing for themselves. We don't want to get . . . tied down to a land war in Asia."[35]

While it was widely reported in 1968 that candidate Richard Nixon had a "secret plan" to end the war in Vietnam, Nixon never used those words himself and disavowed them in his memoirs.[36] But he raised no objection during the campaign to reports of his secret plan and when asked for details would usually respond that to provide details would be to tip his hand and interfere with the negotiations underway in Paris.[37]

In 1980, Ronald Reagan promised a balanced budget within three years and a 30 percent decrease in tax rates over that same period. He promised as well to eliminate the Department of Energy.

George H. W. Bush, channeling Clint Eastwood, assured his party's convention that "My opponent won't rule out raising taxes. But I will. And the Congress will push me to raise taxes, and I'll say no, and they'll push, and I'll say no, and they'll push again, and I'll say, to them, 'Read my lips: no new taxes.'"

Bill Clinton promised to end the ban on military service by gays and lesbians "with the stroke of a pen." "When it comes to AIDS," he also said, "there should be a Manhattan Project." He suggested that "With the dwindling Soviet threat, we can cut defense spending over a third by 1997." "Vote for me," he told a campaign audience in Dallas, "and we'll conserve more energy all over America."[38]

In his second debate with Al Gore, George W. Bush described his foreign policy philosophy by saying,

> I'm not sure the role of the United States is to go around the world and say this is the way it's got to be. I want to empower people. I want to help people help themselves, not have government tell people what to do. I just don't think it's the role of the United States to walk into a country and say, we do it this way, so should you . . . we can't be all things to all people in the world. I am worried about over-committing our military around the world. I want to be judicious in its use. I don't think nation-building missions are worthwhile.[39]

In 2008, the website PolitiFact.com (which won the Pulitzer Prize for national reporting on the election) carefully counted Barack Obama's campaign promises: 510 in all.[40]

So one powerful contributor to citizens' expectations of presidential performance is the inflated promises that candidates make when they seek that office. Candidates set a bar much higher than the real powers of the presidency permit them to hurdle once in office.

But the promising and elevating of expectations doesn't end with the campaign. Presidents, once in office, are as likely to make unrealistic and often unfulfillable promises as they did when campaigning. Lyndon Johnson's State of the Union Address in 1965 affords an example of this kind of over-promising:

> I propose that we begin a program in education to ensure every American child the fullest development of his mind and skills. I propose that we begin a massive attack on crippling and killing diseases. I propose that we launch a national effort to make the American city a better and a more stimulating place to live. I propose that we increase the beauty of America and end the poisoning of our rivers and the air that we breathe. I propose that we carry out a new program to develop regions of our country that are now suffering from distress and depression. I propose that we make new efforts to control and prevent crime and delinquency. I propose that we eliminate every remaining obstacle to the right and the opportunity to vote. I propose that we honor and support the achievements of thought and the creations of art. I propose that we make an all-out campaign against waste and inefficiency.[41]

The difference between this presidential address and most State of the Union Addresses is one of degree, not kind. Presidents always make promises that exceed their capacities to deliver on them. As the Washington journalists Spencer Rich and David Hess have noted, "Every year, presidents deliver a State of the Union message describing their hopes, goals and plans for the nation. Millions of Americans tune in to the televised speech and listen attentively, believing the chief executive will succeed in all his aims. Many are certain it will happen. But they are bound to be disappointed. Just because the president mentions a proposal does not mean it will be enacted—or even that he will really push it."[42]

It is incumbent upon presidents—or so they have all believed—that they be optimists in their public presentations, that they must have auspicious goals and convey the sense that government can accomplish those goals. When Jimmy Carter took the unusual step in a national address in 1979 of suggesting the reality of national limits, noting that "all the legislation in the world can't fix what's wrong with America," and suggesting a "crisis in the growing doubt about the meaning of our own lives and in the loss of a unity of purpose for our nation," he was widely criticized, even by many in his own administration.[43] Vice President Walter Mondale thought the tone and approach of the speech a "dead end."[44] Reread now, that speech seems like a statement of contemporary conservative philosophy, but Ronald Reagan hastened to join the chorus of its critics in 1979 and during his campaign in 1980. He told the Republican Convention that nominated him,

> The . . . Democratic Party leadership, in the White House and in the Congress . . . tell us they've done the most that could humanly be done. They say that the United States has had its day in the sun, that our nation has passed

its zenith. They expect you to tell your children that the American people no longer have the will to cope with their problems, that the future will be one of sacrifice and few opportunities. My fellow citizens, I utterly reject that view.[45]

The citizen disappointment that often afflicts contemporary presidents is, in no small part, self-inflicted. They raise hopes that they cannot fulfill, make promises that they cannot deliver. In so doing, they set standards for achievement that nearly always yield incompletion, shortfall, or failure.

Presidents are also haunted by the legacy of their most prominent predecessors, often a legacy freighted with mythology. Since his administration ended several generations ago, the Franklin Roosevelt image has haunted his successors, especially the Democrats. Roosevelt swept into office on a popular tide, repeatedly fired up the citizenry with his speeches, conquered the Great Depression, and then vanquished the Axis devils in a war. His efforts exhausted and ultimately killed him, and he died a hero's death. At least that's the image that lingers—an image that later presidents could not escape.

John Kennedy's legacy looms large in another way. Kennedy's, we are reminded, was an era of glamour and style. The handsome president, the beautiful young wife, the delightful children, and the surrounding cast of family, celebrities, and athletes all effect an image that no modern president—no real president—can match. We long for a time when problems seemed definable and solvable, as they did then, when national resources were growing at a record pace, when Americans in large percentages trusted the government in Washington.

Ronald Reagan's legacy is an additional burden for his successors. We are reminded, especially by Republican candidates for the office he once held, of the "Reagan revolution": that he won the Cold War, cut taxes, and shrunk the national government. The reality is much more complex, but the lingering image of Ronald Reagan is built, as the journalists Lou Cannon and Carl Cannon suggest on a good deal of "selective amnesia."[46] The contours of the Reagan revolution are hard to define, perhaps even hard to perceive, but it persists as rhetorical reality. "Each of Reagan's successors," political scientist Stephen Skowronek writes, "has been subject to political expectations that he set."[47]

Each of these presidents—and a few others who survive and shine in memory—struggled much harder with the tasks they faced and succeeded much less often than our recollections admit. Yet we permit them to set the standard for any contemporary president—without a nuanced appreciation for the full story of their administrations. As political scientist Thomas Cronin suggests, "Those we remember as 'great presidents' are remembered primarily for their military victories and humanitarian vision, though—looking through our rose-tinted retrospective glasses—we remember even these presidents on their best days."[48]

Then there is the president of film and fiction: Josiah Bartlet of TV's *The West Wing*, James Marshall in the film *Air Force One*, Andrew Shepherd of *The American President*, Jack Ryan in Tom Clancy's novels *Executive Orders* and *The Bear and the Dragon*. There are many fictional depictions of incompetent and corrupt presidents, but the books that sell best and the films that gross the most typically treat presidents as humans with, if not super powers, remarkable wisdom, patience, courage, integrity, compassion, and good looks. They have beautiful wives and exemplary children or—in the case of President Shepherd in *The American President*—they are widowers with extraordinary romantic possibilities (a first date at a State Dinner, a weekend of courting at Camp David. . . .) They avoid anything that smacks of dirty politics, their political opponents are usually devious and craven, their aides suggest shortcuts around constitutional limits which they brush aside. They make decisions without dithering and implement them forcefully. Their actions and policies always turn out for the best and serve the American people well.

Mike McCurry, a political analyst and press secretary to President Clinton, said of the fictional Josiah Bartlet, who appeared each week on *The West Wing* and against whom Clinton was judged: "President Bartlet is, I think, every American's idea of what they think the president should be. He has the compassion and integrity of Jimmy Carter; he's got that shrewd decision-making and hard-nosed realism of a Richard Nixon; he's got the warmth and amiability and the throw-the-arm-around-the-shoulder of a Bill Clinton; and he's got the liberal passion of a Teddy Kennedy."[49]

Real presidents can't live up to these fictional counterparts. The burdens they bear, the opposition they face can't be scripted away. But the comparisons are inevitable, and the real presidents are never elevated in the public mind as a consequence.

Presidents in reality rarely equal the image of the ideal president that endures in the public mind. However often Americans are disappointed by the presidents they elect, they persist in believing that presidential possibilities and capacities are far more expansive than historical experience demonstrates. If only Franklin Roosevelt or Ronald Reagan could rise from their graves and return to the White House, many citizens believe, these problems we face now could be solved.

But it not's that simple. "We make it hard, if not impossible, for presidents to live up to our expectations, yet we are unforgiving critics when presidents disappoint us," Thomas Cronin writes. "Presidents have, on occasion, been tremendously consequential for this nation, yet we generally exaggerate the capacity of presidents to shape their times."[50] Indeed we do, yet we are undeterred in our expectations.

THE EXPECTATIONS-REALITY GAP

We began this chapter by tracing the expanding role of the federal government over the past century. We then noted the enlargement of the institutional presidency that coincided with the growth in presidential responsibilities in this ever-larger federal enterprise. We enter the twenty-first century with a presidency that has large and diverse resources.

Yet, contemporary presidents are in a constant and often unsuccessful struggle to provide the kinds of leadership that the American people demand and the American government requires, especially in domestic and economic policy. The expansion of the presidency, in role and resources, has not yielded an equal expansion in presidential power or capacity.

The president envisioned by many Americans is much more powerful and sure-handed than the president in reality. And when presidents in office fail to live up to these unrealistic expectations, they become discredited. They lose popular support—a primary resource for overcoming their constitutional limitations. With the erosion of popular support, presidential capability rapidly diminishes, not infrequently to the vanishing point.

Summarizing an extensive literature on popular expectations of presidents, political scientist Richard W. Waterman and his colleagues conclude: "expectations are seen as shaping evaluations. Since expectations are excessive and contradictory, evaluations of presidential performance are negatively affected, which then constrains actual presidential performance (i.e., the president's ability to get things done)."[51]

For more than half a century, the Gallup Poll has asked a sample of the American people each month to rate the job the incumbent president is doing. These job approval ratings are not a perfect measure of popular perceptions of the president, but they are a consistent and reliable indicator of patterns of support over time. The characteristic trend in eight of the ten administrations since 1960 is that popular approval of the president's performance has declined over the course of an administration. In nine of those ten administrations, the president at some point during his term has commanded the support of less than half the respondents.

We should not be surprised. We are always disappointed in people who don't live up to our expectations. Presidents are no different—except, perhaps, that our expectations are so out of line with the real abilities of the people we elect and the real character of the powers with which we invest them. As political scientist Charles O. Jones has written: "expectations of a president often far exceed the individual's personal, political, institutional, or constitutional capacities for achievement. Performance seldom matches promise."[52]

The gap between real capacity and public perceptions is a major contributor to the disappointment that Americans commonly feel in assessing their presidents. Presidents frequently fall short of public expectations because the expectations are unrealistic.

But the problem is not simply that popular expectations are too high or unrealistic. It is not unreasonable that Americans should expect competent leadership and effective job performance from their presidents. But for many of the tasks they face, presidents either lack the authority necessary to meet popular expectations or find themselves encased in a system of governance that constantly thwarts their best efforts to meet the expectations of the people who elected them. Louis Brownlow, the chair of Franklin Roosevelt's Committee on Administrative Management, wrote more than thirty years after the publication of the Committee's report, "The nation expects more of the President than he can possibly do, more than we give him either the authority or the means to do. Thus, expecting from him the impossible, inevitably we shall be disappointed in his performance."[53]

David Gergen, who served on the White House staffs of four contemporary presidents, describes the problem this way: "Expectations of what a president can accomplish have escalated dramatically, while his capacity for action has diminished even more."[54]

Historian James MacGregor Burns sees a similar problem:

> Historians have been too critical of recent presidents. Kennedy was right: scholars have little grasp of the complexity of the hour-to-hour problems that stream into the White House. But the problem is deeper—it is institutional. . . . American political leaders are trying to govern through an eighteenth-century constitution that frustrates collective action and diffuses accountability.[55]

This is the central problem of governance confronting America in the twenty-first century. How do we align the expectations of the American people, the long-term needs of the country, and the leadership capacities of the presidency? The American people want more from their government than government can deliver. They want more from their presidents than presidents are able to provide. Popular disappointment in government, and eventually disaffection and contempt, are the common result.

NOTES

1. Herbert Croly, *The Promise of American Life* (Boston: Northeastern University Press, 1989), 17, 270, 274–75.

2. Marc Allen Eisner, *From Warfare State to Welfare State: World War I, Compensatory State Building, and the Limits of the Modern Order* (University Park, PA: Penn State University Press, 2000), 34.

3. U. S. Bureau of the Census, *Statistical Abstract of the United States, 1925* (Washington, DC: Government Printing Office, 1926), 157.

4. U. S. Bureau of the Census, *Statistical Abstract of the United States, 1941* (Washington, DC: Government Printing Office, 1942), 168, 179.

5. U. S. Bureau of the Census, *Statistical Abstract of the United States, 1947* (Washington, DC: Government Printing Office, 1948), 316.

6. U. S. Bureau of the Census, *Statistical Abstract of the United States, 1947*, 325.

7. Section 2, *Public Law 79-304*, "The Employment Act of 1946."

8. Hugh Rockoff, "By Way of Analogy: The Expansion of the Federal Government in the 1930s," in *The Defining Moment: The Great Depression and the American Economy in the Twentieth Century*, edited by Michael D. Bordo, Claudia Goldin, and Eugene N. White (Chicago: University of Chicago Press, 1998), 131.

9. Hugh Rockoff, "By Way of Analogy: The Expansion of the Federal Government in the 1930s," 147.

10. James Q. Wilson, *American Politics, Then & Now, and Other Essays* (Washington, DC: AEI Press, 2010), 8.

11. Edmund Morris, *Theodore Rex* (New York: Random House, 2001), 125.

12. John P. Burke, *The Institutional Presidency: Organizing and Managing the White House from FDR to Clinton*, 2nd ed. (Baltimore: Johns Hopkins University Press, 2000), 4.

13. On the Taft Commission in general, see Robert S. Kravchuk and James W. Douglas, "The Centennial of the Taft Commission: The Executive Budget as a Milestone in American Political Development" (Paper presented at the Annual Meeting of the Association for Budgeting and Financial Management, Omaha, Nebraska, October, 2010).

14. Commission on Economy and Efficiency, *The Need for a National Budget* (Washington, DC: Government Printing Office, 1912), 141.

15. Jonathan Kahn, *Budgeting Democracy: State Building and Citizenship in America, 1890-1928* (Ithaca, NY: Cornell University Press, 1997), 59.

16. D. Roderick Kiewit and Matthew D. McCubbins, *The Logic of Delegation: Congressional Parties and the Appropriations Process* (Chicago, IL: University of Chicago Press, 1991), 170.

17. Quoted in Fred Siegel, "Liberalism," in *The Reader's Companion to American History*, edited by Eric Foner and John A. Garraty (Boston: Houghton Mifflin, 1991), 654.

18. Eric Foner, *The Story of American Freedom* (New York: W. W. Norton, 1998), 196.

19. W. Dale Nelson, *Who Speaks for the President?: The White House Press Secretary from Cleveland to Clinton* (Syracuse, NY: Syracuse University Press, 1998), 55.

20. History.com, "Radio and Television," accessed October 3, 2015, http://www.history.com/topics/radio-and-television.

21. U. S. President's Committee on Administrative Management, *Administrative Management in the Government of the United States* (Washington, DC: U.S. Government Printing Office, 1937), 5.

22. Harold C. Relyea, "The Executive Office of the President: An Historical Overview," *CRS Report for Congress*, March 17, 2008 (Washington, DC: Order Code 98-606 GOV), 6–8.

23. Executive Office of the President, "Fiscal Year 2012 Overview," 6, http://www.whitehouse.gov/sites/default/files/2012-eop-budget.pdf.

24. Bradley H. Patterson, *To Serve the President: Continuity and Innovation in the White House Staff* (Washington: Brookings, 2008), 393–97.

25. Matthew J. Dickinson and Matthew J. Lebo, "Reexamining the Growth of the Institutional Presidency, 1940-2000," *The Journal of Politics* 69 (2007): 206–07.

26. Burke, *The Institutional Presidency*, xviii.

27. Richard Neustadt, "Presidential Leadership: The Clerk Against the Preacher," in *Problems and Prospects of Presidential Leadership*, edited by James Sterling Young (Lanham, MD: University Press of America, 1982), 33.

28. George W. Bush, *Decision Points* (New York: Crown Publishers, 2010), 117.

29. Gerald R. Ford, *A Time To Heal* (New York: Harper and Row, 1979), 185.

30. William S. Cohen and George J. Mitchell, *Men of Zeal: The Inside Story of the Iran-Contra Hearings* (New York: Viking, 1988), 5.

31. Jimmy Carter, "Clinton, Massachusetts Remarks and a Question-and-Answer Session at the Clinton Town Meeting," March 16, 1977, accessed October 3, 2015, http://www.presidency.ucsb.edu/ws/index.php?pid=7180#axzz1Y1WwRFVh.

32. "Hillary Clinton Ad—3 AM White House Ringing Phone," accessed October 3, 2015, http://www.youtube.com/watch?v=7yr7odFUARg.

33. Gene Healy, "The Cult of the Presidency," *Reason*, June 2008, http://reason.com/archives/2008/05/12/the-cult-of-the-presidency.

34. Stanley A. Renshon, *The Psychological Assessment Of Presidential Candidates* (New York: Routledge, 1998), ix.

35. The Miller Center, "American President: A Reference Resource," accessed October 3, 2015, http://millercenter.org/president/lbjohnson/essays/biography/5.

36. Richard M. Nixon, *RN: The Memoirs of Richard Nixon* (New York: Grosset and Dunlap, 1978), 298.

37. H. W. Brands, *The Devil We Knew: Americans and the Cold War* (New York: Oxford University Press, 1993), 118.

38. "Bill Clinton's Campaign Promises," accessed October 3, 2015, http://www.theforbiddenknowledge.com/hardtruth/bill_clinton_promises.htm.

39. "Second Debate Between Al Gore and George W. Bush," Wake Forest University, October 11, 2000, accessed October 3, 2015, http://www.debates.org/index.php?page=october-11-2000-debate-transcript.

40. PolitiFact, "Tracking politicians' promises," accessed October 3, 2015, http://www.politifact.com/truth-o-meter/promises/obameter/.

41. Lyndon B. Johnson, "Annual Message to the Congress on the State of the Union," January 4, 1965, accessed October 3, 2015, http://www.presidency.ucsb.edu/ws/index.php?pid=26907#axzz1Y1WwRFVh.

42. Spencer Rich and David Hess, "State of the Union promises often go unfulfilled," *Congress Daily*, January 27, 2003, accessed October 3, 2015, http://www.govexec.com/dailyfed/0103/012703cdam1.htm.

43. Jimmy Carter, "Energy and the National Goals—A Crisis of Confidence," July 15, 1979, accessed October 3, 2015, http://www.americanrhetoric.com/speeches/jimmycartercrisisofconfidence.htm.

44. Walter F. Mondale, *The Good Fight: A Life in Liberal Politics* (New York: Scribner, 2010), 235.

45. Ronald Reagan, "1980 Republican National Convention Acceptance Address," accessed October 3, 2015, http://www.americanrhetoric.com/speeches/ronaldreagan1980rnc.htm.

46. Lou Cannon and Carl M. Cannon, *Reagan's Disciple: George W. Bush's Troubled Quest for a Presidential Legacy* (New York: Public Affairs, 2008), 27.

47. Stephen Skowronek, *Presidential Leadership in Political Time* (Lawrence, KS: University of Kansas Press, 2008), 4.

48. Cronin, *On The Presidency* (Boulder, CO: Paradigm, 2009), 2.

49. Beth Nissen, "A Presidential Sheen: Fans of West Wing say Bartlet character has right stuff," CNN.com, August 18, 2000, accessed October 3, 2015, http://b4a.healthyinterest.net/news/archives/2000/08/a_presidential.html.

50. Cronin, *On The Presidency*, vii.

51. Richard W. Waterman, Hank C. Jenkins-Smith, and Carol L. Silva, "The Expectations Gap Thesis: Public Attitudes Toward an Incumbent President," *The Journal of Politics* 61 (1999): 945.

52. Charles O. Jones, *The Presidency in a Separated System* (Washington, DC: Brookings, 1994), 2.

53. Louis Brownlow, "What We Expect the President to Do," in *The Presidency*, edited by Aaron Wildavsky (Boston: Little, Brown, 1969), 35.

54. David Gergen, *Eyewitness to Power: From Nixon to Clinton* (New York: Simon and Schuster, 2001), 344.

55. James MacGregor Burns, *Running Alone: Presidential Leadership JFK to Bush II: Why It Has Failed and How We Can Fix It* (New York: Basic Books, 2006), 189–90.

3

Becoming President

The simple theory of democracy goes something like this: the people have an election to form a government, the government does its work for a fixed period of time, then the people have another election to hold the government accountable—retaining it if satisfied, replacing it if not.

No such theory operates in America today. The American people hold elections almost constantly. They rarely choose a government, at least not one with policy or ideological coherence. And they are unable to hold their leaders accountable because it is impossible to fix credit or blame for the policies that citizens like or dislike.

The American political process has evolved over the past half century from one in which political parties and party leaders managed relatively short campaign "seasons" to one dominated by special interests and the mass communications media. Campaigns have become a permanent feature of the contemporary political landscape, and the constant pursuit of election and reelection shapes the dynamics of American public life.

The character of modern electoral politics is one of the major difficulties that presidents face in leading the country and meeting the expectations imposed on them. They do not have the support of coherent, unified, and potent political parties. The interests that oppose them are multiple and diverse, well-funded and highly sophisticated. Every presidential initiative is colored by its perceived impact on electoral politics. No election is ever more than two years away. And the news media have no larger preoccupation than who will win the next election. Government and politics have become indistinguishable, and this burdens presidents by forcing them to manage intense political complexities as they try to drive and direct the policy-making process.

The character of the contemporary election system discourages talented Americans from seeking public office, yields far too many candidates who lack useful experience or appropriate personal traits to succeed in high office, ensures that legislative-executive relations will be combative—often brutally so—and significantly shortens the policy horizons of the national government. It is hard to imagine an election process less conducive to the efficient formation of a government or its successful performance in office. It is especially hard to imagine one less conducive to effective executive leadership.

A rational election process should generate candidates who are properly qualified for the offices they seek, allow voters to make thoughtful choices among them, and yield leaders and coalitions that are adequate to the governing challenges they will face. The American political system in the twenty-first century does none of those things.

GETTING ELECTED: THE NEW POLITICS IN AMERICA

Perhaps there was a time when one could reasonably say when elections end and government begins. But not now. Elections never end. Government and politics are so intertwined that they defy disentanglement. "Americans have developed *a unique conception of democracy* that requires frequent citizen participation," notes a leading American government text, "with the result that *elections are plentiful* and *politicians are permanently campaigning*. The need to please a fickle and demanding electorate therefore drives political behavior across the nation's institutions."[1]

In the twenty-first century, nearly every American over the age of eighteen is eligible to vote. And their opportunities to vote are frequent and demanding. There are more than a half-million people holding elective office in the United States. Choosing them is one of our great national preoccupations. We have national general elections every other year and the primary elections to choose the candidates for those. Municipal and state elections often occur on a different timetable. And when citizens go to vote they are confronted by ballots that are lengthy and bewildering. In no other country do citizens vote for as many offices, on as many substantive questions, as often as in the United States.

And these elections are not one-day affairs. Each contest for office, each referendum question is decided after a lengthy campaign in which voters are bombarded with information and advertising seeking to shape their decisions. These campaigns require time and money, and they fill up most of the months that elapse between elections.

So government doesn't begin where politics ends; government is merely what politicians do to prepare for the next election.

So Many Elections

The frequency and constancy of elections is a notable characteristic of the contemporary political process in the United States. When an American president is elected for the first time and looks out over the gathered multitudes on Inauguration Day, the nagging thought in the back of his or her mind is that the next election—one that may significantly determine the fate of that administration—is only twenty-one months away. But, of course, the primary contests that all members of Congress face in the run-up to that next election are not much more than a year away. So the political gears have already begun to grind. Indeed, they never stopped. All that happens in that administration, from that day forward, will be shaped and conditioned by the electoral realities that confront the president, members of Congress, and all of the other constituencies that compose the political universe.

Presidents, of course, are political veterans. They begin running for the office at least a year and a half previous and, in all likelihood, began planning for it much earlier than that. There was a time in American politics, not so long ago, when candidacies for president were confined to the election year. Dwight Eisenhower announced his decision to seek the presidency on March 12, 1952, but only after the "Draft Eisenhower" movement had placed his name on the New Hampshire primary ballot and he had received 50 percent of the vote. The incumbent, Harry Truman, chose not to seek reelection that year, but did not announce his intentions until March 29 at the Democrats' annual Jefferson-Jackson Day dinner.

In 1960, John Kennedy received some criticism for his brashness in announcing his candidacy on January 2 of that year. Lyndon Johnson, his chief rival for the nomination, worked privately with party leaders and did not make a public announcement of his candidacy until July 5, 1960. Johnson's decision not to seek reelection in 1968 was not announced until March 31.

The tide began to turn in December 1967 when Senator Eugene McCarthy announced that he would challenge President Johnson for the 1968 Democratic nomination. That began an evolution in which presidential elections were no longer confined to the election year. And over the decades that followed, candidacies have been determined earlier and earlier, and campaigns have gone on longer and longer. When Barack Obama announced in January 2007 the formation of a committee to explore his candidacy for the presidency in 2008—a year earlier in the calendar than Kennedy's announcement in 1960—the timing seemed not the least unusual to most observers.

Changes in the role of presidential primaries are an important part of the explanation for the elongation of presidential campaigns. Prior to 1972 most candidates saw primaries as little more than isolated opportunities to test a candidacy and demonstrate its merits. They carefully selected the primaries in which they would compete. John Kennedy in 1960, for example, recognized the need to prove his electability as a Roman Catholic. So he chose to run in the primary in West Virginia, a heavily Protestant state. Barry Goldwater, the eventual Republican nominee in 1964, similarly chose to compete in a few primaries, notably in Illinois, Indiana, and California, to demonstrate that a political conservative from the Southwest could be competitive nationally.

But those primaries did not determine the nominee. None did. The real decisions were made at political conventions still very much dominated by the most powerful leaders in the Republican and Democratic Party: the people whom the conventional parlance called "the bosses." Candidates entered primaries to show their stuff to the bosses.

But the old system in which the bosses dominated died in 1968. In that remarkable political year, the Democratic Party nominated Hubert Humphrey, the incumbent vice president, as its presidential candidate. Humphrey had not competed in a single primary or caucus, and his eventual defeat by Richard Nixon in the general election and the bruised feelings of supporters of candidates he bypassed for the nomination convinced many Democrats of the need to change the rules that governed the way they chose their presidential nominee.

Among the several changes that followed was a new rule requiring that each state's delegates to the Democratic National Convention had to be selected by a process that "fairly reflected" the presidential candidate preferences of that state's citizens. This meant in practice that the bosses could no longer hand pick the delegates from their states to the national convention nor control their votes for a nominee.

One boss, Mayor Richard J. Daley of Chicago, paid no heed to this new rule and came to the Democratic convention in Miami Beach in 1972 with an Illinois delegation chosen by and loyal to him. But the party's credentials committee refused to seat Mayor Daley's delegation and sent him packing. There could not have been a clearer statement of the magnitude of the change that was happening in presidential politics.

In 1968, fifteen states had held presidential primaries. In the decade that followed, primaries and caucuses became the norm in every state and the mechanism for selecting the vast majority of delegates to both Republican and Democratic conventions. But this was not a process devised by some central body seeking to improve the qualifications and quality of American presidents. In fact, one could hardly have dreamed up a nominating process less likely to ensure those objectives. Political scientists Steven Smith and Melanie Springer have noted the complexity and illogic of the nominating process that subsequently unfolded:

Choosing presidential candidates is the most bewildering process in the American electoral system, if we dare call it a system. . . . Since the early 1970s, many, but not all, state legislatures have stepped in to establish by state law the timing of primaries and caucuses, eligibility to vote in primaries, the placement of candidates' names on ballots, and the process by which delegates are named by candidates. No two states have identical processes. No federal law governs the process of selecting delegates to the parties' national conventions, at which the presidential candidates are officially nominated.[2]

For those who sought the presidency, the emergence of this decentralized, constantly evolving, often chaotic process had profound effects. It meant, first of all, that they had to compete in a large number of contests conducted in different places, under different ground rules, at different times. Doing so was expensive and required that they raise large sums of money to be competitive. That, in turn, required that they announce and begin their campaigns much earlier than in the past in order to have time to raise money, form organizations, and lay the groundwork for victories in a significant number of states.

Jimmy Carter, among the first candidates to understand fully the impact of these new rules, announced his candidacy for the White House in December 1974, nearly two years before the election. He later confessed that he had actually made the decision to run two years prior to that.[3] Carter's success in winning the Democratic nomination in 1976 helped to make this the dominant model for candidates in subsequent years.

Money Matters

The elongation of the nomination process has yielded two accompanying phenomena. One is the role that campaign contributions now play in the nominating process. The growth in the raising and spending of money in presidential campaigns since the current reporting requirements went into effect in 1976 is startling only to those who have found some secret shelter from the ceaseless bombardment of political messages. All presidential candidates in 1976 spent $66.9 million. In 2012, the total was $1.1 billion, with an additional $1.2 billion spent by parties and outside groups. The $716 million that President Obama raised for his reelection campaign in 2012 was an amount unprecedented in American history—a sum equivalent to twenty times the cost of an entire British general election.[4] And so it grows.

It is now clearly understood by potential presidential candidates that raising large amounts of money and doing it early in the process, before the voting begins, is a key to winning a presidential nomination. Analysts now refer to this as the "money primary." "While many factors influence the outcome of presidential nominations," write political scientists Randall

Adkins and Andrew Dowdle, "early fundraising activities are among the most important."[5] Since the beginning of the modern campaign finance regime in the 1970s, candidates who won the money primary have nearly always ended up as the nominees of their party.

While federal matching funds have been provided in every presidential election since 1976, they have not significantly diminished the importance of private contributions, especially from large donors and the political action committees of special interest groups. In fact, in recent years, the leading candidates have often turned their backs on federal matching funds and the constraints that come with them in order to raise unlimited total amounts with private contributions. The need to raise large sums of money to be competitive in the longer and vastly more complex nominating process distracts candidates from the substantive aspects of campaigning and inevitably ties them into networks of enduring obligation to those who have supported their campaigns with large financial contributions.

The Press Calls the Shots

The second characteristic of the contemporary nominating process is the predominant role played by the communications media. In many ways, the contest for the presidential nomination is a competition not so much to gain the support of party leaders or even voters as to gain favorable coverage in the news media—on the theory that the latter is the best way to secure the former. Jimmy Carter understood this in 1976, spending more time with journalists in his travels around the country than with party leaders. Subsequent candidates have followed suit. "The news media do not entirely determine who will win the nomination," wrote the political scientist Thomas Patterson in his detailed study of the role of the media in contemporary elections, "but no candidate can succeed without the press. The road to nomination now runs through the newsrooms."[6]

The ascendancy of the news media and the decline of political party regulars have produced a presidential nominating process very different from what prevailed earlier in American history. And it has significant consequences for the kinds of people who seek the presidency and the kinds of people who win it.

The role of the news media has grown because the character of the news media has changed. We will discuss these changes in some detail in chapter 4. They are clearly evident to any close observer of modern campaigns.

The leading candidates are trailed everywhere by their media entourage. Often, the journalists ride in the candidate's plane and interact constantly with the campaign staff and the candidate. The planes land at airports which often serve as the venue for local appearances. A local band plays to fire up the "crowd" that has been gathered by the campaign advance team. The candidate gives the standard stump speech with a few local references, briefly works the rope line at the edge of the audience, then returns to the plane—journalists in tow—to head off to the next similar event.

The purpose of all this is not to connect with voters in any meaningful way, but to mount local events in critical states, to gain some coverage from local media, and to create backdrops for photo opportunities that will get wider play. Often, the selection of venues follows a story-of-the-day strategy. A candidate who wants to demonstrate sensitivity to Hispanic voters will make appearances at a Cinco de Mayo celebration. An appearance at a weapons manufacturing plant will emphasize the candidate's commitment to national security. When John Kerrey "took a day off" from campaigning in 2004 to go hunting, the obvious purpose was to show him as a gun owner. And when George H. W. Bush campaigned in 1988 at a flag factory and gave a speech in front of a giant American flag, it had much more to do with emphasizing his patriotism and his record as a war hero than any pursuit of the seamstress vote. The audience in the presence of the candidate is a prop. The audience seeing an event through the media is the target.

A typical television news report on a campaign appearance is rarely more than a few seconds long. There is little opportunity for the candidate to offer or the viewing audience to digest significant, substantive discourse. So the images matter, and campaigns often put as much emphasis on the placement and surroundings of the candidate as on the words that are spoken.

The best way to control the portrayal of the candidate on television is to use campaign funds to purchase time for positive ads about the candidate and negative ads about his or her opponents. Nothing so forcefully drives up the costs of modern presidential campaigns as their television budgets. Television time is very costly and candidates are usually limited to messages no longer than thirty or sixty seconds—nowhere near enough time to delve into the complexities of issues. The focus instead is on the purported personal characteristics of the candidate and—more often—of the opponent. In fact, more than half of modern presidential campaign ads are negative attacks on the opponent's record, ideas, or personal traits.[7]

In this era of all-news cable channels, talk radio, and Internet blogs, it is essential that no candidate lose control of the message or the news cycle. So an important component of the modern presidential campaign is the "war room." Here a watchful staff fields every criticism or rumor or innuendo about its candidate and prepares and issues an immediate response. "A lie can make it half way around the world before the truth has time to put its boots on," Mark Twain is reported to have said. But in our time, lies spread much faster than that, and candidate war rooms never take their boots off.

The constancy of attack and response, of brief television ads that afford little opportunity for the discussion of complex issues, and what Patterson describes as the "antipolitics bias of the press"[8] yield a process from which no heroes emerge and few citizens feel deeply bonded to the president they have chosen. The media through which our campaigns are now primarily conducted are not neutral in their effects. The valence is clear and consistent, and the valence is negative.

THE CANDIDATES

Who does run for president and why? This is a question of no small consequence for those who seek to understand the capacities and deficiencies of the contemporary presidency. What we get out of that office is determined in no small part by whom we get in it. But whom do we get in it, and why do we get them?

In most large organizations—corporations, nonprofits, universities, and hospitals—the selection of a new leader follows a rational process in which the needs of the organization are carefully defined, the skills and experience desired in a leader are specified, and a comprehensive search is initiated to find the person who best fits the organization's needs outlined in the profile it has developed. Professional search consultants—"headhunters"—are frequently employed to assist in defining those needs and in identifying and recruiting candidates, many of whom would be unlikely to present themselves for consideration voluntarily. This is not a perfect science, and misfits sometimes occur. But the success rate is significant, and this has become the leadership selection template for many large organizations.

Most democratic governments follow a different model. They allow the majority party in the legislature to choose the chief executive of the country. The person who becomes chief executive is usually the party leader. And he or she became the leader of the party through years of toil in the legislature, first on the back benches, then in a junior ministerial position, perhaps in the shadow government, then in a more senior ministerial position in which the eventual party leader demonstrated to fellow party members his or her readiness to be prime minister. A decade or more of relevant national government service always precedes accession to the highest political office.

How different those two models are from the one that now dominates the selection of American presidents. A visitor from another planet, observing the way Americans choose their presidents, might easily draw the following conclusions:

1. Experience in the national government is not necessary and might even be a burden for one seeking the presidency.

2. Evidence of successful accomplishment in prior office is unnecessary.
3. Hard-working members of Congress who have ascended to leadership positions in their party rarely seek and are rarely sought as candidates for the presidency. When they do run, they rarely succeed.
4. Experienced administrators in the federal government, even the leaders of the most important cabinet departments, are not in the on-deck circle for the presidency.
5. No one seems to be in charge of this process.

When Barack Obama became president in January 2009, he had spent only four years in the national government as a junior member of the Senate. He never chaired a major committee nor introduced any significant bills that became law. He held no leadership positions in his party. His real legislative experience was further truncated by the two years he spent away from the Senate campaigning for the presidency. Yet, he had more experience in the national government than four of his five immediate predecessors. Jimmy Carter, Ronald Reagan, Bill Clinton, and George W. Bush all came to the presidency with no experience in the national government. Indeed, all of them trumpeted that fact as an argument *for* their election: that they were not part of the "Washington establishment."

All four had been governors before coming to the presidency, but their effectiveness as governors of their states was rarely analyzed during their campaigns and not determinative in any of them. They did not rise to the level of presidential candidate because they were the best governors in the country. The quality of that experience was largely irrelevant, just as Obama's prior political experience in Illinois and Washington offered little justification for his candidacy or his election.

All of them, like virtually all presidential candidates these days, became presidential candidates for two reasons. First, there were no barriers to prevent them from doing so. No group of party leaders or party elders controls the nominating process or has any significant say in who is eligible to enter the process. As the political scientist Hugh Heclo has noted, "The cumulative effect of many changes from the late nineteenth century onward—ending the 'spoils' system in public employment, electoral reforms in party primaries, suburbanization, and television, to name a few examples—was largely to destroy the parties' control over recruitment and nomination of candidates for office."[9] With no gatekeepers, the gates have been wide open.

Why then did this particular group of individuals become presidential candidates? No one chose them for that enterprise. In many cases, there was minimal encouragement to run. To the question "who chose them?" the only answer can be that they chose themselves. People run for president because they want to, irrespective of whether anyone else wants them to.

Alan Ehrenhalt, a journalist who studied this issue with great diligence and insight, concluded that the dominant dynamic in the emergence of contemporary presidential candidates is personal ambition.

> The skills that work in American politics at this point in history are those of entrepreneurship. At all levels of the political system, from local boards and councils up to and including the presidency, it is unusual for parties to nominate people. People nominate themselves. That is, they offer themselves as candidates, raise money, organize campaigns, create their own publicity, and make decisions in their own behalf. If they are not willing to do that work for themselves, they are not (except in a very few parts of the country) going to find any political party structure to do it for them.[10]

Americans have little choice but to select their presidents from among those candidates who present themselves to the electorate. But that is precisely the point: candidates present themselves. Nobody chooses them. They do not get their names on a ballot by surviving any careful scrutiny by people who might be in a position to judge who is qualified and who is not qualified to be an appropriate candidate for the presidency of the United States. Nobody does that. Their names appear on ballots because they possessed the personal ambition necessary to do the things that one must now do to mount a campaign for the presidency.

In 1968, Richard Nixon won the Republican nomination for the presidency. Nixon, who had announced his intent to disappear from politics at his "last press conference" in 1962, was back in the fray not because there was any great demand for his return to politics, in his party or in the country, but because he saw an opportunity among another group of self-selected candidates to satisfy his own personal ambition to be president.

In 1992, five candidates sought the Democratic nomination for the presidency: Paul Tsongas, Bob Kerrey, Tom Harkin, Jerry Brown, and Bill Clinton. All five of them followed the same path to candidacy: they were pursuing their personal ambitions. No one picked this particular group to contest for the nomination of the Democratic Party. Few knowledgeable insiders that year would have had most of them on a list of the party's best potential presidents. Public opinion polls on the eve of the 1992 nominating contest found that three-quarters of American citizens knew nothing about any of these candidates.[11] As Ehrenhalt notes:

> We have taken the decision out of the hands of an elite and given it, in theory, to the electorate. In practice, what we have done is given it to the candidates. They decide what the array of choices will be. The voters are asked merely to make distinctions among the field, to sort out the qualifications of a set of contenders who may not differ very much and whose messages may be almost

identical . . . we have dismantled the structure of peer review, the screening process, that used to guarantee that qualities besides ambition, stamina, glibness, and face-to-face charm would be counted in the selection of leaders.[12]

Ambition is not necessarily a bad thing, especially in political leaders whose ambition is to develop and implement public policies that will meet the challenges faced by their government and their country. But there is little benefit to a nation when the dominant form of ambition in its politics is personal, the simple desire to win office. That, however, seems to be what the contemporary nominating process permits, even encourages. Ambition is the driving force in the presidential nominating process, but as Thomas Patterson notes, "the electoral reforms of the early 1970s have served to channel ambition in the wrong direction."[13]

What, for example, drove Jimmy Carter—a man with the thinnest of political resumes—to seek the presidency in 1976? What did he stand for? In a moment of candor—and no small insight into this entire process—his close aide Gerald Rafshoon said "Carter stood for getting elected."[14] In that, among contemporary presidential candidates, he did not stand alone.

THE NON-CANDIDATES

If the task of getting elected to the presidency now requires a two year or longer slog through endless coffees, speeches, hand shaking, debates, and fund-raising calls; and if the only way to get to be a candidate is to decide to do it on your own, we should not be surprised that many Americans with significant qualifications for the presidency choose not to run. In fact, in any election year, it would be easy to construct a list of people who are not running for president who possess many more qualifications for that office than the people who are.

Some would say that this has long been a characteristic of American politics—that the people best qualified to be president rarely become president. More than a century ago, the distinguished British observer, James Bryce, struggled to explain "why the best men did not become president." He offered several suggestions: that public life in the United States is not as exciting or meaningful as in European countries, that many people of talent find more satisfaction in the private sector, or that the "the best people" are turned off by the "the bad company they would have to keep, the general vulgarity of tone in politics, the exposure to invective or ribaldry by hostile speakers and a reckless press."[15]

No doubt, some of Bryce's explanations, especially the last, still obtain. But Bryce was writing at a time when the process of securing a party nomination and running for president was much shorter, much less demanding on the candidates, and nearly fully controlled by party leaders. No candidates for the presidency in his time or any time before our own had to endure a process that lasted two years or more and required competition in dozens of state contests to secure the nomination. Two explanations beyond Bryce's catalog help us understand why we get the presidents we do.

One is simply that the nature of the nominating process is a turn-off to many potential candidates. To make the decision to run for president is a choice that requires putting one's personal life aside for several years at a time. A candidate's family will be deeply affected by the decision to run, the ability to earn an income will be diminished, and there will be little opportunity to hold or work at any other job.

Then there are the obligations of candidacy: endless travel, constant fund-raising, pandering to special interests and extremist activists, personal attacks from one's opponents, and fatigue. To some potential candidates the burdens of running for president outweigh the desire to be president. They rationally decide that their chances of winning the nomination are too small to justify its pursuit. Others, however, may believe they have a realistic chance of winning the nomination contest but simply choose not to impose its burdens on themselves or their families.

In 2012, with the economy still in a tailspin and President Obama looking increasingly vulnerable, the field of candidates for the Republican nomination reflected most of the problems that now beset this process. Republicans held twenty-nine of the country's governorships, but only one sitting governor—Rick Perry of Texas—chose to be a candidate and he entered the race only after the weakness of the others was demonstrable. Mitt Romney, a former one-term governor of Massachusetts and out of public office for five years, was a candidate. There were forty-seven sitting Republican senators, but none of them chose to run. Republicans held a majority in the House of Representatives, but none of their leaders were candidates for president and the two House members who did choose to run—Ron Paul and Michelle Bachmann—had produced little in their tenures in the House that suggested leadership qualifications. A disgraced former Speaker of the House, Newt Gingrich, who had not held public office for twelve years, decided to run. So did Rick Santorum, a former senator who had lost his 2006 reelection effort in Pennsylvania by a margin of 18 percent. And there were several other candidates with even fewer significant credentials than these.

Throughout the year leading up to the first primaries and caucuses in 2012, public opinion polls consistently showed a lack of broad knowledge of these candidates or of significant enthusiasm for them among the Republican rank-and-file. That is no surprise since most of them were strangers even to fellow Republicans and few of them had a track record that inspired enthusiasm for their candidacies. Throughout 2011, some party leaders sought to entice other, perhaps more attractive, candidates into the race: Haley Barbour, governor of Mississippi; Mitch Daniels, governor of Indiana; Chris Christie, governor of New Jersey; and Paul Ryan, a bright young congressman from Wisconsin. But all of them demurred, in a pattern reminiscent of other recent election years. Potentially good candidates and potentially good presidents are far too often reluctant to enter a nominating process they find repellent.

Another explanation for why we get the candidates that we do is that American politics lacks a leadership succession system. There is no meaningful staging ground or on-deck circle for presidential candidates. Successful large corporations pay a good deal of attention to grooming future leaders. The military services emphasize this very heavily. Parties in parliamentary democracies operate a kind of escalator system that moves future leaders through steadily increasing levels of responsibility to prepare them for the highest office. Even the houses of Congress tend to choose leaders who are experienced and have been tested in lower-level leadership offices before becoming party leaders. But no such system exists for preparing or identifying future presidents.

There has long been a kind of myth that the Senate is a breeding ground for future presidents or at least future presidential candidates. But the evidence suggests otherwise. Of the forty-four presidents of the United States, only three have come directly from the Senate: Warren G. Harding, John F. Kennedy, and Barack Obama. In the fifty-seven presidential elections from 1789 through 2012, current or former senators won only seventeen. And the track record of recent Senate veterans nominated for president by their parties—Barry Goldwater (1964), Hubert Humphrey (1968), George McGovern (1972), Walter Mondale (1984), Bob Dole (1996), John Kerry (2004), and John McCain (2008)—strongly suggests the unreliability of that body as an incubator of presidents.[16]

The House of Representatives has an even weaker record as a source of presidential candidates. James A. Garfield in 1880 was the only president elected while serving in the House. No sitting member of the House has been the presidential candidate of a major party since that year. Those who rise to leadership positions in the House are rarely regarded as presidential timber by party leaders, journalists, or—it would seem—themselves.

Even the vice presidency has rarely proved to be a natural source of presidential succession. In fact, only four incumbents in the vice presidency have ever been elected president, only one—George H. W. Bush—since 1836.

By default then, most new presidents tend to come from governorships. Four of the six presidents elected prior to 2012 had been governors before their election. There is some logic to this in that governors hold executive offices that are in some ways analogous to the office of president. They have to be politically sensitive to succeed, they have to make a host of appointments, they have to deal with varied constituencies, and they have to work with state legislatures.

But the analogies are more hypothetical than apt. No governor has foreign policy obligations. No governor bears the daily scrutiny of thousands of reporters and commentators that a president does. No state legislature resembles the Congress in anything other than its formal structure. Service as a state governor, even success as a state governor, may be relevant preparation for some aspects of the presidency, but there are no guarantees that a former governor will be well prepared for what awaits him or her in Washington.

CONSEQUENCES

It is hard to imagine that any rational group of citizens, charged with creating a selection process for an able national leader, would come up with anything like the system now in place. "From right, left, and center, pols and pundits and scholars have lambasted the protracted, byzantine, and confusing array of fund raisers, forums, straw polls, precinct caucuses, primaries, and conventions that characterize campaigns for presidential nominations," writes political scientist John Haskell. "It is safe to say that there has not been a single persuasive defense offered of this process of nominating presidential candidates."[17]

Where parties once dominated in a system that was—at least by the standards of democratic politics—relatively stable, compressed, and predictable, we now have a long, individualized, money-laden, ambition-driven process for choosing the two candidates from whom the American people must select their president. This process repels potentially strong candidates. It sheds many of those candidates who do choose to run long before most Americans have an opportunity to participate. It grants undue importance to a few small and unrepresentative states. It allows a small group of activists to play a disproportionate role in determining who runs the country. Intelligent, substantive discussion of issues is often pushed aside by oversimplification, hyper-partisanship, and character assassination.

Efforts to reform the election process often produce outcomes quite opposite from their intentions. The campaign spending reforms of the 1970s have neither reduced the impact of money on elections nor corralled the influence of special interests. Money is more important than ever and there has been a steady escalation in special interest electioneering.

The reforms of the nominating process begun by the Democratic Party in the aftermath of the 1968 election were aimed primarily at broadening popular participation in the selection of the nominees. But the sequential, front-loaded system of primaries and caucuses that emerged has often made it difficult for most Americans to participate in a meaningful way. Even in the most vigorously contested nomination contests, as in 2008, fewer than 30 percent of adults take part.[18]

Elections should give presidents more than just the keys to the White House. They should provide the newly elected leader with ample opportunities to lead. But in many ways the contemporary process of choosing presidents fails to accomplish that. It winnows out too many people who possess strong qualifications for the presidency and winnows in too many people who don't. It rarely provides the successful candidate with a coherent or effective governing coalition. And it does too little to connect citizens to government and to establish them as stakeholders in the success of the president's administration.

The Presidents We Get

Some devotees of the contemporary election process claim that its rigors are a good test for people who want to be president. The historian Gil Troy writes that "presidential campaigns are nasty, long and expensive because they should be. Many aspects of campaigns that Americans hate reflect democratic ideals we love."[19] Requiring the candidates to raise millions of dollars, endure the slings and arrows of hundreds of reporters and opposition researchers, and deliver the same speech a half dozen or more times a day for months on end, they argue, separates the strong personalities from the weak, the tough from the soft. "Campaigns are like an MRI for the soul," said Obama campaign advisor David Axelrod; "whoever you are eventually people find out."[20]

Such comments whistle past the graveyard of failed and disappointing modern presidencies. The contemporary election process is a stamina test, to be sure, and it opens the soul and every other organ of the candidates to endless scrutiny. But does it really test the qualities that matter in chief executives: wisdom, relevant experience, judgment, political sensitivity? Hardly.

The quaint notion that the modern nominating process places heavy emphasis on "retail politics," that voters make their choices after face-to-face meetings with the candidates, is simply inaccurate in all but a few cases. Candidates for the nomination, with any hope of success, mount national campaigns costing millions of dollars focused primarily on the television audience, the news media, and the political commentators. The so-called debates—often with a half dozen or more candidates limited to one-minute responses to questions posed by grand-standing "moderators"—play a large role in shaping early impressions and eventual outcomes. These put a premium on personal appearance, the occasional bon mot, and slipups by one's opponents. Instead of digging deeply and thoughtfully into the policy issues that vex the nation, candidates for major party nominations offer simplistic, catchy program ideas that may appeal to core constituencies but bear little resemblance to reality and little hope of ever being enacted.

"America gets bad Presidents," notes *The Economist*, "because it gets bad candidates, and it gets bad candidates because they are now chosen chiefly in a series of primary elections in which voters put a premium on superficial qualities televisually conveyed, with little consideration of the attributes needed to run the most powerful country in the world."[21]

The news media contribute to the problem by portraying the contest for a party's nomination as a horse race in which the candidates constantly jostle for position. One moves ahead, another falls behind. Success in fund-raising pushes you ahead; disappointing receipts force you back. A quick riposte in a debate and you move up; a misstatement and you fall back. Little of this has much to do with the qualities we seek in a successful president. "The press," writes Thomas Patterson "magnifies certain aspects of politics and downplays others, which are often more central to issues of governing."[22]

Instead of testing qualities desirable in a president and sorting those who possess them from those who don't, the contemporary selection process awards candidates who may be good at running for president but lack the skills and experience to be good at being president. "To become president takes a determined, and even a driven person," write political scientists Thomas Cronin and Michael Genovese, "a master fund-raiser, a person who is glib, dynamic, charming on television, and somewhat hazy on the issues. But, once president, the person must be well-rounded, careful in reasoning, more transparent, and more specific in communications."[23]

And there is, of course, a natural burden for people who come to the presidency with no Washington experience, as most governors do. They try to "hit the ground running," but quickly realize they have never met many of the most powerful people in Washington, that their networks of acquaintance are inadequate to the task of staffing their administrations, and that so many demands for action and attention press upon them so persistently that setting priorities is often the most difficult challenge they face—and one that most of them fail. They must acquire understandings of the folkways of Washington, the substantive details of public policy, and the vagaries of international relations that only experience can bring. For most of the presidents we have tended to elect over the past few decades, the presidency has been on-the-job training.

Take the example of Bill Clinton and the deficit crisis of 1993. Clinton's campaign speeches had constantly cited his desire to "grow the economy." Avoiding the pejorative term "spending," he had talked instead about "investing" in new programs. But in an initial meeting with his new team of economic advisers on January 7, 1993, he suffered a hard lesson about economic reality. Led by Robert Rubin, who would head the

National Economic Council and later the Treasury Department, the advisers informed Clinton that he would have to abandon much of the economic program he had advanced during the campaign because of its potential effects on the deficit and the reaction that would produce in the bond markets. As Bob Woodward reports:

> At the president-elect's end of the table, Clinton's face turned red with anger and disbelief. "You mean to tell me that the success of the program and my reelection hinges on the Federal Reserve and a bunch of fucking bond traders?" he responded in a half-whisper.
> . . . It was no longer a political campaign. They faced new economic realities and had to start all over again.[24]

Of this and other realizations, Clinton later wrote "in the critical early months, both the staff and I would do a lot of on-the-job learning, and some of the lessons would prove to be quite costly."[25]

A secondary but very important effect of the character of the nominating process—its length, its heavy dependence on fund-raising, and the frequent incivility and imbecility of its discourse—it is to discourage well-qualified individuals from seeking the nomination. They stay home. We all suffer collectively when we are forced to choose our leader from among a handful of self-selected politicians who may be telegenic and aggressive fund-raisers but who too often lack relevant experience in the national government, essential personal contacts with members of Congress, substantive knowledge of the policies they must pursue, and skills to manage more than a hundred executive departments and agencies.

David Broder, one of the most respected political journalists of the post-World War II period, articulated in 1973 what has become known as Broder's Law: "Anybody that wants the presidency so much that he'll spend two years organizing and campaigning for it is not to be trusted with the office."[26] Strong words. But, of course, we have an election process that guarantees that those are precisely the people who will become president of the United States.

The Governing Coalitions We Don't Get

Government in any democracy is not a solo act. In America, in our system of multiple institutions sharing power, nothing gets accomplished without a broad base of support for action. James MacGregor Burns, an historian who spent a long career studying political leadership, points out that "true collective leadership, which combines the power to lead with accountability, means that the president governs together with a broad and united coalition of Americans."[27]

But where do those coalitions come from? A reasonable expectation is that elections will produce them. Candidates for president would present their differing ideas for the direction of the country and the policies they support. A majority of voters would choose the president and the majority party in Congress to implement the plans that drew broadest support. Presidents could take office knowing that they had the confidence and support of a large number of Americans and that they shared values and goals with the majority in Congress. There would be, if not an overwhelming mandate, a majority coalition upon which the president in most instances could rely.

That, of course, is a fantasy. Not a fantasy in most democracies where elections do yield a government that can govern through a majority party or coalition, but a fantasy in contemporary America where elections yield no such thing. In the nominating process and the general election, presidential candidates run their own campaigns with little substantive policy connection to their party or to their party's congressional candidates. The platform the parties draft at their national conventions is usually forgotten before the ink dries. No candidate for any office is obliged to support or conform to any collective set of principles or policy promises. And parties in America today have no power to impose even a limited orthodoxy on their candidates or their members in Congress.

The breakdown of political parties in America has yielded a politics of personalism: it's everyone for themselves. When the dust settles after an election, there is no guarantee—indeed there is little likelihood—that a majority in the country or in Congress is lined up to support the new president. "It is now possible to become president without a stable constituency or set of allies even in one's own party," notes Alan Ehrenhalt. "It is very difficult to govern effectively that way. To campaign for president as an individualist, as someone who has risen above factions, interest groups, and entangling alliances, is to court eventual frustration in office."[28]

Compounding the contemporary difficulties facing presidents in their pursuit of majority coalitions is the lack of competitiveness in most House and Senate elections. In the House, especially over the past several decades, districts have been redrawn and incumbents fortified in ways that virtually ensure that most members of Congress will win in a landslide. In the vast majority of congressional districts in any election year now the winning candidate will get a larger percentage of the vote, often far larger, than the winning presidential candidate. Even in winning a significant victory in 2008 with 53 percent of the popular vote, Barack Obama drew a greater percentage of the vote than the winner in only 36 (14 percent) of the 257 districts carried by Democrats.[29]

The concept of presidential coattails has become quaint. Rare indeed is the member of Congress these days who feels obligated to a president for carrying him or her into office by sweeping the district. No president can call in his electoral chits in policy battles these days—because he has so few.

Combine these ingredients of the election process in America—self-selected candidates for the nomination driven by personal ambition, a nominating process that places high value on carving out a narrow but passionate constituency, the constant election of presidents with little or no Washington experience, and the vast and growing distance between presidential and congressional elections—and you have a recipe for governance that is bound to fail. Our elections don't produce a government. They yield a ticket to a dogfight.

Citizens as Spectators

To most Americans, electoral politics is something they watch, not something they do. In fact, many Americans don't even watch.

When they do watch, what they see is a seemingly endless spectacle of men and women they barely know, promising the moon, hurling negative charges against each other, and saying the same words over and over and over again. It is not a pretty sight, and to a great many Americans the natural reaction is to turn away. The nominating process of the major parties, which now consumes the bulk of the time and energy in our election process, directly engages only a small percentage of American citizens. The percentage of citizens who say they are following the campaign very closely barely exceeded 20 percent in the 2008 and 2012 nominating seasons, according to polling by the Pew Research Center.[30] The general election attracts more attention, but even many of those who vote are left with a bad taste.

"The ever-extending duration of the campaign and the 24/7 intensity of the media coverage that surrounds it systematically encourage distortion and denigration," writes the journalist Ron Brownstein. "The need to break through the constant chatter and drive the daily media narrative—the imperative to win each news cycle—encourages the campaigns to portray policy disagreements as character flaws and to reduce the candidates' differences to garish stereotypes (Plutocrat! Socialist! Warmonger! Appeaser!). . . . Months of this sniping tend to harden the country's divisions and diminish the eventual winner's ability to govern."[31]

Candidates in America have always criticized their opponents, sometimes brutally. But since the advent of television campaigning, those negative attacks have become more common and sophisticated, reach a much broader audience, and are repeated constantly. Negative advertising is now the most common form of television advertising in presidential campaigns.[32] A regular television viewer in campaign season will nearly drown in a steady rain of ugly pictures, out-of-context statements, and disinformation about candidates for national office.

The political science literature on negative advertising suggests that such ads have become the norm because they work; they help the candidates who deploy them, encouraging all candidates to go negative.[33] But their cumulative effect is corrosive. "The change in the tone of election coverage has contributed to the decline in the public's confidence in those who seek the presidency," notes Thomas Patterson.[34] He's right, of course. If McDonald's and Burger King advertised the way that presidential candidates do, no one would ever again eat a hamburger.

One candidate is left standing at the end of a campaign and he becomes the president. But that candidate has for so long been the target of so much invective, innuendo, and distortion that it is hard for citizens who were not hardcore supporters to feel much connection to their president. They have watched him become president, but have played little if any role in that process. The typical president today takes office with nearly three-quarters of the American people never having voted for him. Citizens feel no ownership of the administration that tries to govern in Washington because they played no role in putting it there. It's hard to be a spectator and a stakeholder simultaneously.

The absence of stakeholders imposes a heavy burden on presidents. When a president needs the steady support of the people who elected him, it's often not there—either because most people had nothing to do with his election or because many of those who voted for him did so with little passion or conviction. And citizens who feel little direct or personal connection to their government or their president are ripe for cynicism and disaffection.

It is hard to build effective, durable governing coalitions on a flimsy foundation of popular support. The measures of citizen disaffection—trust in government, personal efficacy, beliefs that the government is responsive to average citizens—have all been at perpetually low levels over the past several decades.[35] A complex of factors contributes to that pattern of decline. But very important among them is the failure of national elections to inspire and sustain popular support for the government and the leader that they produce every four years.

NOTES

1. Morris P. Fiorina, Paul E. Peterson, and D. Stephen Voss, *America's New Democracy* (New York: Longman, 2002), 5.

2. Steven S. Smith and Melanie J. Springer, *Reforming the Presidential Nominating Process* (Washington: Brookings, 2009), 1.

3. Cronin and Michael A. Genovese, *The Paradoxes of the American Presidency* (New York: Oxford University Press, 2010), 65.

4. Center for Responsive Politics, "2012 Presidential Race," accessed October 3, 2015, http://www.opensecrets.org/pres12/; "Fundraising and spending in U.S. presidential elections from 1976 to 2012," accessed October 3, 2015, http://www.statista.com/statistics/216793/fundraising-and-spending-in-us-presidential-elections/.

5. Randall E. Adkins and Andrew J. Dowdle, "The Money Primary: What Influences the Outcome of Pre-Primary Presidential Nomination Fundraising?" *Presidential Studies Quarterly* 32 (2002): 257.

6. Thomas E. Patterson, *Out of Order* (New York: Random House, 1994), 33.

7. Darrell M. West, *Air Wars: Television Advertising in Election Campaigns 1952–2008* (Washington: Brookings, 2010), 67.

8. Patterson, *Out of Order*, 18.

9. Hugh Heclo, "Campaigning and Governing: A Conspectus," in *The Permanent Campaign and Its Future*, edited by Norman Ornstein and Thomas Mann (Washington, DC: Brookings and the American Enterprise Institute, 2000), 19.

10. Alan Ehrenhalt, *The United States of Ambition: Politicians, Power, and The Pursuit of Office* (New York: Random House, 1991), 17.

11. Nate Silver, "A Brief History of Presidential Polling, Part II," *New York Times*, May 6, 2011, accessed October 3, 2015, http://fivethirtyeight.blogs.nytimes.com/2011/05/06/a-brief-history-of-primary-polling-part-iii/.

12. Ehrenhalt, *The United States of Ambition*, 266–67.

13. Patterson, *Out of Order*, 49.

14. Quoted in Joe Klein, *Politics Lost: How American Democracy Was Trivialized By People Who Think You're Stupid* (New York: Doubleday, 2006), 38.

15. James Bryce, *The American Commonwealth*, vol. II (New York: Macmillan, 1919), 73.

16. See Barry C. Burden, "United States Senators as Presidential Candidates," *Political Science Quarterly* 117 (2002): 81–102.

17. John Haskell, "Reforming Presidential Primaries: Three Steps for Improving the Campaign Environment," *Presidential Studies Quarterly* 26 (1996): 380.

18. The Pew Center on the States, *2008 Primary in Review*, July 2008, 10, accessed October 3, 2015, http://www.issuelab.org/resource/2008_primary_in_review.

19. Gil Troy, "Nasty, Brutish, and Long: The Brilliance of the Modern Campaign," *New York Times*, November 6, 2011, accessed October 3, 2015, http://campaign-stops.blogs.nytimes.com/2011/11/06/nasty-brutish-and-long-the-brilliance-of-the-modern-campaign/.

20. Quoted in Troy, "Nasty, Brutish, and Long."

21. "Only Freaks," *The Economist*, May 9, 1987.

22. Patterson, *Out of Order*, 29.

23. Cronin and Genovese, *The Paradoxes of the American Presidency*, 20–22.

24. Bob Woodward, *The Agenda: Inside the Clinton White House* (New York, New York: Simon and Schuster, 1994), 84.

25. Bill Clinton, *My Life* (New York: Alfred A. Knopf, 2004), 467.

26. *Washington Post*, July 19, 1973.

27. Burns, *Running Alone*, 5.

28. Ehrenhalt, *The United States of Ambition*, 268.

29. Rhodes Cook, "Obama and the Redefinition of Presidential Coattails," *Rasmussen Reports*, April 17, 2009, accessed October 3, 2015, http://www.rasmussen-reports.com/public_content/political_commentary/commentary_by_rhodes_cook/obama_and_the_redefinition_of_presidential_coattails.

30. Pew Research Center for the People and the Press, "GOP Candidates Hardly Household Names," October 5, 2011, accessed October 3, 2015, http://www.people-press.org/2011/10/05/gop-candidates-hardly-household-names/?src=prc-headline.

31. Ronald Brownstein, "Reconcilable Differences," *Atlantic* (September 2008), accessed October 3, 2015, http://www.theatlantic.com/magazine/print/2008/09/reconcilable-differences/6942/.

32. West, *Air Wars,* 66.

33. See: West, Air Wars; Emmett H. Buell, Jr., and Lee Sigelman, *Attack Politics: Negativity in Presidential Campaigns Since 1960,* 2nd ed. (Lawrence, KS: University Press of Kansas, 2009); and John G. Geer, *In Defense of Negativity* (Chicago: University of Chicago Press, 2006).

34. Patterson, *Out of Order,* 22.

35. See data on trust in government and political efficacy from recent national polling by the American National Election Studies, accessed October 3, 2015, http://www.electionstudies.org/nesguide/toptable/tab5a_1.htm.

4

The Myth of the Bully Pulpit

The most famous presidential address of all time was delivered on a crowded outdoor platform from folded handwritten notes without a microphone or a teleprompter. Because the crowd numbered in excess of 10,000 and there was no sound amplification, many in the audience could scarcely hear what the president said. No film or television cameras were present, and no still photograph of the speech was ever produced. The few reporters present scrambled to write down the president's words; their transcriptions varied, and the actual words spoken by the president are still debated.

The legend persists that the speech was hastily written by the president on the train on the way to the place of delivery. Not so. It was prepared in advance, but the words he spoke were those he wrote himself.

The president was on the platform for several hours that morning, but almost entirely as a spectator. The featured oration lasted two hours, but the president spoke for barely two minutes. Newspaper stories in the following days often reprinted the remarks of all the speakers, but rarely featured the president's. The Republican newspapers of the time reported his speech with satisfaction, the Democratic papers with dismay.[1] Objective reporting had yet to be invented.

The Gettysburg Address was meant to be a purposeful use of words by the president of the United States. It was meant to shape the national political debate and to influence the opinions of American citizens. That has always been the goal of presidential speeches and public appearances. But the reach of the president's voice and the impact of his words have always been conditioned by two things above all others.

One of those is technology, especially the technologies of communications and travel that connect presidents to the American people. Those technologies have evolved over the history of the American republic. Washington traveled on horseback and his words were spread by mail. Lincoln had trains to travel long distances, the telegraph to spread his words rapidly across the land, and photography to provide an occasional image. Presidents today function in a universe of communications and travel technology full of marvels and wonders. What was once science fiction is fiction no more.

The second factor conditioning presidential communication with the American people is strategic competence: the president's ability to use available technologies to convey powerful and persuasive messages to American citizens, to aid his efforts to convince them to support his actions and policy initiatives. Technology is no inherent guarantor of success; it only affords opportunity. Presidents must seize that opportunity and put it to their own purposes. Some do, some don't.

The history of the American presidency, especially over the past century, is in large part a story about adaptation to technological change. It is also the story, of how technology has enlarged and altered the behavior of the presidency. The flow of technological change has been a tide so strong that no president could swim against it. All—some faster, some slower—have gone with the flow.

At times in that long process of technological modernization, presidents found great natural advantages. Their ability to reach a large audience, with little interruption or opposition, reached its zenith in the middle decades of the twentieth century. But newer developments eroded and eventually demolished that foundation of presidential dominance of the nation's public space. For a time, the state of technology appeared to elevate the presidency, seeming to make it easier to be an effective national leader. But that time has passed. The contemporary state of technology has a different impact, a more negative impact for the presidents of our time.

Those changes and those impacts are the story of this chapter.

TECHNOLOGY AND THE EMERGING MASS AUDIENCE

For the first century of its existence, the presidency was not a public institution. Indeed, it was not an institution at all. For most Americans, the president was just a person, one who often inhabited their imaginations through characterization not presence—"Old Hickory," "Tippecanoe," "Honest Abe." Most Americans never heard nor saw the president except in newspaper line drawings and political broadsides. He was a distant figure, like a Japanese emperor.

President James Polk, not atypically of presidents in the early days, was isolated in Washington for long stretches. With little staff, the work was often overwhelming. Travel was difficult and hazardous. Polk rarely appeared in public or addressed an audience. He socialized almost entirely with Washington politicians. In the summer of 1848, he complained to his diary that for more than a year: "I have not been three miles from the White House."[2] Public attention to the president occurred only through partisan newspapers, but was almost never the result of direct reporting.

Even in the final decades of the nineteenth century, news stories about the president were as likely to focus on the details of his personal life as on any of the limited ways he was involved in public policy. As political scientist Stephen Ponder noted in his history of presidents and the press, "In the 1870s and 1880s, presidents were regarded as newsworthy when they died, were married, made important speeches, or traveled around the country. They responded regularly to inquiries. But they rarely sought publicity overtly, and few senior members of the Washington press corps called at the Executive Mansion to receive news on a routine basis."[3]

As earlier chapters indicate, presidents became more important figures when the national government expanded its role in American society and economy. Their visibility increased along with their activity as new opportunities arose for presenting and publicizing the president. Three overarching technologies have shaped and conditioned the relationship between presidents and the American people.

The first is print. In the early days of the American republic, newspapers and pamphlets were the primary form of public communication. But print itself was an evolving technology, and in the second half of the nineteenth century, national magazines began to appear and improvements in the operation of printing presses permitted more rapid publication of large numbers of newspapers. The "penny press" became possible after the Civil War, and new business models, driven by advertising and mass circulation, freed newspapers from their partisan ties. Newspaper oligopolies developed and the press became a highly competitive enterprise. In the search for stories that would sell newspapers, the industry began to focus more attention on the American president. Reporters began to follow the president's activities and policy views more closely; the White House became a journalist's "beat."

The second evolution in communications technology came in the third decade of the twentieth century when wireless, or radio, became a consumer product. As radios became a common item in more and more homes, new radio stations sprung up across the country to broadcast news and entertainment for the home audience. Networks began to tie these stations together and to provide universal programming for citizens everywhere. Politicians took note.

Three decades later, broadcasting came to include sight as well as sound. Television spread across the landscape even more rapidly than radio had.

The radio networks quickly became television networks as well. By mid-century, Americans were linked together by communications technologies in a single national audience. Politicians took note.

The third wave of evolution came in the last decade of the twentieth century with the simultaneous spread of personal computers and the link that tied them all together: the Internet. Broadcasting began to give way to narrowcasting. The mass audience fragmented and became a vast and eclectic collection of niche audiences. Americans who had largely been consigned to the role of news consumers now found themselves with technologies that allowed them to be news producers. Politicians took note—but often found themselves struggling to master these new technologies in which communication traveled up as well as down.

For American presidents each of these technological evolutions was a sea change. And despite their expansive efforts to adapt, technological development accelerated too rapidly, eventually outpacing the ability of contemporary presidents to dominate or even control. Their opportunities for connecting with the American people—indeed their opportunities as national leaders—were at first dramatically expanded and then rapidly diminished. And in the twenty-first century, American presidents function in a public environment as hostile to their purposes as any of their predecessors ever faced.

THE PUBLIC PRESIDENCY

The idea that the presidency should be a public institution—one that emphasized communication with the American people as an important responsibility and the manufacture of supportive public opinion as an essential strategy—preceded the capacity to implement it. In his scholarship before entering politics, Woodrow Wilson argued that public opinion was an important potential cure for the constitutional weakness of the president in his relations with Congress. If the public supported the president's initiatives, it would be hard for congressional majorities to oppose them. "He has no means of compelling Congress except through public opinion," Wilson wrote in 1908.[4]

But the challenge for Wilson and his contemporaries was how to persuade the American people to support the president's objectives and initiatives. One answer was a bolstered party system. Wilson envisioned the federated political parties of his time, not simply as electoral machines, but as continuing political vehicles as well. The party that got a president elected, in Wilson's view, should also help him succeed in governing.

But Wilson also saw potential in an "aggressive style of popular rhetoric."[5] The president's role, Wilson argued in his scholarship (and later sought to realize in office), was to be more than a mere executive officer; he must be a political leader as well. The president had to be the embodiment of the will of the people and their agent in bringing that will to bear in shaping the country's public policies.

Wilson may have been the first to establish the philosophical underpinnings of what political scientist Jeffrey Tulis has called "the rhetorical presidency."[6] But his fellow Progressive, Theodore Roosevelt, preceded him in putting the notion to work. Roosevelt traveled the country frequently as president, he sought publicity for his persona and his policies, he was an indefatigable public speaker, and he never shied from an opportunity to build public support for his policy priorities. The aggressive style of popular rhetoric for which Professor Wilson sought to build a theoretical justification was already being practiced by President Roosevelt from his self-described "bully pulpit" in the White House. The idea and the practice would soon become the norm as the twentieth century unfolded.

But there was a problem. In fact, there were several. One was that the technologies of the time provided little support for implementing the concept of a public presidency. The emergence of national newspaper chains and magazines had brought more reporters into regular contact with the White House. Presidents at the end of the nineteenth century had begun to regularize their contacts with reporters, to see them as useful vehicles— indeed the only vehicles—for significant communication with American citizens. But newspapers and magazines were controlled by people who didn't always agree with the president. There was no guarantee that the president's availability to reporters would produce stories that served his purposes.

The only alternative for a president of the time was to travel to the people and to speak to them directly. But travel was hard and slow. A cross-country train trip was a venture requiring more than a week coming and going. And even when the president appeared before an audience, the absence of sound amplification limited the reach of his voice to those in shouting distance.

There is no better evidence of the contemporary constraints on a public presidency than Woodrow Wilson's effort to reach out to the American people to build support for the League of Nations treaty in 1919. Arduous travel and constant speech-making were to little avail. The treaty failed in the Senate. And an exhausted Wilson collapsed in Pueblo, Colorado, suffered a subsequent cerebral hemorrhage, and never fully recovered.

In the decade that followed, however, new opportunities emerged for the fuller flowering of a public presidency. Momentum has long been a powerful force in the institutional development of the presidency. And the Republican presidents of the 1920s, while not bullish on expansions of the federal government, could not resist the momentum their predecessors had built for a more assertive and public presidency. Theodore Roosevelt had established the practice of presidential press conferences. Wilson, at least before the outbreak of war, had continued it. Harding, Coolidge, and Hoover followed suit. The relationship between the president and the press was becoming institutionalized.

THE BROADCAST AGE

Harding was elected in 1920, the year that the first commercial radio station, KDKA in Pittsburgh, went on the air. A novelty at first, radio quickly became a powerful mass medium of communication. On December 6, 1923, Calvin Coolidge delivered an address to Congress that was the first speech by a president to be broadcast on radio. On the previous day, the *New York Times* had declared: "The voice of President Coolidge, addressing Congress tomorrow, will be carried over a greater portion of the United States and will be heard by more people than the voice of any man in history."[7] A few months later, the 1924 Republican and Democratic national conventions were broadcast to stations across the country. And by the time Hoover was elected in 1928 there were national radio networks and an audience the dimensions of which no president could disregard.

As the public character of the presidency developed, presidents had a growing need for help. There were constant reporters' queries in need of response, press conferences for which to prepare, more speeches to deliver, new talents to acquire. The president's secretary had been the primary daily contact with reporters starting in the final administrations of the nineteenth century. But that responsibility soon became too large for a single person with other duties. By the end of the 1920s, superintending the president's relationship with the press became the full-time responsibility of an aide known informally as the press secretary. Speech writers began to appear in the White House in the 1920s as well. There would not be a formal EOP until 1939, but the demands of an expanding public presidency were shaping presidential staff arrangements more than a decade before their institutional formality was fully certified.

As Stephen Ponder notes: "To seek increased news coverage, presidents from McKinley forward altered their own activities and the responsibilities of their assistants; encouraged the hiring and use of publicists in the White House and in executive agencies, and tried to adapt their messages to the technological and organizational changes taking place in the media of mass communications."[8]

Radio, of course, was the harbinger of a new age of presidential communication, the broadcast age. Print would continue to be important, as it does into our own time. But increasingly presidents and their staffs would look to radio and its technological successors as the primary focus of their efforts to build public support for the programs of the president.

By 1933 that process was well underway. For Franklin Roosevelt, president at a time of great national distress, radio was a godsend. Two-thirds of homes had radios when FDR took office, national networks enabled a single broadcast source to reach them all. Many of the country's major newspapers were owned by Republicans who had opposed Roosevelt's election and would even more vigorously oppose the New Deal. Roosevelt and his press secretary, Stephen Early, worked hard at cultivating good relations with the press. The 998 press conferences he held testify to the diligence of that effort. But radio freed Roosevelt from dependence on reporters and editors. And it empowered him to deploy his skills of rhetoric and persuasion to build public support for his domestic and economic policies—and later for his leadership in a world war. These were lessons that no subsequent president would disregard.

The broadcast age came to full flower as television spread with unprecedented rapidity through the American population. The first consumer sets came on the market and the first TV stations on the air in the late 1940s. By the end of the 1950s, more than 50 million television sets had been sold and nearly 80 percent of American homes possessed at least one.[9]

Again, the technology drove new forms of experimentation and eventually new forms of institutional structure and activity in the White House. Television advertising had played a small role in Dwight D. Eisenhower's election in 1952; it would play a steadily growing role in his eight years in office. Many of Eisenhower's press conferences were filmed and made available for delayed television broadcast. He embraced the practice of requesting—and getting—free air time from the national networks for televised addresses to the American people. And, at the urging of press secretary James C. Hagerty, his staff began to respond to the working rhythms of the network newscasts.

Eisenhower was not a natural television performer. The 1952 television advertisements in which he appeared are notable primarily for their woodenness. But he understood how important the broadcast media had become to the presidency and set out to master them—even hiring Robert Montgomery, a well-known television actor of the time, to coach him in honing his skills before the camera. Emmet John Hughes, a member of Eisenhower's staff, wrote of this new instrument of communication: "No more favorable medium could be devised to allow a president to carry his cause beyond the White House gates to the farthest reaches of the Republic. . . . He can command at his chosen hour a wider audience than anyone else in the nation. And the very nature of the medium allows one man to summon attention in a way that no group can hope to match, for how can a legislature collectively answer the Chief Executive, or how can an opposition party collectively refute him, on the television screen?"[10]

By the early 1960s, television had fully penetrated the American population. When campaigning in the 1960 primary in West Virginia, John Kennedy had noted with astonishment the television antennae on the rooftops of even the poorest shanties in the hill country. Once in office, he and his staff moved aggressively to use television as a central component of the president's efforts to build support for his program initiatives—and not incidentally—for his reelection. Television was, said top aide Theodore Sorensen, "his greatest weapon."[11] In light of the frequent opposition of major newspaper publishers, Kennedy himself believed that "we couldn't survive without TV."[12]

But the medium was not static. Television, and especially television news, was evolving rapidly in the 1960s. Technological advances shrunk the size and weight of cameras. Communications satellites permitted transmission from remote sites. Television stations could broadcast in color. And the news divisions of the national networks were eagerly implementing all of these improvements in their broadcasts. By the end of 1963, CBS and NBC had expanded their evening newscasts to thirty minutes. Their news anchors and some of their reporters had become national celebrities. And for the first time in 1963, a majority of Americans reported that television was their primary source of news.[13]

America had entered what contemporary political scientists now call the "golden age" of television.[14] What does that mean? For American presidents, it meant an era in which the broadcast connections between them and the American people were few in number, readily accessible, and vast in reach. Television signals came into American homes over the airwaves. Only a few hundred television stations had a license to use those airwaves and nearly all of them were part of the three major national networks: ABC, CBS, and NBC. On any evening, citizens in a majority of American homes were tuned into one of those three networks because there were no other choices.

For American presidents of the time, this was a captive audience. Once Kennedy began the practice of permitting live television broadcast of his press conferences, all of his successors were forced to follow suit. The use of prime-time national addresses to speak to the nation on important issues became a common practice during this period. From 1953 through 1985, presidents addressed the nation in prime time on more than 100 occasions.[15] If Americans were watching television during one of these press conferences or prime-time addresses, they were watching the president. There was no alternative.

This "golden age," we now know, was an historical anomaly. It was a time of unique centralization of major news sources in the United States. The three television networks and a handful of newspapers and national magazines dominated the production and reporting of the news and set the standards for the entire news business. They had unprecedented resources for doing so, they cultivated teams of well-educated reporters and demanding, conscientious editors—many of whom became popular and highly trusted public figures. A commitment to objective reporting of the news and clear separations between news and opinion took hold as the dominant standards of the journalism profession.

Nearly all of this was good news for American presidents. In addition to their extraordinary access to the national audience through television, it was an era in which news coverage of the president was ample and generally positive. And it was an era as well in which the president's political opponents could not begin to match his communications opportunities. In the battle for influence over public opinion, they were out-gunned.

Political scientist Jeffrey E. Cohen, a leading expert on presidential uses of the communications media, has noted that

> during the golden age of television . . . the news media were highly concentrated and produced a comparatively high volume of news about the president. News about the president tended to be favorable during this era, and the relationship between presidents and journalists was generally civil and respectful. The mass public, while not notably interested in politics, tuned into television news broadcasts in relatively large numbers and held the news media in relatively high regard. Presidents, during this age, spoke to the public directly on nationally televised addresses but also provided the news media, especially television, with material to use in their news stories. Through these direct and indirect routes of access to the mass public, presidents enjoyed an ability to lead the public as never before.[16]

This was different from the eras of the partisan press and yellow journalism and even the early days of radio broadcasting. And it would be different from the fracturing of public communications that would follow. But even the "golden age" was far from golden. Television, in reality, provided little more than opportunity to presidents. It was soon evident that the value of that opportunity depended on a president's skill and creativity in using it. Sensing this, presidents began to build staffs of people who were media savvy, and they and those staffs began to experiment with strategies designed to yield the potential benefits that access to the national audience and the evolving characteristics of news reporting provided.

More and more senior advisors to presidents came from backgrounds in advertising, marketing, and public relations, rather than politics or policy. In many ways, making news was almost as important to the president as making policy. The public presidency became an end in itself. If the president's day ended with positive stories on the evening network news, if his job approval rating inched higher, those were good days in the White

House. And growing portions of the president's time were being spent in travel, public appearances, ceremonies and speeches designed to accomplish those ends. A primary task for every White House in the broadcast age was to manufacture spectacles that would enhance the visibility and, presumably, the influence of the president.[17]

It became the conventional wisdom in the White Houses of the "golden age," and especially after the congressional reforms of the early 1970s eroded the consummate bargaining power of the committee chairs and party leaders in Congress, that the way to accomplish presidential objectives in Washington was to build public support for them in the country. Political scientist Samuel Kernell captured the change incisively in a book titled *Going Public*. "'Going public' . . . is a strategy whereby a president promotes himself and his policies in Washington by appealing directly to the American public for support. . . . Going public should be appreciated as a strategic adaptation to the information age. . . . If the public ruminations of politicians are to be believed, the president's effectiveness in rallying public support has become a primary consideration for those who do business with him."[18]

What was happening here was a coalescence of political reality, leadership strategy, and technological imperative. Presidents found it increasingly difficult to succeed at the insider's game of elite political bargaining that had dominated in the middle decades of the twentieth century. Effective bargaining partners were harder to find as the influence of party bosses and once-dominant congressional committee chairs waned.

Presidents came to believe that individual members of Congress had become decreasingly dependent on their party leaders and increasingly responsive only to their constituents. The way to win the support of members, therefore, was to win the support of their constituents. And these alterations of political reality were occurring just as presidents were acquiring new resources for reaching out to those constituents and urging them to push their representatives in Congress to support presidential initiatives.

Even the consummate insider, Lyndon Johnson, recognized the new reality. "When traditional methods fail," he wrote, "a President must be willing to bypass the Congress and take the issue to the people. By instinct and experience, I preferred to work from within, knowing that good legislation is the product, not of public rhetoric but of private negotiations and compromise. But sometimes a President has to put Congress's feet to the fire."[19]

Ronald Reagan held a similar view. In his memoirs he recalled his efforts to neutralize the opposition of Dan Rostenkowski, a powerful Democrat who opposed many of his economic initiatives:

> I . . . used my visit to the district of Dan Rostenkowski, chairman of the House Ways and Means Committee, to point out to his constituents that he held the fate of the tax-cut proposals in his palm. I urged them to write to him: "If all

of you will join with your neighbors to send the same message to Washington, we'll have that tax cut and we'll have it this year." I was told that the speech generated hundreds of letters to Rostenkowski, who subsequently became something of a conciliatory voice among the Democratic leaders in the House.[20]

The reality, however, rarely fit the fantasy. It is hard to imagine that any president could have wished for or designed a communications environment more conducive to effective presidential leadership than this. Direct access to a large, national audience. Little interference or intermediation from editors or commentators. Overwhelming advantages over political opponents in dominating the public discourse. And yet in this era, Kennedy struggled to get the most important elements of his legislative program through Congress, Lyndon Johnson fell from grace and gave up on reelection, Richard Nixon was driven out of town, Gerald Ford failed to win reelection, and Jimmy Carter suffered the same fate. All of the presidents of the "golden age" left office with lower job approval ratings than they began with.

Television in this era was a marvelous instrument for pulling the country together at times of great danger or challenge—the Cuban Missile crisis, the Kennedy assassination, the civil rights turning points in Birmingham and Selma, the Nixon resignation. But as a day-to-day instrument of presidential leadership, the record is mixed. Presidents in the broadcast era were certainly more prominent than ever before, but often more prominent than powerful. Even with an instrument of such vast reach and deep penetration as television, even in the hands of presidents who were telegenic and rhetorically skillful, even when the rules of journalism granted presidents unprecedented deference, presidents could not overcome with great frequency the constitutional and political impediments to effective executive leadership. Where presidents sought to lead, the American people—and their representatives in Congress—were often unwilling to follow.

"Presidents typically do not succeed in their efforts to change public opinion," wrote political scientist George Edwards at the beginning of the twenty-first century. "Even 'great communicators' usually fail to obtain the public's support for their high priority initiatives....Presidents usually fail to move the general public and are frustrated in their attempts to move those who should be most attuned to their messages."[21]

And soon it got worse.

THE MODERN MEDIA ENVIRONMENT

Again it is technological evolution that reshapes political reality. In the 1980s, two technological changes began to erode the captive audience that presidents had enjoyed for the previous thirty-five years. One was video recording and the production and rapid consumer adoption of video cassette recorders (VCRs). Only one percent of American homes had VCRs in 1980, but by 1986, ownership had swelled to a third of homes and by the end of the decade to more than half.[22] This is the first of what would be many challenges to real-time viewing of television broadcasts, or of what some call "time shifting." Equipped with a VCR, Americans could record programs at one time and watch them later. Or they could go to the local video store and buy or rent a movie to watch at home.

Simultaneous with this development was the spread of cable television, the replacement of broadcasting over the airwaves with transmission by wires. Cable improved the quality of television reception in many places, but more importantly to consumers it enlarged the number of available television channels. Cable had been around almost since the beginning of commercial television. But the addition of satellite technology and the incentives of new programming options like HBO and ESPN spurred rapid growth in the early 1980s. By 1985, 41.5 million households—nearly half of American homes—received their television signals over cable.[23] The three-decade oligopoly of the major networks was coming to an end. New cable networks popped up everywhere, and soon home viewers had dozens of choices when they turned on their sets.

One of those new choices was the first all-news network, Cable News Network (CNN), which appeared in 1980. CNN's home studios were in Atlanta but it had correspondents and affiliate stations across the country and around the world. For twenty-four hours every day, it reported the news. But it was soon apparent that there wasn't enough news on most days to fill twenty-four hours with unique stories, so CNN began to develop programming that provided commentary on the news by journalists, academics, and political insiders. The model for these programs was one called _Crossfire_ in which liberals and conservatives, Republicans and Democrats, would argue, often in vehement shouting matches, about current events— and not uncommonly about the performance of the president.

In the 1990s, satellite broadcasting became a commercial option. By the end of that decade, there were nearly 10 million subscribers to DirectTV, one of the satellite providers.[24] DirectTV, the Dish Network, and others sent television signals from satellites to home antennae and further multiplied the number of channels available to Americans.

The twenty-first century brought a rapid expansion of new entertainment and news options for Americans. The Internet had emerged as an important new form of communication in the 1990s, but in the following decade it exploded, penetrating the population faster than any previous communications technology. By the beginning of 2014, 87 percent of American adults reported that they used the Internet, and more than half owned a smart phone that allowed them to connect to the Internet anytime, anywhere.[25]

Internet content mushroomed as well. In 1998, there were 26 million pages of Internet content. A decade later there were one trillion and the number of new pages was growing at a rate of several billion each day.[26] No longer confined to the offerings of three television networks, an American could watch a recorded show or a streaming movie, listen to selected music on an iPod, e-mail or text with acquaintances, follow the exploits of friends on Facebook, read a blog, or watch one of the new ideologically tinted cable channels like MSNBC or Fox News.

The news business was still a business, but it barely resembled its character in the earlier broadcast age. It had decentralized to the point of fragmentation. Instead of a few primary news sources, there were hundreds, perhaps thousands. You didn't need a printing press nor a broadcast station to produce "news" anymore; you just needed a computer and an Internet connection. The old rules about objective reporting and separation of news and opinion, while still honored by the legacy networks and a few newspapers, had been challenged and overwhelmed by people named Matt Drudge, Sean Hannity, and Chris Matthews.

Bloggers of every ideological stripe multiplied constantly. As Elliot King noted about the growth of blogs in his study of the impact of the Internet on journalism: "From fewer than one hundred Web sites that might be called blogs in 1999, it was estimated that there were close to 500,000 blogs by 2002, and a blog was being started every 40 seconds. By 2004 . . . there were more than 4 million blogs. That year blogs were being added at the rate of 12,000 a day, or one every 7.2 seconds."[27] A consumer of blogs never had to leave his or her ideological comfort zone.

Opinion polling, once the province of a few esteemed and methodologically cautious organizations like those founded by George Gallup and Louis Harris, became common currency in the news and political advocacy businesses. When polls became news, the news organizations began to produce their own. And political advocates soon followed suit, often with methodologically questionable polls they hoped to insert into national debates.

Radio that seemed to have been bypassed by television in the latter decades of the broadcast age, recovered dramatically in the late twentieth and early twenty-first centuries, riding the wave of popularity of a programming format called talk radio. About 400 stations carried talk radio programming in 1990; by 2010 that number had grown to nearly 3,000.[28] Talk radio was little more than a host offering his or her opinions on current events and taking phone calls from listeners nearly all of whom cheered on the host. Rush Limbaugh, with an audience of millions,[29] perhaps tens of millions, soon became the most prominent of these talk radio hosts. But others—Sean Hannity, Michael Savage, and Laura Ingraham, for example—also typically reached millions of listeners each week.

The talk radio business was highly competitive. And the key to success seemed to be anger and indignation. The more provocative the host, the more extreme his or her commentary, the larger the audience that tuned in. This business model, concludes one careful study of the impact of talk radio, "represents the growth of an industry that makes profits in large part by peddling political outrage and fueling the fires of polarization."[30]

The earlier broadcast age was characterized by a concentration of elite news sources similar in the subjects and tone of their news coverage, a national audience nearly all receiving their news from the same small number of sources, a commitment to objective and accurate reporting and separation of news and opinion, civility in the normal relations between the press and government officials, high levels of public trust of the news media, and generally favorable news coverage of American presidents.[31]

The new media age bears none of these characteristics. News sources have multiplied and diversified. The news audience has fragmented into thousands of different parts. Journalistic standards are in disarray, and the separation of news from opinion is no longer widely honored. Factual accuracy often gives way to ideological bent. Incivility, even hostility, often characterizes the relations between journalists and commentators, on the one hand, and government officials on the other. Public trust in the news media is in steep decline.[32]

What, then, is the impact of this evolution in media environments on presidents of the United States? Nothing good, it now appears.

The end of the broadcast age has yielded an escalation in competition among news organizations. But it is in many ways a race to the bottom. Instead of succeeding in the competition by adopting the highest standards of professional journalism, by carefully verifying the accuracy of stories before reporting them, by focusing on matters—even complex matters—of greatest importance to the American people, large segments of the news media have turned in the opposite direction.

There is less hard news than in the past, news about government, public policy, official actions. And there is consequently more soft news: lifestyle reports, "human interest" stories, updates on the activities of celebrities, high-profile crimes, and criminal trials. An impact, according to every recent study of the phenomenon, is that there is less news about American presidents than in the past. For example, an examination of news patterns by political scientists Matthew Eshbaugh-Soha and Jeffrey S. Peake con- cluded: "The decline in hard news among the three networks broadcast is striking. In 1977 about two-thirds or more of broadcast news stories dealt with government and policy, the hard news categories. That dropped to about 40 percent by 1997. . . . No matter which data we inspect, we find declines in presidential news that began sometime in the late 1970s or early 1980s."[33]

This has two secondary impacts. One is that the reduction in news reporting about the president makes it more difficult for presidents to reach the American people, to tell their story, to influence public opinion, to build support for their policy initiatives. The other is that the news hole left by the diminished reporting on the president is now available to those who would oppose the president or his policies. The less the president dominates the news, the more room there is for dissenting or critical views.

Another impact of the altered media environment has been a steady increase in negative news about presidents and in open and often hostile criticism of presidents and their actions. "Increasingly the coverage of the president (and other political leaders) is negative from the initial campaign through their term in office," writes political scientist Richard Pious. "Reporters dissect and question the president's strategies and motivations. Any maneuver, any rhetorical shifting of ground that can be detected over the course of an entire term, any attempt to exercise the art of political compromise, becomes a bad-news story, with a negative valence: The president is waffling, pandering, or posturing."[34]

The common civility of the broadcast era no longer prevails. Reporters, even those working for the elite media, now make their reputations by baiting and challenging public officials, by seeking to put them on the defensive, by engaging them in verbal combat. Presidential press conferences, for example, were initiated in the early years of the twentieth century as opportunities for presidents to enrich the understanding and thus the reporting of journalists. They were often conversational and educational. More often now they resemble a combat zone, with only a lectern separating the combatants.

The all-news networks have relatively small audiences by national television standards, but the composition of those audiences makes them more important to the national discourse than the numbers would suggest. In a recent study of the new media environment, journalism professor Elliot King noted the impact of CNN in its early days when it "came to be monitored continually by the power elite in Washington, DC, including reporters for other media outlets. Offices in the Pentagon, the State Department, and the White House reportedly had CNN turned on at all times."[35] The all-news networks have become the forum in which politicians and opinion leaders talk to each other—and to their funding sources and leading constituents.

These networks have adopted a standard programming approach intended to suggest a "balanced" discussion of the day's news stories. For every guest who supports a president's actions, there must be one who opposes or attacks them. Some of these "commentators" have become well known and well compensated for their skill in provocation and oversimplification. James Carville, Laura Ingraham, Pat Buchanan, and Donna Brazile are among those who have become celebrities as a result of their frequent appearances on cable news and their skills at invective and criticism, at standing their ground even on the slipperiest factual footing. Some of the hosts and commentators are failed politicians—Sarah Palin, Mike Huckabee, and Eliot Spitzer—who come directly from combat in the political arena to combat in the media. To the commentators on the left, no Republican president ever did a praiseworthy thing; neither did any Democratic president to those on the right. Presidents come out on the short end at least half the time.

Public policies are often complex and the compromises necessary to enact them often difficult to explain. But the prevailing notion in contemporary television news is that the audience has little patience for discussions of complexity or sometimes even of facts. Audiences, it seems, are drawn to controversy and that's what the news networks aim to provide. Heat replaces light. And presidents get scorched more than any other victims.

The negativity is even greater and more frequent on talk radio and the scheduled evening programming of the all-news networks. Hardly a day passes without audio snippets taken out of context, edited quotes and misquotes, urban legends spreading like wildfire across the talk radio airwaves, and host-generated anger directed at the incumbent president. The president is the biggest target in politics and every talk radio host knows that listeners relate most strongly (and tune in most often) to indignant criticism of his actions or statements.

Talk radio leans right. Surveys by the Pew Research Center for the People and the Press found that "the audience for political talk radio remains more conservative and more Republican than the public at large. Among those who listen to these shows regularly, 44% describe themselves as conservatives, while only 19% consider themselves liberals."[36] Hence this is a free-fire zone when there is a Democrat in the White House as there has been for most of the resurgent talk radio era. But even George W. Bush received a good deal of bruising from talk radio hosts who found him not conservative enough for their tastes, too willing to compromise on education and welfare issues, too reluctant to exercise veto powers, too ineffective in fighting for Social Security privatization.

Even when the political invective is aimed at government in general rather than the president in particular, the president is no innocent bystander. It is simply too difficult for most news or commentary consumers to separate the one from the other. Criticism of the government must be criticism of the leader of the government. "There are plenty of bad-news stories in the antipolitics era," notes Richard Pious. "In the 1960s, less than one-third of the media's evaluations of top national political leaders were negative; that figure rose to more than two-thirds by the 1990s."[37]

One of the most debilitating consequences for presidents of the new media environment is the culture of durable falsehoods that it encourages.

The Whitewater "scandal" and the suicide of presidential aide Vincent Foster in the Clinton presidency, the accusations that George W. Bush had pulled political strings to avoid the Vietnam draft or had been a heavy drug user in college, the persistent charge that Barack Obama was not born in America and was thus ineligible to be president: these are stories that crop up at the extreme edges of politics but are then given credence by constant repetition on talk radio, Internet blogs, and the all-news networks. "The gossip that comes across the Internet comes in precisely the same format as does professional news, Wall Street reports, and important other factual information," notes Matthew Wald of the *New York Times*, "thus ordinary scuttlebutt at the water cooler . . . is now for the whole world to read and believe."[38]

The "birther" issue in the Obama presidency is an apt example. In a mid-2009 survey by the Pew Research Center, 80 percent of Americans responded that they had heard about the claims that President Obama was not an American at birth and thus ineligible to be president.[39] A number of other polls found that among Republicans often a third or more believed the claims.[40] Evidence provided by the White House—official birth certificates, contemporary news reports of Obama's birth, evidence of his mother's U.S. citizenship—were insufficient to extinguish the incessant retelling of falsehoods by those who opposed him.

The constancy of criticism of their actions and motives is only one of the challenges that the new media environment poses for presidents. Presidential credibility, a highly important asset to presidents, is hard to sustain in the face of those assaults. But this environment also affects the other actors with whom the president has to deal in seeking to secure policy objectives. It is harder now, for example, for presidents to recruit and retain highly qualified executive branch officials. Too many are reluctant to enter the swamps of the modern media environment, to risk the reputations they have spent a lifetime acquiring. Those who have to review and confirm them in the Senate are often urged to delay or oppose the president's personnel choices by the hanging judges in the blogosphere and talk radio. The nomination and confirmation processes for presidential appointees have become yet another combat zone of modern politics, complicating the administrative tasks of every president.[41]

Members of Congress whose support the president needs often have their negotiating latitude narrowed by the close observation of bloggers, talk radio hosts, and the all-news networks. It is simply more difficult to work with a president, let alone follow his lead, if any appearance of compromise or consent is likely to bring the sword of Damocles (or Rush Limbaugh) down on one's political neck. Firestorms of outrage and opposition spread with remarkable speed in contemporary politics, and no reelection-minded politician wants to be a burn victim.

In 2006, for example, the Bush administration supported the purchase of the rights to manage six American cargo ports by DP World, a state-owned company based in the United Arab Emirates. This was a business deal of the sort that is increasingly common in a global economy. The rights had previously been owned by a British company. But once some political bloggers got wind of the story—An Arab company! Running American ports!—they pushed it into the vast echo chamber of the modern media environment. Soon politicians from both parties joined the debate; newspapers and talk show hosts took sides, and Bush found himself under multipronged attack. When the Congress threatened to pass legislation to void the deal, Bush threatened to veto it.

Eventually, DP World agreed to turn management of the ports over to an American entity and the fracas died down. But not before diminishing the president's standing in the eyes of his constituents. "In the aftermath of the Dubai ports deal," noted a report from the Pew Research Center, "President Bush's approval rating has hit a new low and his image for honesty and effectiveness has been damaged."[42] "We should have seen the uproar coming, and we didn't," lamented Secretary of State Condoleezza Rice.[43]

Nearly all of the apparent advantages that the broadcast era provided to American presidents have vanished in the new media environment. There is less news about presidents and the news itself is often more negative. There is much less public trust of the news media, so even positive stories are often discounted. The president's critics and opponents have many more outlets and avenues to public opinion than ever before and those are less regulated by law, policy, and common decency than in the past. It is, for all of these reasons, simply harder than it was in the past for presidents to be effective and persuasive leaders.

THE WHITE HOUSE RESPONDS

Presidents adapt to reality. When their environment changes, their behavior changes. That's a basic rule of survival in politics as in biology.

Presidents adapted to the emergence of vast national newspaper chains by cultivating the growing Washington press corps with printed advance copies of their speeches, designated aides to respond to news queries, and press conferences. The concept of a public presidency took root. As the broadcast era unfolded, presidents learned to use radio and then television for their purposes. They built staffs of people who understood modern advertising and public relations. When jet planes facilitated wider presidential travel, presidents left Washington more often, to the countryside and abroad, often to create events that would attract broadcast coverage.

The new media age has had its own extensive impacts on the organization of the institutionalized presidency and the behavior of incumbents.
But this new age came so quickly, with so many facets, and with such frequent reinvention that it has been a constant scramble for presidents of the
past few decades to make sense of the communications environment and
to find their footing within it.

Presidents have responded in a number of ways to the changes that have
washed over them. The style of "going public," of using the high visibility of
the White House and presidential dominance of the news to build national
public support for presidential initiatives, could not survive the diminished
visibility and less frequent and more negative news coverage that have
characterized the contemporary era. Presidents travel more than in the past
and give more speeches than ever. But the formats and the purposes are
different.

The prime-time television address, the principal weapon in the president's arsenal during the broadcast era, is close to obsolescence now.
Prime-time addresses to the nation are rarer in number, the audience much
smaller than in the past, and the impact much weaker.[44] Presidents in our
own time simply cannot gain from them the kind of political traction that
these addresses afforded their predecessors. Most have given up trying.

A similar fate has befallen the televised presidential press conference. The
casual conferences that Franklin Roosevelt held twice a week in the Oval
Office and the dignified affairs that President Kennedy held twice a month
for national television audiences in the State Department auditorium have
passed into history. Press conferences are still a part of the relationship
between the president and the press; presidents in the new media age
have averaged more than two a month.[45] But often these occur now with
little advance scheduling and infrequent coverage by the major broadcast
networks. Where Roosevelt and Kennedy saw press conferences as valuable
opportunities for shaping and leading public opinion, presidents in our
time tend to see them as necessary evils that avail them of little political
advantage and much risk.

With leadership of national public opinion posing such enormous challenges for contemporary presidents, they have looked elsewhere for leverage
and opportunity. A number of recent and excellent studies of presidential
communications strategies have determined that they have replaced the
broad strategy of "going public" with much more targeted strategies of
"going local."[46]

Presidents now leave Washington often to address audiences in strategically located states or cities or to reach out to strategically important organizations. Their goal is to try to shift or strengthen public opinion in areas
where it might be a tipping point in national debates. Sometimes, their target is independent or undecided citizens who might be potential supporters

of presidential initiatives. More often the target is known supporters whose enthusiasm and activism the president seeks to sustain or heighten.

This is not so much a change in the game as in the way it is played. Presidents still believe that their best opportunity for building winning legislative coalitions is through triangulation: winning the support of members of Congress by building support among their constituents. But instead of seeking to do this in broad strokes to a national audience, presidents seek to cobble together national coalitions by building regional and interest-based pockets of support. The new approach is more difficult and demanding than the older one, but the older one is no longer available.

So presidents give more speeches than ever before. They travel more often and appear more often in public when they do. They engage in more interviews and other controlled interactions with reporters, both local and national. And they spend more time raising money for their political parties and for congressional candidates who have in the past or are likely in the future to support their policy priorities.

The numbers tell a clear and powerful story about these changes in presidential behavior. From 1949 to 1992, presidents averaged thirty-nine appearances per year outside Washington. Presidents since then have averaged more than a hundred. In the 1950s and 1960s, presidents averaged about 154 speeches per year. From 1974 to 2009, the average was 351 a year.[47] And, while press conference numbers have remained reasonably steady over time, individual interviews and other more controlled meetings with national and local reporters have escalated in number and strategic importance. According to one study, for example, President Clinton had the same number of formal press conferences as President Eisenhower (193), but in addition he met with reporters in other venues 1,500 times.[48]

Supporting these new forms of presidential behavior has required new structures and more personnel in the institutional presidency. Because presidents give more speeches, there are more speechwriters. Because travel is more common, there is a large staff of planning and advance people to prepare for the president's trips and ensure that each event occurs in the proper setting with the proper audience for the purpose the president hopes to accomplish. Because presidents are more consistently active in party and electoral politics, even outside the normal election season, political staffs in the White House have grown in size and importance as well.

Martha Joynt Kumar, a political scientist who spent several years directly observing communications operations from an office within the White House press room, has calculated the dimensions of those operations:

Contemporary communications operations involve several units and many people. The domain of [George W.] Bush's first two communications directors extended from the Offices of Communications, Media Affairs, Speechwriting, and Global Communications to the Press Office and the Photography Office. In 2005, after the Office of Global Communications was eliminated, the remaining offices had sixty-three full-time employees. Add another twenty-one working on communications and the press in the Office of the Vice President, the Office of the First Lady, and the National Security Council. Include also the twenty-four staff members working in communications for ancillary operations in the Executive Office of the President (who are not White House staff members), at the Office of Management and Budget, the Council on Environmental Quality, the Office of National Drug Policy, and the United States Trade Representative.

In addition to these 150 front-line employees, there were nearly 200 people working in communications-related support operations . . . scheduling public appearances, making travel arrangements, and analyzing all of the public correspondence (paper or electronic) that arrives at the White House.

A conservative estimate at the beginning of his second term has approximately 350 people in the Bush White House working in communications and supporting operations.[49]

Kumar goes on to note that the communications staff in just the White House itself was almost twice as large as the combined staffs of the economic and domestic policy operations in the executive office. But even these numbers don't fully reveal the emphasis that communications and public relations command in the contemporary presidency. Mike McCurry, a press secretary for President Clinton, notes that "just about everybody who has any serious, consequential role at the White House, from the chief of staff on down, has to be mindful of, cognizant of playing a role in how are we going to communicate, how are we going to present our message, how are we going to put our best argument forward?"[50]

The Permanent Campaign

The task of being president these days closely resembles the task of becoming one. All of the accouterments of a presidential campaign are now characteristics as well of White House operations: constant travel, frequent speech making, endless fund-raising, and war rooms for rapid response to opponents and critics. As political scientist Charles W. Dunn has noted, "Presidents in the twenty-first century must master the art and science of weaving their campaigning and governing together as an undivided whole."[51]

When Jimmy Carter took office in 1977, a young aide, Pat Caddell, wrote him a long, prescient memo in which he said, "governing with public approval requires a continuing political campaign."[52] Thus was born the permanent campaign that has been a feature of every White House since then. When presidents travel it is often to "battleground states" where tipping points in legislative battles (and reelection contests) are most likely to reside. Trips featuring presidential speeches or events are also likely to include at least one fund-raiser for the president, his party, an organization that supports him, or congressional candidates who, more often than not, are on his side. Careful calculations by political scientist Brendan J. Doherty found that between 1977 and 2011, presidents held 4,526 events outside the Washington metropolitan area and that 26 percent of these were fund-raisers and another 14 percent were events related to fund-raisers.[53]

Dick Morris, a political consultant with a bird's-eye view of Bill Clinton's political activities, described the burden of fund-raising that weighs on all contemporary presidents:

> During the Clinton presidency, fund-raising consumed about a third of the president's public schedule when he was in the United States. Almost every night would include a trip to a fund-raiser; on travels around the country, there would often be several events on the same day. In scheduling the president, we looked first at his fund-raising schedule, building public and press events around the receptions, fitting them in between a fund-raising luncheon and the evening campaign finance events, so that Clinton could justify making the poor taxpayers—rather than the Democratic Party—pay for his travels.[54]

The president's daily schedule is full of positive valence events that have little direct impact on the real tasks of a national chief executive but may contribute to the halo effect that is presumed to sustain or enlarge public support. And they consume a lot of precious time. Presidents now meet in the White House with championship athletes and athletic teams in virtually every sport, college or professional. They have become the nation's mourners-in-chief, appearing regularly at funerals and memorial services for symbolic national figures and victims of fires, violence, or tragedy.

Pseudo-events fill presidential travel. When Bill Clinton visited Normandy in 1994 to celebrate the 50th anniversary of the D-Day invasion, he was repeating an event from which Ronald Reagan had reaped favorable publicity a decade earlier. During his time there, the television audience at home was treated to what appeared to be a lonely and pensive walk by Clinton along Omaha Beach where at one point he came across a pile of stones and stooped to arrange them in the shape of a cross. To the innocent home viewer, it appeared as a spontaneous moment. To the White House staff that had collected the pile of stones, prepped the president, and alerted the photographers, it was just another event that went as planned.

Polling is now a constant in White House operations as it is in presidential campaigns. Few presidential initiatives see the light of day until their acceptability has been carefully polled and tested in focus groups and tactical leaks sometimes called "trial balloons." Consultants with political backgrounds play a key role in deciding what policies presidents will embrace, what battles they will engage, and what activities will fill their day. People like Dick Morris, Karl Rove, and David Axelrod become primary advisers to modern presidents not because they are skilled in the legislative process or well tutored in the details of public policy, but because presidents rely on them to manage the permanent campaign which is now at the heart of every president's leadership strategy. "Rove," noted one study of the relationship between George W. Bush and his primary political adviser, "is shaping policy based on politics. He reads the polls and studies political trends then argues for policies that point in the same direction."[55]

"Leading the public is at the core of the modern presidency," writes political scientist George Edwards. "Even as they try to govern, presidents are involved in a permanent campaign. . . . The division between campaigning and governing has become obscured. Indeed, governing often seems little more than an extension of the campaign that won the president his office in the first place."[56]

CONSEQUENCES

The broadcast age changed the presidency, but it also changed public perceptions of the presidency. Presidents came to believe that television and the frequently benign news environment afforded them unprecedented opportunities for national leadership. Fred Friendly of CBS captured the period's prevailing view when he said of presidents: "No mighty King, no ambitious Emperor, no Pope, no prophet ever dreamt of such an awesome pulpit, such a magic wand."[57]

In response, presidents took to the airwaves. Every major policy initiative, every crisis, every dark national moment came with a prime-time television address. Press conferences became presidential show and tell. The White House swimming pool was converted to a press room so that reporters could be at the ready, a few feet from the Oval Office. Caravans of cameras and journalists followed presidents whenever they traveled and, oh, did they travel.

An unsurprising consequence of this was that the broadcast age made presidents celebrities in ways they had never been before. Their lives were our lives, their families extensions of our own. To many Americans the enlarged visibility of the president seemed to signal an enlarged importance. Surely a public figure of this prominence must be a very powerful person indeed.

But even in the broadcast age, presidents struggled to convert their prominence into power. The prime-time addresses, the masterful press conferences, the glamorous state dinners, the spectacles often did little to broaden public support, to improve presidential relations with Congress, to accomplish presidential objectives. Ronald Reagan, for example, made it a high priority of his administration to provide American support for the Contra rebels in Nicaragua in their struggle to overthrow the leftist-leaning Sandinista government. He spoke of their cause on television, calling them "freedom fighters"[58] and comparing them to American patriots of the revolutionary war. He traveled the country to drum up congressional support for aid to the Contras. But he never succeeded—a failure he admitted in his memoirs: "Time and again, I would speak on television, to a joint session of Congress, or to other audiences about the problems in Central America. . . . But the polls usually found that large numbers of Americans cared little or not at all about what happened in Central America."[59]

The broadcast age never fulfilled its promise for presidents. The opportunities for national leadership it seemed to dangle in front of them were more mirage than miracle. Television and radio broadened the president's reach, but rarely his grasp.

The visibility and celebrity of the presidents in the broadcast era did, however, raise public expectations about presidential performance. It created a new illusion of presidential power. Americans came to expect that presidents could get things done precisely, because they had such wondrous instruments of communication and persuasion. They expected constant and effective leadership from the president because presidents, more than any other actors in national politics, commanded the tools of the trade. That presidential leadership often fell short of presidential objectives contributed to the growing gap between expectations and performance that has confounded the modern presidency.

When the broadcast age evolved into the contemporary media environment, expectations did not diminish. The illusion of presidential power did not evaporate, but opportunities did. And the pattern of disappointment became more persistent than ever. Presidents continue to struggle to communicate with the American people, to build public support for their policy priorities. They work very hard at this—with the help of hundreds of people on the White House staff. It consumes vast portions of presidential time. But communication is more difficult, the audience more fragmented, the news media more hostile, and the opposition more empowered than in the past. And for contemporary presidents the task of national opinion leadership is often overwhelming.

All of this matters, and greatly. In a political realm where elections do not deliver governing coalitions nor settle policy disputes, where partisanship has a very sharp edge, where executive powers rarely equal executive responsibilities, presidents depend heavily on public support. As their tools for building that support deteriorate and the opposition and resistance to their efforts multiply, the leadership capacity of the presidency diminishes, the government dawdles, and the country suffers.

NOTES

1. Garry Wills, *Lincoln at Gettysburg: The Words That Remade America* (New York: Simon and Schuster, 1992).

2. Allan Nevins, ed., *Polk: The Diary of a President* (New York: Capricorn Books, 1968), 340.

3. Stephen Ponder, *Managing the Press: Origins of the Media Presidency, 1897-1933* (New York: St. Martin's, 1998), xiv.

4. Wilson, *Constitutional Government in the United States*, 70–71.

5. Ronald J. Pestritto, ed., *Woodrow Wilson: The Essential Political Writings* (Lanham, MD: Lexington Books, 2005), 19.

6. Jeffrey K. Tulis, *The Rhetorical Presidency* (Princeton, NJ: Princeton University Press, 1988).

7. "A Million Persons Will Hear Coolidge's Voice When He Addresses Congress This Afternoon," *New York Times*, December 5, 1923.

8. Ponder, *Managing the Press*, xv–xvi.

9. U.S. Bureau of the Census, *Historical Statistics of the United States, Colonial Times to 1970* (Washington, DC: Government Printing Office, 1975), Part 2, 792ff.

10. Emmet John Hughes, *The Living Presidency* (New York: Penguin Books, 1972), 160.

11. Theodore C. Sorensen, *Kennedy* (New York: Harper and Row, 1965), 328.

12. Quoted by John A. Barnes, *John F. Kennedy on Leadership* (New York: AMACOM, 2007), 35.

13. University of Minnesota, *Media History Project*, accessed October 15, 2015, www.mediahistory.umn.edu/timeline/1960-1969.html.

14. See, for example, Matthew A. Baum and Samuel Kernell, "Has Cable Ended the Golden Age of Presidential Television?" *American Political Science Review* 93(1), (1999): 1–16.

15. Calculated by the author from data in Samuel Kernell, *Going Public: New Strategies of Presidential Leadership*, 4th ed. (Washington: CQ Press, 2007), 116–18.

16. Jeffrey E. Cohen, *The Presidency in the Era of 24-Hour News* (Princeton, NJ: Princeton University Press, 2008), 27–28.

17. See Bruce Miroff, "The Presidential Spectacle," in *The Presidency and the Political System*, edited by Michael Nelson, 9th ed. (Washington, DC: CQ Press, 2010), 210–35.

18. Kernell, *Going Public*, 1–2.

19. Lyndon B. Johnson, *The Vantage Point: Perspectives on the Presidency, 1963–1969* (New York: Holt, Rinehart and Winston, 1971), 450.

20. Ronald Reagan, *An American Life* (New York: Simon and Schuster, 1990), 286–87.

21. George C. Edwards III, *On Deaf Ears: The Limits of the Bully Pulpit* (New Haven, CT: Yale University Press, 2003), 241.

22. Center for Media Literacy, "Video is Here to Stay," accessed October 15, 2015, www.medialit.org/reading-room/video-here-stay.

23. Gareth Marples, "The History of Cable TV—Can You Remember?" accessed October 15, 2015, www.thehistoryof.net/history-of-cable-tv.html.

24. "DirecTV," accessed October 15, 2015, www.en.wikipedia.org/wiki/DirecTV.

25. Pew Research Internet Project, "Internet Use Over Time," accessed October 15, 2015, http://www.pewinternet.org/data-trend/internet-use/internet-use-over-time/.

26. Bill Kovarik, *Revolutions in Communications: Media History from Gutenberg to the Digital Age* (New York: Continuum, 2011), 294.

27. Elliot King, *Free for All: The Internet's Transformation of Journalism* (Evanston, IL: Northwestern University Press, 2010), 234.

28. Kovarik, *Going Public*, 232.

29. The size of radio audiences is difficult to determine with precision because not all networks carry programs at the same time and some carry only a portion of the original program. Most estimates of Limbaugh's weekly audience put the size at greater than 10 million.

30. Jeffrey M. Berry and Sarah Sobieraj, "Understanding the Rise of Talk Radio," *PS* (2011): 767.

31. For support of these characterizations, see Kernell, *Going Public*; Jeffrey E. Cohen, *Going Local: Presidential Leadership in the Post-Broadcast Age* (New York: Cambridge University Press, 2010); Matthew Eshbaugh-Soha and Jeffrey S. Peake, *Breaking Through the Noise: Presidential Leadership, Public Opinion, and the News Media* (Stanford, CA: Stanford University Press, 2011).

32. Jonathan M. Ladd, *Why Americans Hate the Media and How It Matters* (Princeton, NJ: Princeton University Press, 2012), 6.

33. Cohen, *The Presidency In The Era of 24-Hour News*, 64, 70.

34. Richard M. Pious, *Why Presidents Fail* (Lanham, MD: Rowman and Littlefield, 2008), 268.

35. King, *Free for All*, 51.

36. "Key News Audiences Now Blend Online and Traditional Sources: Audience Segments in a Changing News Environment," Pew Research Center for the People and the Press, August 17, 2008, accessed October 15, 2015, http://www.people-press.org/2008/08/17/watching-reading-and-listening-to-the-news/.

37. Pious, 268.

38. Matthew Wald, "Cyber Mouse That Roared, Implausibly," *New York Times*, Week in Review, October 10, 1996.

39. "Many Fault Media Coverage of Health Care Debate: Partisan Divide Over Coverage of" Pew Research Center for the People and the Press, August 6, 2009, accessed October 15, 2015, http://www.people-press.org/2009/08/06/many-fault-media-coverage-of-health-care-debate/.

40. These polls are summarized at https://en.wikipedia.org/wiki/Barack_Obama_citizenship_conspiracy_theories, accessed October 15, 2015.

41. See G. Calvin Mackenzie, ed., *Innocent Until Nominated: The Breakdown of the Presidential Appointments Process* (Washington, DC: Brookings, 2001) and David E. Lewis, *The Politics of Presidential Appointments* (Princeton, NJ: Princeton University Press, 2008).

42. "Bush Approval Falls to 33%, Congress Earns Rare Praise: Dubai Ports Fallout," Pew Research Center for the People and the Press, March 15, 2006, accessed October 15, 2015, http://www.people-press.org/2006/03/15/bush-approval-falls-to-33-congress-earns-rare-praise/.

43. Condoleezza Rice, *No Higher Honor: A Memoir of My Years in Washington* (New York: Random House, 2011), 435.

44. Baum and Kernell, "Has Cable Ended the Golden Age of Presidential Television?" 110.

45. Average for the years 1989–2012 calculated by the author from data provided by the American Presidency Project, accessed October 15, 2015, http://www.presidency.ucsb.edu/data/newsconferences.php.

46. Note especially Eshbaugh-Soha and Peake, *Breaking Through the Noise*; Kernell, *Going Public*; Cohen, *Going Local*; and Brendan J. Doherty, *The Rise of the President's Permanent Campaign* (Lawrence, KS: University Press of Kansas, 2012).

47. Eshbaugh-Soha and Peake, *Breaking Through the Noise*, 6, 156.

48. Martha Joynt Kumar, *Managing the President's Message: The White House Communications Operation* (Baltimore: Johns Hopkins University Press, 2007), xxx.

49. Kumar, *Managing the President's Message*, 4–5.

50. Quoted in Kumar, *Managing the President's Message*, 5.

51. Charles W. Dunn, "The Presidency in the Twenty-first Century: Continuity and Change," in *The Presidency in the Twenty-First Century*, edited by Charles W. Dunn (Lexington, KY: University Press of Kentucky, 2011), 4.

52. Quoted in Joe Klein, *Politics Lost*, 38.

53. Doherty, *The Rise of the President's Permanent Campaign*, 98.

54. Dick Morris, *Because He Could* (New York: Regan Books of HarperCollins, 2004), 173.

55. James Moore and Wayne Slater, *Bush's Brain: How Karl Rove Made George W. Bush Presidential* (Hoboken, NJ: John Wiley and Sons, 2003), 10.

56. Edwards, "The Limits of the Bully Pulpit," in *Readings in Presidential Politics*, edited by George C. Edwards III (Belmont, CA: Wadsworth, 2006), 184.

57. Fred Friendly, "Foreword," in *Presidential Television, A Twentieth Century Fund Report*, edited by Newton N. Minow, John Bartlow Martin, and Lee M. Mitchell (New York, New York: Basic Books, 1973), vii.

58. Ronald Reagan, "Televised Address to the Nation," May 9, 1984.

59. Reagan, *An American Life*, 479.

5

Forces of Resistance

No president is an island. The task of governing the American democracy is a collective enterprise where power is divided and shared—often widely and without clear borders or rules of engagement. To lead in such an environment requires vision and skills of persuasion and negotiation. But it also requires authority, for no person is sufficiently skilled to forge enduring majority coalitions amid the cacophony of disparate interests in a diverse democracy.

Every American president has confronted the reality that power has limits. But for contemporary presidents, the reality has often been overwhelming. It is no longer simply the case that power is shared, but that it is shared among an ever-widening group of institutions and interests, ever-more sophisticated in the tactics they employ, and with ever-more frequent intentions to prevent presidents from accomplishing even their limited objectives.

The Republican presidents of the 1920s inhabited a Washington with few competitors for power. The press corps was small and tame, interest groups were few and mostly cooperative, the Congress was dominated by a small oligarchy of party leaders and committee chairs with whom presidents could form relationships of mutual benefit. Many of the players were different a few years later when the New Deal swept into town, but for Franklin Roosevelt only the Supreme Court succeeded in holding back the tides of change.

Even into the early postwar decades, as the Washington community grew and diversified, the old rules continued to hold. Governance remained largely an insiders' game where critical negotiations took place out of public view. Party leaders and committee chairs in Congress could deliver support to a president who sought it effectively. Interest groups most often pursued their objectives through the medium of political parties, and the old hands of Washington—some in government and some on the periphery—could keep the wheels turning. It was far from perfect and hardly pretty, yet Washington was a place where things could get done and where a determined president could play the lead in determining what those things would be.

But that Washington no longer exists.

The presidential scholar Richard Neustadt wrote of the Washington community at mid-century that "all of its members are compelled to watch the President for reasons not of pleasure but vocation. They need him in their business just as he needs them."[1] But those were not eternal verities. The city in which Neustadt learned his politics as an aide to Harry Truman has evolved far beyond the dimensions he described. His recipe for presidential power—that presidents depend on their popular support and their political reputations—no longer fits contemporary realities. Presidents must still function in the Washington community. It's where government gets done. But today's Washington is a place so full of political polarities and procedural roadblocks that the only prevailing force is inertia.

Presidents rarely have opportunities to lead because they are so bereft of followers. Instead, in all of their efforts, they must compete. And their competitors have been growing steadily more numerous, more diverse, more sophisticated, and more obdurate. Presidents, even while expanding their own resources, have fallen further and further behind.

"To study one branch of government in isolation from the others is usually an exercise in make-believe," wrote Louis Fisher, a leading expert on legislative-executive relations.[2] The state of the presidency is inevitably a reflection of the state of the Congress. But the Congress and the presidency also reflect and absorb other characteristics of the political universe. In earlier chapters, we explored the impact of constitutional design and of changes in the electoral process and the communications media on the American presidency. Here, we must look more directly at the Congress and at the networks of special interests and policy activists that now envelop national policy making.

What we will see, more clearly than anything else, is a steady thickening of the governing process. On its way to enactment, every presidential initiative must pass more formal reviews, endure more scrutiny, fend off more opponents, and require more executive energy than ever before. From the White House perspective, it always seems like the defense has too many players on the field. And well it should, for Washington has become a place where the defenders of the status quo have enormous procedural and resource advantages over the proponents of change.

How that came to be and what it now means are the story of this chapter.

THE EMBOLDENED CONGRESS

On March 4, 2014, President Barack Obama submitted his annual budget recommendations to Congress for the coming fiscal year. The submission came more than a month after the deadline established by law for a president to send a budget proposal to Congress. But this was an improvement over the previous year when the president's budget for Fiscal Year 2014 was submitted on April 10, 2013.

In reality, these late submissions didn't much matter. Why would timeliness matter for an act of no consequence? The president's budget request has become a sham, little more than an opportunity for the president to make a political statement, documenting priorities and potential expenditures to appeal to his political base. President Obama's budget, like all recent presidential budget requests, was widely described as "dead on arrival."

Government budgets have always been political documents. Budgets reflect political choices. But until recently, budgets were not solely political documents. Nor were they sunk by the weight of their political cargoes. Presidents proposed budgets to Congress; then they hammered out the details with congressional appropriators. There was plenty of politics in these budget battles, but the politics sought a conclusion, one usually built on a foundation of compromise. The budget passed, government moved forward.

Not so in our time. It wasn't simply that the 113th Congress disagreed with the substantive recommendations of the incumbent president and intended to pass a budget reflecting its own priorities. The second session of the 113th Congress would pass no budget—just like the first session of that Congress and the several Congresses that preceded it. Most of the government would be funded, as it had been for years, by a series of continuing resolutions—a peculiar legislative device for acting without making decisions. Not since 1997 had the Congress passed all the regular appropriations bills on time. Through years in which the U.S. government was hemorrhaging debt in greater amounts than at any time in its history, the American Congress was incapable of performing the most basic act of any legislature: enacting a government budget.

Awkwardness has always been a dominant characteristic of the relationship between the president and the Congress. The Constitution bears primary responsibility for that because it creates a set of interlocking forms of power sharing. Over the course of American history, there have been ebbs and flows in this relationship. Sometimes, though rarely more than briefly, presidents prevailed. Most of the time, the Congress has been a frustration for presidents. Most, no doubt, would share Teddy Roosevelt's lament: "Oh, if I could only be president *and* Congress together for just ten minutes."[3]

But it is far too glib to view the current state of evolution in this relation-ship as just another one of those ebbs or flows. The kind of Congress we have today is without precedent. And there is little in its behavior or mood that portends any significant change in its operations in the foreseeable future.

The three great functions of any legislature are these: to represent citizens at the seat of government, to make laws to serve the common good, and to oversee the actions of the other branches of government and hold them accountable, that is, representation, legislation, and oversight. Over the course of its history, the Congress has varied in the way it has carried out these functions and varied the balance among them. In times of political ferment, in the first, fourth, and seventh decades of the twentieth century, for example, it has legislated vigorously. In times of war, it placed enhanced emphasis on its oversight activities.

But in our time, the representative functions of the Congress have come to dominate—one might even say to obliterate—all of its other behaviors. Today's Congress has become an aggregation of parts that do not sum. Its collective identity can only be described as the product of the individual identity of its 535 members. They inhabit the same institution, but instead of adapting their behavior to institutional purposes, they have adapted institutional behavior to their individual purposes. And they all share the same individual purpose: to get reelected.

Getting reelected, in the eyes of individual members, is not accomplished by passing laws. Nor is it accomplished by diligent and even-handed oversight of other branches. Getting reelected is deeply grounded, however, in acting as a faithful, unwavering representative of the defined interests of one's geographical constituents and of the cash constituents who fund reelection campaigns. The widely shared understanding on Capitol Hill is this: Be a good representative, do the bidding of those who vote for you and those who fund your campaigns, and your tenure in Congress is secure. It matters not whether you are a creative legislator or uncompromising overseer.

Congress today is little more than a confederation of 535 small busi-nesses. Their motive is not profit, but career maintenance. Each of them is headed by an elected member of the House or Senate whose actions are shaped by that motive. Each employs a staff whose primary purpose is to support the accomplishment of that motive (and to preserve their own jobs in the process). All of their resources from the federal treasury are spent in service to that motive through such things as trips home where the voters reside, self-advertisement, and constituency casework.

This has had potent consequences, nearly all of them negative, for the Congress as an institution. By 1990, as the journalist Alan Ehrenhalt reported:

It had become clear that too many of the 535 representatives and senators had locked themselves into a vicious circle of political responsiveness. As national problems grew more complex and less tractable, members of Congress sought to secure themselves in office by focusing on local interests and demands. However, the more they pursued this strategy, the further they sank into stalemate on national issues, fostering public disappointment and discontent with the institution as a whole. The members, growing ever more concerned about their political survival, responded with still further efforts at local responsiveness, which in turn generated even more deadlock, seemingly with no end in sight.[4]

Many members of Congress are honorable people. They believe in public service. They seek public policies that enlarge the common good. But they also believe that their continued presence in Congress is a key element of national progress. And they shape their behavior around that belief above all others.

We all do that. The desire to keep our jobs informs and guides everything we do. It's the reason we get to work on time and follow organizational protocols and try to do the things that will please our employers. Members of Congress are no different, except that their real employer is not the Congress, not the government of the United States of America. It is the people in their states and districts who vote for them. Those are the only employers who matter.

There is nothing new about this, about members of Congress placing their connection with the people they represent above all others. What is new, however, are several things that account in large part for the difference between the contemporary Congress and its predecessors.

Party Dynamics: The South Goes Red

On the night that he signed the Civil Rights Act of 1964 into law, Lyndon Johnson told his press secretary, Bill Moyers, "I think we just delivered the South to the Republican Party for a long time to come."[5] It was a prescient observation. At that time, Democrats controlled 90 percent of the southern seats in the House and 95 percent of those in the Senate. All of the southern state legislatures had overwhelming Democratic majorities and all of the southern governors were Democrats. The "solid south" of that era and the century that preceded it was solid for Democrats.

But they were not much like the Democrats who came to Washington from the rest of the country. Most of the southerners composed the conservative wing of the party, especially on matters of race and social welfare. So, on many issues, the Democratic Party of the 1960s and early 1970s was a party divided against itself. The measure used by the nonpartisan Congressional Quarterly service to assess party unity reported the lowest unity scores in its history in those years.

Things were only slightly less divided in the Republican Party of that time. Tight-fisted Republican conservatives from the Midwest bore the same party label as liberals like Jacob Javits of New York, Clifford Case of New Jersey, and Robert Stafford of Vermont. Republican party unity—at 60 percent in the Senate and 56 percent in the House in 1970—was not very different from the disunity across the aisle.

This produced a Congress in which bipartisanship was essential to accomplish anything. On important issues, majorities could not be formed without votes from both parties. Members of Congress formed the habit of working with each other without much regard to party labels. As Ira Shapiro has noted in a recent book, the Senate before 1980 "worked on the basis of mutual respect, tolerance of opposing views, and openness to persuasion in the search for bipartisan solutions. . . . [A] commitment to pursuing the national interest and making the Senate work acted as powerful constraints on partisanship.[6]"

But the civil rights revolution, it turned out, was also a revolution in American party identity. "The southern realignment left both congressional parties with more politically homogenous electoral coalitions reducing internal disagreements and making stronger party leadership tolerable," wrote political scientist Gary Jacobson, a leading analyst of American voting trends.[7] The South turned Republican, eventually almost entirely so. And the moderate wing of that party, drawing largely from districts in the Northeast and Midwest, began to shrink as Democrats made steady inroads in those areas. The House delegations from New England, the bastion of moderate Republicanism, were pretty evenly divided between the parties in the early 1960s. By the beginning of the twenty-first century, Republicans held only eleven of the thirty-five New England seats in Congress.

What was happening in the decades surrounding the pivot into the twenty-first century was an ideological purification of the two major political parties. The Democrats became a party of the left, the Republicans a party of the right. Bipartisanship—the prevailing dynamic of legislative accomplishment in the middle decades of the twentieth century—had essentially disappeared by the beginning of the twenty-first century. The parties had gone to war.

For presidents, this would not have been the source of frustration it became were it not for another enduring characteristic of contemporary Washington: divided government. In parliamentary democracies, intense partisanship is normal, even desirable. An election produces a parliamentary majority which chooses a government. That government sets its agenda and disciplined party members in the legislature dutifully vote that agenda into practice. The same majority party controls both the legislature and the executive. The minority party (or parties) forms a loyal opposition. Democratic theorists often call this "responsible party government."

The American constitution creates a different system where the president and the congressional majorities bear the same party label only by coincidence. Yet, for much of American history before the second half of the twentieth century, coincidence prevailed. Presidents could, with but rare exceptions, count on their parties holding the majority in Congress. This pattern of unified government occurred 86 percent of the time between 1900 and 1946. But then Americans began to split their tickets with a vengeance and the revolution wrought by the Supreme Court in its decisions on congressional apportionment yielded districts increasingly safe for one party's candidates and immune to the tides of presidential elections. From 1946 through 2016, divided government became the norm. In those years, the party of the president controlled a majority of both houses only 37 percent of the time.

So the intensifying ideological purity of the major parties occurred in an era in American history when neither party dominated the government. And, given the widening ideological divide between them and the vanishing interest in cross-aisle cooperation, Washington became a city where it was extremely difficult to get anything done. As political scientist James Sundquist noted, divided government had enormous consequences for presidential leadership:

> If the president is tied through the party mechanism only to the minority, presidential leadership cannot become a fact, because the Congress is controlled by the opposing party. Leadership cannot exist without followership, and the members of Congress will never accept as their leader the head of the opposition party, whom they tried to defeat at the last election and whom they will strive again to defeat in the next election. Parties exist to oppose one another, and by their very nature they seek to undermine and discredit one another. In times of divided government, this healthy competition between parties is transmuted into a conflict between the elements of government themselves.[8]

Contemporary presidents are not less ambitious than their predecessors in the goals they set for their country. They are not notably less clever nor less skilled in the arts of political negotiation and bargaining. But they are encumbered by a political system trapped in the escalating intensity of its own cross-purposes. When the opposition party is committed to nothing more deeply than the defeat of the president and that opposition party controls one or both houses of Congress, leadership opportunities are crammed into a very narrow channel—one that few recent presidents have navigated with much success.

Partisan polarization is simply a fact of life in contemporary Washington. "[The] narrowing and anti-deliberative propensities of the permanent campaign are exacerbated by the increasing ideological distinctiveness of the two major parties," writes the political scientist George C. Edwards, "which encourages presidents and members of Congress to view those on the other side of the aisle as enemies to defeat rather than opponents with whom to compromise."[9]

Bill Clinton, George W. Bush, and Barack Obama all came to office promising efforts to bridge the partisan divide in Washington. In campaign speeches throughout 2008, for example, Barack Obama regularly promised that he would "turn the page on the ugly partisanship in Washington, so we can bring Democrats and Republicans together."[10] Each of the recent presidents made some initial efforts to accomplish this. But each came to believe that reaching out to the opposition party was an exercise in futility and soon abandoned the exercise. An aide reported of Bush's early efforts to hold meetings with Democrats: "He thought the meetings were a waste of everyone's time. Plus, it was uncomfortable for everyone concerned to sit around a table and pretend to be friendly, and then they would go back to the Hill and blast us. They can't even pretend to be a constructive force anymore, so why even have the meeting?"[11]

This polarization has come to focus not so much on policies as on presidencies. Whatever the president is for, the opposition party is against—even if they were once for it. When a president sees an opportunity to side with an idea supported by the opposition, the opposition abandons it. Occasionally divided government briefly recedes and a president enjoys a rare moment of unified government. Clinton did in his first two years in office, George W. Bush for the first year and middle four years of his administration, and Barack Obama for his first two years. Taking advantage of those opportunities, each of them pushed significant initiatives through Congress: Clinton's 1993 economic program, Bush's 2001 tax cut, Obama's 2010 Affordable Care Act. Thirteen House Democrats and twelve Senate Democrats voted for Bush's tax cut proposal. No Republicans voted for Clinton's economic program nor Obama's Affordable Care Act.

Legislation passed on party-line votes is troublesome, however. Such legislation, as the journalist Ronald Brownstein has noted, "cannot incorporate ideas that divide the majority party's coalition, which means that many policy tools are left out because they are ideologically impure. As a result, we are asked, for example, to choose between energy legislation that either focuses almost solely on new drilling or tilts overwhelmingly toward conservation and subsidizing renewable energy. This is like trying to cut a piece of paper with one scissor blade."[12]

And programs enacted by party-line majorities do not easily become settled matters of public policy. Instead of accepting defeat and moving on to other issues, the opposition continues to refight old battles in subsequent elections, in the media echo chambers, and in their fund-raising efforts. John Kerry in 2004 and Barack Obama in 2008 made Bush's "tax cuts for the rich" a recurring element of their campaign rhetoric. Four years after the passage of the Affordable Care Act—and more than fifty House votes to repeal it—Republicans still hoped to make their criticisms of it the central issue of the 2014 midterm elections.[13]

In an era of intense partisan polarization and frequent divided government, presidents may occasionally win significant legislative victories. But such victories are rare, they are not often complete, and they never yield closure on policy debates.

THE EVER-LOOMING MIDTERM ELECTION

Once in the office they worked so hard to earn and eager to pursue their programmatic goals, American presidents soon encounter a painful reality. The horizon is not four years away, but only twenty-one months. Their "window of opportunity" is already half shut before they have spent a day in office. A presidential election is a minor point of punctuation in the permanent campaign that envelops contemporary Washington—a comma, not a period. Members of Congress hardly pause to enjoy one election before beginning their efforts to secure the next.

It takes time for a new presidential administration to get up to speed. The lingering image of the headlong legislative rush of Franklin Roosevelt's first hundred days is still a yardstick widely used for measuring the early performance of new administrations. But it's invalid in almost every way. Roosevelt had almost six more weeks of postelection transition than any of his successors. The country was in a state of dire crisis and profoundly ready for action. Roosevelt's party had overwhelming majorities in both houses of the 73rd Congress. And staffing a new administration was a much smaller and simpler task than it is now.

In our time, a newly elected president takes office seventy-five days after the end of an exhausting election campaign. If the Congress elected with him has majorities of his own party, they are likely to be slender. Presidents must fill hundreds of administrative positions, many of them requiring advanced technical skills. And the process of nominating and confirming those appointees has become so thick that in most cases it lasts for six months or more. The first year in office ends before many of those positions are filled.

But the larger drag on the accomplishments of new administrations is the opposition or indifference of Congress. It is a rarity these days for any more than a few of the newly elected members to believe that they owe their election to the president's victory. Electoral fashions have changed and presidential coattails are no longer in style. As Rhodes Cook wrote, "Dwight D. Eisenhower in 1956, Lyndon Johnson in 1964, and Richard Nixon in 1972, all ran ahead of more than 100 victorious House candidates of their own party. Only one candidate since then (Ronald Reagan in 1984) has run ahead of more than 40." In 2008, Barack Obama ran ahead of only thirty-six victorious House Democrats.[14]

In fact, presidential elections do alter the shape of the electorate. It's not so much that people will switch away from their normal party loyalty to vote for a candidate of the other party. That happens rarely. In recent presidential elections Republican and Democratic candidates have both gotten around 90 percent of the votes from their party's identifiers. The shape changing comes in the form of turnout. Much larger numbers of people vote in presidential elections than in the midterm elections that follow. And often the characteristics of presidential election voters are different from those of midterm voters.

In 2008, for example, Barack Obama won 52.9 percent of the popular vote. But his victory was in no small part the result of unique surges in turnout among African Americans and young voters. They voted in larger than normal numbers and they voted overwhelmingly for Obama. There was no evidence that this represented a long-term change in voting habits among those groups. It was an Obama surge. And as part of that surge, the Democrats retained control of both houses of Congress.

But two years later, in 2010, the surge ebbed. African Americans and younger voters regressed to their more normal patterns, and Republicans regained control of the House and gained seats in the Senate. It was a familiar sight. A president elected on a wave of popular enthusiasm, barely into his first term, with an agenda still unfolding had run aground on the cruel shoals of midterm elections.

There was nothing new about this. The Democratic gains in the midterm elections of 1982 effectively ended the Reagan revolution in domestic policy. The Republican tsunami that rolled over the Clinton administration in 1994 had even more devastating effects on that president. At a postelection press conference, Clinton was asked "Are you still relevant?" It was the right question.

Here, the data tell the story, and it is a story that almost always ends unhappily for the president. Presidential elections have produced Congresses controlled by the president's party 38 percent of the time since 1950. After midterm elections the president's party has controlled Congress only 29 percent of the time. On an average in midterm elections the president's party has lost twenty-six seats in the House and four in the Senate since 1946.

But it isn't simply the loss of seats by the president's party at midterm elections that diminishes presidential leadership capacity. Midterm elections change the legislative dynamic as well, imposing a kind of near-sightedness on members of Congress. A newly elected president, especially one with a full agenda of desired policy changes, finds it difficult to compel the attention, let alone the support, of members of Congress. Their primary focus is not on the president's goals or needs, but on the personal challenges they face in the midterm election ahead. And more than anything else, anticipation of those elections will shape their relations with and support for a president. Members of the president's party will feel little strong obligation to him, because he did little to help them win their own seats and in nearly every case won fewer votes than they did in their districts. Many of them as well may be strangers to the new president because of the recent American habit of electing presidents with little or no prior service in Washington.

Members of the opposition party, having just lost a bitter election to the new president, will not now have any interest in hatchet burying. The rallying cry of the opposition seems to be, "If you can't beat them, thwart them." Their dominant goal will be to prevent the new president from succeeding in any of his initiatives, so that they can gain seats at the midterm election and regain the White House at the next presidential election. The substance of presidential policy initiatives matters little. Elections are all that really matter. And the first election members will face is usually a primary in which a challenge, if any, will come from an opponent with even more extreme views than their own. There is simply no political benefit for career-minded members of Congress in supporting or acquiescing to an opposition-party president. To do so has become the political equivalent of treason.

In recent Congresses, it hasn't been enough for opposition party members simply to withhold their support for the president. They have undertaken aggressive strategies to build public opposition to his agenda and public disappointment with his performance. Coordinated efforts by opposition party leadership in and out of Congress take constant aim at the president, often using the newer communications media to do so. As political scientists Gary Lee Malecha and Daniel J. Reagan have noted:

> Contemporary presidents who "go public" confront a strategic context different from that of their predecessors. Although presidents still command considerable attention on the public stage and have at their disposal many new ways to communicate their views, they now share that stage with multiple actors who can also tap the power of new technologies and coordinate their public relations efforts to create an echo chamber that can on occasion significantly constrain the White House's ability to shape public support for its positions, in ways they would have been unable to in the past.[15]

Because the opposition party seeks advantage in defining them that way, midterm elections usually become a referendum on the performance of the incumbent president. But it is a peculiar referendum because the president is not a candidate and the voters are offered no alterative with whom to compare him. And it is a referendum in which the vast majority of Americans do not participate. Turnout in midterm elections is consistently lower than in presidential elections and it has been so for more than 150 years.

The profound reality is this: midterm elections weaken presidents. Indeed, it is hard to imagine a more efficient device than they have become for diminishing the accomplishments of presidential administrations. They consistently weaken the president's hold on Congress. And as Sarah Binder, a leading contemporary student of Congress, has noted, "Split party control increases the likelihood that more issues on the agenda will end in stalemate. We can think of divided government as a force that erects another barrier in the legislative process: it traps bills that might've been enacted had control of government been unified in a single political party."[16]

Procedural Chaos

No one ever said the legislative process was pretty. Bismarck famously compared it to sausage making. But most legislatures over time develop something approaching a regular order of business. To manage the complexities of law making, they create committees and develop rules of procedure. The committees specialize in certain subject matters and develop a degree of expertise. They hold hearings to permit public input. They draft bills and then, with the approval of a majority of their members, send those bills to the "floor" where the full membership can deliberate, debate, and ultimately vote on their passage. The rules determine scheduling, participation in floor debate, and the permissibility of amendments.

Both houses of Congress began developing rules of procedure when they first met in 1789 and have been elaborating and institutionalizing those rules as their experiences have accumulated. Committees have long played a key role in developing legislation. By the middle of the twentieth century, a regular order was fully emergent in both houses of Congress.

But in the years since then, the regular order has been attacked, evaded, and altered in ways that have turned the legislative process into a mine field through which few proposals, especially those initiated by presidents, have successfully navigated. Much of this has been the response to and the consequence of intensified partisan polarization. As the parties grew more ideologically homogenous and more distant from each other, their leaders in Congress cast aside the regular order in pursuit of legislative—and electoral—advantage.

To Thomas Mann and Norman Ornstein, scholars much concerned about the character of the contemporary Congress, this all yields a worrisome set of outcomes: "The eschewal of the regular order, the abandonment of deliberation, the core value that the political ends justify the legislative means, the lack of concern about legislative craftsmanship—that results in the production of poor laws and flawed policy."[17]

In the House, the majority punishes the minority—disregarding bills introduced by minority party members, excluding it from any meaningful participation in committee consideration of bills, preventing it from offering amendments, appointing no minority members to conference committees. In the Senate, it's often the minority party, through use or threats of filibusters and other tactics of obstruction, that practices a scorched earth policy. No major bill supported by the majority can come to a floor vote without sixty supporters. When an election reverses party control of either house, the perpetrators change but the tactics remain the same.

Nowhere is the procedural chaos of the contemporary Congress more evident than in the budget process. The Budget and Accounting Act of 1921 established a primary role for the president in the creation of the annual government budget. The president would draw recommendations from all the executive agencies, his budget bureau would seek to remove the fat from those and balance them against broad national purposes, and then a budget recommendation would go to Congress early in the calendar year. Then Congress would divide the president's proposals among its appropriations subcommittees where defenses by agency heads would be carefully and often aggressively reviewed. The appropriations bills would come forward thereafter and be enacted before the beginning of the fiscal year to provide government agencies with funding for the year ahead.

Most of the time, the alterations of the president's budget proposals by Congress were incremental.[18] The president's budget recommendations shaped the nation's finances in a very significant way. As political scientist Aaron Wildavsky noted in a classic study of the "old budgetary order": "These partly cooperative and partly conflicting relationships existed within a general framework of informal understandings. The budget would be balanced, the level of taxing and spending would not grow rapidly, and agreements on the amount and distribution of public monies would be maintained."[19]

But the Congress always struggled to get its budget work done on time. To extend that time and to ensure a greater coordination of the work of the appropriations committees with consensual targets for overall expenditures and revenues, the Congress in 1974 enacted a significant reform of the budget process. This moved the start of the fiscal year from July 1 to October 1, created new budget committees in each house, and established a new procedure of setting budget goals in April to discipline the appropriations process and then confirming them in September. It also created a nonpartisan Congressional Budget Office to provide independent analyses of financial issues.

But the new budget process accomplished few of its objectives, especially the broader one of controlling budget deficits. In the forty years following the 1974 reforms, there were deficits in all but four federal budgets, and the magnitude of the deficits grew rather than diminished with the new budget procedures in effect. The new deadlines in the budget process were often missed—in the first twenty-five years, for example, the April 15 deadline for the first budget resolution was missed twenty-one times, by an average of forty-one days.[20] Subsequent reforms—the Balanced Budget and Emergency Deficit Control Act of 1985 and the Budget Enforcement Act of 1990, for example—added more complexity but not much more rationality to the process.

By the twenty-first century, the budgetary process was in near-total disarray. Any concept of a federal fiscal year with carefully considered agency budgets developed before it begins had been totally obliterated. The fundamental problem was this: members of Congress could not align their collective procedures and goals with their individual objectives. No process could successfully discipline the desires of members to spend more for the programs they liked and to avoid raising revenue to the level of their spending.

Their efforts to discipline themselves with ingenious new procedures were bound to fail. Process is no substitute for will, and members lacked the will to accomplish what their procedural reforms sought to effect. Unable to reconcile spending and taxing goals, members turned to the one available escape from a harsh political arithmetic: debt.

These budget reform efforts may have failed to curb congressional spending appetites or to introduce timeliness to the budget process, but they did have one significant effect: a weakening of the president's role in determining the finances of the federal government. "Presidential responsibility for the budget was undermined by the Budget Act of 1974," wrote Louis Fisher, "because the nation now had not one budget but two: the presidential budget and the congressional budget."[21]

The Budget Reform Act of 1974 centralized the budget process in Congress, albeit unevenly. Where once the president's budget proposal had been the baseline for all congressional action—spending more than the president recommended was over-budget, spending less was under-budget—now the figures in the congressional budget resolution came to be viewed as the baseline or starting point. The president's budget was shoved to the sidelines. While presidents continued to go through the motions of submitting an annual budget recommendation to Congress, these submissions grew increasingly irrelevant to decisions—and non-decisions—on Capitol Hill.

The creation of a Congressional Budget Office further diminished the president's role by limiting the impact of the Office of Management and

Budget in developing information about underlying economic realities and scenarios. Congress now had its own capacity for that and often used CBO projections to shape its budget decisions where it had once had little choice but to use those provided by the president's budget agency.

And the 1974 legislation curbed presidential influence in yet another way. Its full name was the Congressional Budget and Impoundment Control Act. It imposed significant new curbs on the president's role in spending appropriated funds. Since the beginning of the republic, presidents had sometimes delayed or accelerated the expenditure of appropriated funds. At other times, they had rescinded such expenditures altogether. Often this was for perfectly valid and widely supported reasons. A war may have ended between the appropriation of funds for war material and the surrender of the enemy. Declining to spend those funds was a prudent exercise of executive management. Every modern president found reasons to exercise control over the expenditure of appropriated funds.

But sometimes, too, presidents rescinded spending simply because they did not support the purposes for which Congress had appropriated funds. Richard Nixon, for example, used the power of impoundment to curtail a wide swath of domestic programs with which he disagreed. He defended this presidential power in a news conference on January 31, 1973: "The constitutional right for the President of the United States to impound funds . . . is absolutely clear . . . I will not spend money if the Congress overspends, and I will not be for programs that will raise the taxes and put a bigger burden on the already overburdened American taxpayer."

The Impoundment Control Act was in some ways a response to Nixon's aggressive exercise of presidential spending powers. But it imposed significant constraints on the ability of all presidents to defer or rescind expenditures, activities that presidents had long pursued with far fewer constraints than those now affecting their contemporary counterparts.

Overall, the changes enacted in the budgetary process and the chaos that now envelops it have severely weakened the president's hand in managing the finances of the nation. "The president has not been eliminated from the budget process," notes political scientist Keith Whittington, "but his role has been substantially altered and reduced. . . . Congress is now designed to replicate executive budget analysis and decision-making in order to meet the president in budgetary negotiations rather than rely on presidential guidance and initiative in setting budget priorities."[22]

The budget's real leverage over public policy is small to begin with. Nearly 70 percent of expenditures are now tied up in nondiscretionary spending: Social Security, Medicare, Medicaid, veteran's benefits, debt service, and the like. Because most federal payments to individuals are indexed to inflation, cost of living adjustments, not political decisions, influence their annual alterations. Of the remainder of the budget that is discretionary, a substantial portion, more than half in recent years, is in the Defense budget and largely untouchable for political reasons. So even if the president somehow dominated the budget process, there would be little room to effect significant changes in the nation's priorities.

But the changes in the budget process in the past few decades, intentional and unintentional, have muted even what little impact remains to presidents. In virtually every other American organization and institution, from state governments to corporations to universities, the chief executive plays a critical role in shaping the budget and in thus setting institutional spending priorities. In few other places is the chief executive's routine influence in financial matters so limited as it is now in the federal government of the United States.

Oversight by Enemies

In May 2014, the Republican leadership in the House announced the formation of a special committee to review the events surrounding the murder of several American diplomats in Benghazi, Libya. In normal times, this might have seemed a prudent exercise of congressional oversight responsibilities. The central questions of the inquiry might have been "What went wrong in Benghazi?" and "What can be done to prevent such tragedies in the future?"

But they weren't. Like so many of the oversight investigations now conducted in Congress, this one had a primarily political purpose: to shine a harsh, negative light on the president and others in his administration. Not the least of those others was Hillary Clinton, the secretary of State at the time of the attacks and widely presumed to be the Democratic presidential nominee in 2016.

In fact, the House Committees on Armed Services, Foreign Affairs, and Oversight and Government Reform, all dominated and chaired by Republicans, had been investigating the Benghazi affair almost continuously since its occurrence on September 11, 2012. Darrel Issa, the chair of the House Oversight Committee, refused to let the matter die. That the millions of dollars his committee spent on these investigations turned up little new evidence mattered little. What mattered was keeping the issue in the spotlight—and the Obama administration on the defensive.

The context is important here. Congressional interest in genuine, bipartisan oversight has been declining for decades. Political scientist Joel Aberbach tracked a steep decline in the number of oversight hearings by congressional committees in both houses in the last two decades of the twentieth century.[23] Routine oversight—the kind that requires serious investigation of government programs and the development of needed reforms—holds little appeal for individual members of Congress. Few constituents are attentive to it, and it rarely produces newsworthy findings. Hence it doesn't contribute much to the primary goal of most members: getting reelected. And it has opportunity costs. Time spent on oversight is time spent away from other activities that may have a greater electoral payoff.

The majority party in each house of Congress controls the oversight function. And in periods of unified government, when the president's party controls both houses, little oversight is attempted. Why embarrass a president of your own party? But when one or both houses are controlled by the opposition party, presidents are the constant target of oversight investigations. It matters little whether there is a substantive basis for those investigations or whether they produce any meaningful findings of fact. Embarrassment and humiliation, not accountability, have become the primary purposes of oversight in the contemporary Congress. As former Representative Lee H. Hamilton has noted, "Congress has given too much focus to personal investigations and possible scandals rather than programmatic review and a comprehensive assessment of which federal programs work and which don't."[24]

Congressional Democrats, the majority at the time, may have thought themselves obligated to investigate the savings and loan scandals of the late 1980s. But the fact that those occurred during a Republican presidency made the investigation much more attractive to them. It held the promise of negative news for the administration of George H. W. Bush.

When Republicans took control of both houses of Congress after the 1994 midterm elections, they initiated a string of politically motivated investigations of Bill Clinton and his administration. The investigation of the investment by Bill and Hillary Clinton into an Arkansas development on the Whitewater River consumed committees in both houses for years. When Republicans gained control of the Senate in 1995, the Banking, Housing, and Urban Affairs Committee significantly enlarged its Whitewater investigation, eventually holding sixty committee sessions over thirteen months lasting more than 300 hours and yielding 10,000 pages of testimony and 35,000 pages of depositions from nearly 250 people. It produced more days of hearings than most major legislation in that time. And it yielded no evidence that either of the Clintons had acted unlawfully.

But that merely paved the way for the investigations later in the 1990s that led to the House's impeachment of President Clinton. The House Judiciary Committee vote to impeach Richard Nixon a quarter century earlier had been bipartisan. The vote to impeach President Clinton was not. By nearly all accounts it was a partisan effort by the majority party in the House to weaken a president of the opposition party.

In 2007, having just regained control of Congress, Democrats began a major investigation of the Bush administration and, especially of the attorney general, other Justice department officials, and some White House staff members, for their roles in what were characterized as politically motivated firings of U.S. attorneys. The plan to fire the U.S. attorneys had been initiated in 2005 and implemented in 2006. In all likelihood, there would have been no congressional investigation of it, except for one important fact. The Democrats regained control of Congress—and the investigation power—in 2007. And they used it to require many days of testimony by the attorney general and other Bush administration officials.

The Benghazi investigations were no anomaly. They simply reflected what congressional oversight has become: a political tool for weakening the president of the United States. When the president and congressional majorities share the same party label, oversight diminishes almost to the vanishing point. But when party control of government is divided, the oversight machinery cranks up, fueled not by a renewed desire for accountability to law or high purpose but rather by the contemporary intensity of partisan polarization and the permanent campaign.

The Appointments Battleground

George H. W. Bush followed a familiar path when he chose John Tower to be his first secretary of Defense. Tower, like Bush, was from Texas, and they had known each other for years. Tower was a former senator and had for four years chaired the Senate Armed Services Committee. He was an expert on defense issues. He was an utterly unsurprising choice to serve as Defense secretary. And historically presidents had been granted broad leeway in cabinet appointments and senators had a habit of being deferential when former members of their body were nominated for executive positions.

But Senate Democrats in 1989 had little interest in historical imperatives. After harsh and vituperative debate, much of it focusing on the personal character of John Tower, the Senate voted 53–47 to reject the Tower nomination, the first time a cabinet nominee of a newly elected president had ever been rejected. Only one Republican joined fifty-two Democrats in defeating Tower's nomination.

This reflected a trend that had been developing since the mid-1970s: a reinvigoration of the Senate's confirmation power as a tool of partisan combat. It is not a coincidence that confirmation struggles became more frequent and more contentious just as members of Congress came to recognize divided government as a common fact of Washington life. Unable to beat the opposition party's candidate in a presidential election, Plan B became "Let's make it hard for him to govern effectively." And one valuable way to implement that plan was to impede the president's freedom in staffing his administration.

Rejections in formal floor votes, like that suffered by John Tower, remain relatively rare. But other tactics serve the same purpose. For most of

American history, confirmation hearings by Senate committees were a rarity. Now they are an inevitability. And the hearings produce opportunities for senators to question nominees intensively, to criticize them, sometimes to embarrass them, to seek pledges that they will act in certain ways once in office, to scrutinize their past actions and decisions, and to delve in great detail into their personal finances. Nominees must complete long and invasive committee questionnaires. They must respond in writing to questions submitted by senators, sometimes hundreds of questions, sometimes more than a thousand. Gina McCarthy, who was nominated by Barack Obama in 2013 to head the Environmental Protection Agency, was required to answer more than 1,100 written questions by Republicans on the Senate Committee on Environment and Public Works—a tactic that slowed her confirmation for more than four months.

To avoid embarrassments in the confirmation process for themselves and their nominees, presidents now routinely require potential nominees to go through extensive vetting before their nominations go to the Senate: completion of financial disclosure statements, review of potential conflicts of interest, FBI, income tax audits, and responses to a personal data statement that contains more than sixty questions covering every aspect of a nominee's personal and professional life. Even for those nominees who have little to hide and little potential for political attack, the process of White House vetting and Senate confirmation can easily consume six months.

But that doesn't guarantee confirmation. The president's opponents in Congress have several other tools to impede the staffing of an administration. Simple delay is the most common of those, especially when the opposition party controls the Senate. Why hurry to confirm a president's nominee when there is no meaningful pressure to do so? And sometimes, a delay in confirmation can handicap or even stop the activities of an executive agency with few admirers in the opposition party.

The principal tool of delay when the opposition party is in the minority in the Senate is the threat of a filibuster. President Obama and the Democrats in Congress succeeded against Republican opposition in creating a Consumer Financial Protection Bureau in 2010, an agency responsible for consumer protection in the financial sector. When Obama sought to appoint Elizabeth Warren, the consultant who had been instrumental in designing this agency, to be its first director, Republicans in the Senate made it clear they would use a filibuster if necessary to prevent her confirmation. Obama then nominated the attorney general of Ohio, Richard Cordray, to fill this position. Again Republicans declined to act. Without a director, the agency was unable to issue new rules or regulate any institutions other than banks—precisely what Republicans intended. Eventually Obama gave Cordray a recess appointment, end-running the regular order. This led to Republican cries that he was acting like an imperial president.

This is not an unfamiliar scenario. Similar opposition party procrastination in recent years has hamstrung the National Labor Relations Board and the Federal Elections Commission. Sometimes the delay in the confirmation process is caused by a single senator who places a "hold" on a nomination. Holds are a shadowy Senate practice of long standing. Senators merely communicate to their party leader that they are not yet ready to vote on a nomination—for whatever reason they may wish to articulate or not—and delay ensues. Senators are under no obligation to make public the reasons for their hold or even that they have sought one. Sometimes it's a perfectly valid desire to gather more information about a nominee before voting.

More often, however, holds are used to hold nominees hostage to some other political battle with the administration. Senator Jesse Helms (R-NC) once placed a hold on thirty ambassadorial nominations by President Clinton as a tactic to pressure the president to support a reorganization of the State Department bureaucracy.[25] In February 2010, Senator Richard Shelby (R-AL) placed holds on all Obama executive branch nominees to force the administration to review the bidding process for air-to-air refueling tankers that he wanted built in his home state. In frustration over George W. Bush's use of recess appointments to fill seats in the federal judiciary, Senate Democrats in March 2004 put holds on all Bush nominees.

Gary J. Andres, whose position on the legislative liaison staff of George H. W. Bush gave him a keen vantage point on the confirmation process, recalled, "I witnessed many cases in which the nominee's policy preferences had absolutely nothing to do with motivating senatorial delaying tactics. Delays had a lot more to do with senators gaining leverage for advancing their own goals, legislative and nonlegislative."[26]

The impacts of these opposition efforts in the appointments process are broad and substantial. New administrations are in office for more than a year now before they are fully staffed. Excessive time and political capital must be spent in securing confirmation of controversial nominees. Presidents are frequently forced to appoint people to important administrative posts who may not have the skills or experience they want or need but who are confirmable. And recruiting the country's ablest leaders and experts to be public servants is handicapped by the growing reputation of the appointments process as an invasive, brutalizing, and potentially humiliating enterprise.

In the political battles between the president and his congressional opponents, in the permanent campaign, nominees are often like civilians in a free-fire zone. They become victims and hostages for no reason that bears on their qualifications or character. Recognizing this, reluctance to accept a presidential appointment has grown. The ability of presidents to use the appointments process to call on the nation's best talent is diminished—with unsurprising and negative impacts on presidential performance in office.

Imagine if a corporation were to conduct an extensive national search for a new CEO and found one who seemed to possess the right experience, skills, and goals to please the board of directors and the shareholders. And then the board instructed that new CEO to organize the company in the way he or she saw fit and to hire the right managers to ensure increased profitability, hundreds of them if necessary. That would be normal. But then imagine that the board said, "Oh, yes, there is this one caveat: all of your new hires have to be approved by a committee of your worst enemies." But that wouldn't be a corporation—no successful corporation would function like that; that would be the government of the United States.

Curtailing Presidential Authority

In the middle of 1968, Americans could look back over thirty-six years in which there had been only one Republican president and only four years of divided government. Control of the national government by the Democratic Party had become a habit so familiar that it seemed simply normal. A dominant national party, even one with deep fissures like the mid-twentieth-century Democrats, smoothed the awkward institutional separations of the American constitution. It permitted, even encouraged, civility among policy makers. And, on the whole, Americans seemed pleased with the results. The American National Election Studies that year found that 61 percent of Americans trusted the government in Washington to do the right thing always or most of the time.[27]

But in 1968, the *pax Democratica* was coming apart. George Wallace, the Democratic governor of Alabama, was mounting a presidential campaign from the right that would tear open the divide within that party on racial issues. Opposition to the Vietnam War tore at the party from the left. The explosion came in Chicago in August at the party's convention where riots and a brutal police response, not the usual pep rally for the party's nominee, dominated the headlines. Hubert Humphrey, who won that nomination, never recovered. And in November, the country elected Richard Nixon president with 43.4 percent of the popular vote.

Nixon wasn't just another Republican. Democrats had made their peace with Dwight Eisenhower. He was a national hero with no partisan track record before becoming president. And his policy goals posed no great threat to Democratic priorities. Nixon, on the other hand, was the bête noire of many Democrats with a long track record of scorched earth campaigns against them, anti-Communist crusading, and a new political strategy that sought to pry the South away from its traditional Democratic loyalties. Nixon was dangerous to Democrats in a way that Eisenhower never was.

The sharper political analysts in the country also began to see a future in which divided government would become the norm. A book published in the following year by Kevin Phillips explained the looming reality of an emerging Republican majority ensuring the election of more GOP presidents.[28] The new map of presidential politics, with southern loyalties slipping to the Republicans and a growing backlash against the liberal policies of Kennedy's New Frontier and Johnson's Great Society stiffening Republican opposition in the west, would favor Republican presidential candidates, even as Democrats maintained their hold on the Congress. The analysts were right about this, of course; Republicans would dominate the White House for most of the ensuing quarter century.

These new political realities were the context for a series of efforts by Democratic majorities in Congress in the 1970s to curtail the authority and freedom of Republican presidents. In fact, it was not just partisan differences driving these changes. Lyndon Johnson's presidency, especially in his commitment to continue and enlarge the war in Vietnam, had incited a good deal of concern in Congress about its own institutional weakness vis-à-vis the president. It wasn't just that Democrats wanted to constrain Richard Nixon and his Republican successors. Members of Congress in both parties wanted to constrain a presidency that seemed to be reducing them to irrelevance in many areas of policy making.

The war in Vietnam had been initiated and perpetrated, at great cost, without a declaration of war—the Congress's purported constitutional handle on the war power. Richard Nixon used the power of presidential impoundment to prevent the disbursal of nearly $12 billion in congressionally appropriated funds in 1973 and 1974—despite the clear constitutional assignment of the appropriations power to Congress.

It came to light, as well, that Nixon and his predecessors had entered into hundreds of international agreements that were not treaties and therefore not subject to the constitutional requirement of Senate ratification. Many of these were kept secret from the Congress. Intelligence activities had often come to include covert actions around the world of which Congress had no knowledge and over which it had no means to exercise control. Even the intelligence budget was a mystery to most members of Congress. And the Senate's constitutional power to confirm presidential appointments had fallen into such inconsistent and haphazard use that a study by the public interest group Common Cause concluded that "the Senate Confirmation Process is a rubber stamp machine."[29]

Members of Congress in the 1970s set out to change all this. In part, they did so by passing a series of new laws that redefined the relationship between the president and the Congress—and in each case sought to constrain presidential authority and freedom of action. In part, too, they tried to accomplish these same objectives by changing their behavior, by more vigorously exercising the constitutional controls they had allowed to lag or wither.

In 1969, with Nixon now in the White House and focusing heavily on foreign policy, Congress passed the National Commitments Resolution aimed at limiting presidential authority to negotiate international agreements or commit the resources or the armed forces of the United States without treaty authority or the consent of the Senate.

In 1972, the Congress passed the Case Act which, while not preventing the president from entering into executive agreements, did require that the Congress be notified of any executive agreement within sixty days. Knowledge of such agreements gave Congress the ability it did not have when they were secret to vote to cancel them or refuse funding for their implementation.

Congress went a long step further in 1973 when it adopted the War Powers Act. This required presidents to notify Congress when committing troops to hostilities abroad and limited such use of American forces to sixty days without a declaration of war or specific congressional authorization. Richard Nixon vetoed the War Powers Act, but his veto was overridden by a bipartisan two-thirds majority in both houses of Congress.

In other actions during this decade, the Congress limited the president's ability to rescind or delay the expenditure of appropriated funds, created special committees in both houses of Congress to provide more effective and assertive congressional oversight of intelligence activities, required congressional approval for any significant sale of military equipment to foreign countries, enacted over President Ford's veto a broad expansion of the Freedom of Information Act, and established a new set of procedures limiting the president's authority to declare national emergencies. It also passed an Ethics in Government Act that established procedures for the appointment of an independent counsel—beyond presidential control—to investigate potential abuses of power in the executive branch.

The Congress also began to act more assertively in the exercise of existing constitutional prerogatives. A new budget process, created in 1974 gave Congress tools to challenge presidential economic assumptions and budget requests. Senate committees added staff and developed beefed-up procedures to improve the review of nominees for presidential appointments, and senators became more willing to withhold confirmation from those they found objectionable.[30]

At the same time, the Congress was undergoing substantial internal reform in its own operations. The legislative process was opening up to broader participation by more members. The hegemony that congressional committees had enjoyed in earlier decades was diminishing. And old practices like committee meetings closed to the public and congressional voting by voice or teller votes were giving way to "sunshine" practices— open committee meetings, more recorded votes, televising of House and Senate sessions—that opened the Congress to much broader public view and to a wide array of outside influences.

The direct impacts of these efforts to limit presidential authority and free- dom have been mixed. The War Powers Act, for example, has brought about somewhat greater attention by presidents to consultation with Congress and the pursuit of prior authorization before major force commitments in the Persian Gulf and Iraq. But it has provided little impediment to presi- dents of both parties in conducting a multitude of American interventions abroad. Similarly, the creation of House and Senate Intelligence Commit- tees has improved inter-branch communication about intelligence activi- ties, but appears to have imposed little constraint to presidential freedom in this area.[31]

But the creation of authority for independent counsels, the impound- ment controls, the enlarged and sustained assertiveness of the Senate in the confirmation process, and the opening up of the legislative process to pub- lic view and broader participation have all imposed significant constraints on presidential authority and freedom of action.

More than that, they have contributed to a new attitude that now prevails throughout legislative-executive relations—an attitude fueled, of course, by the persistence of divided government. It is that the two branches are caught up in a constant game of procedural chess. An effort to expand its authority by one branch is always met by an effort by the other to check that expan- sion. Daniel Patrick Moynihan, an experienced hand in both branches, described this in what he called the iron law of emulation: "Whenever any branch of the Government acquires a new technique which enhances its power in relation to the other branches, that technique will soon be adopted by those other branches as well."[32]

And so it has been for decades. The response of Congress to any appar- ent expansion of presidential authority has been an expansion of its own capacity to respond to and check that expansion. As the presidential scholar Stephen Skowronek has noted: "A resurgent Congress responded to new assertions of presidential power and independence by attempting to strengthen its own position in the exercise of war powers, budget powers, investigatory powers, prosecutorial powers, appointment powers, and the like. But with the wisdom of the Framers fueling constitutional arguments on both sides, things have grown increasingly unsettled. If anything, recent history has found the presidency engulfed in one constitutional crisis after another."[33]

What is curious about all this has been its ad hoc character. The altera- tions in the relationship between the two branches have followed no grand design, no challenge to the constitutional system itself, no emergent new theory. Politics and especially—one might more precisely note—the politics of the moment have driven these changes. This was less a reform movement than a series of largely disconnected reform actions. They may have followed neither script nor connective theory, but the cumulative result of all of these piecemeal changes has been a steadily escalating stalemate in which the capacity of the presidency for leadership and action has been constrained and diminished.

THE INFLUENCE VORTEX

To fully understand the changing dynamics in the relationship between the president and the Congress, one must consider a third set of actors: Washington's special interest groups. Whether lobbying members of Congress or their executive branch counterparts, filing lawsuits against government agencies, spending hundreds of millions of dollars in election campaigns, waging policy battles with television advertising, or resisting changes in law or regulations, interest groups now suffuse and often dominate the processes of government.

Nowhere is this more apparent than on Capitol Hill. In many ways, the contemporary Congress resembles Vichy France. The members seem to be running their own institution and their own individual careers. But, in their hearts and minds, they know well the very high costs of getting out of line, of voting against the interests of their patrons. The lobbyists often play the tune to which members dance. Career maintenance—getting reelected—is heavily dependent on cultivating and keeping the support of special interests.

Most members learn this lesson before they ever take their seats in Washington. They've had to pursue special interest support to win their nominations and then again to succeed in increasingly expensive general elections. In the 2012 election cycle the average cost of a successful House campaign was almost $1.7 million. A Senate seat cost much more: about $10.5 million.[34] The support of political action committees (PACs) and other forms of special interest largesse is critical to most such campaigns.

When they arrive in Washington, members quickly get to know the representatives of the special interests, especially those whose clients are affected by decisions of committees and subcommittees to which members are assigned. Lobbyists make regular visits to members' offices, fill the best seats in committee rooms when bills are considered, comb the hallways before important votes, attend the fund-raisers, offer travel and golf at luxurious resorts, and provide many kinds of services to members faithful to their causes.

One of the first things to strike new members is the sheer number of lobbyists. It's hard to get a reliable count because only certain lobbyists are required to register with Congress—those who spend more than 20 percent of their time lobbying for a particular client in the previous three-month period. That may be more than the tip of the iceberg, but it's well known that there are many others in Washington who seek to influence Congress without triggering or observing the registration requirements. But the number of registered lobbyists suggests the magnitude of the influence industry confronting members of Congress. According to the Center for Responsive Politics, there were 11,509 active, registered lobbyists in 2014, about twenty-two lobbyists for every member of Congress.[35]

Perhaps the next thing to strike a new member of Congress is how many of these lobbyists on Capitol Hill are congressional veterans with a rich understanding of the nuances of the legislative process. A ten-year analysis by LegiStorm, an organization that monitors congressional staff, found in 2011 that nearly 5,400 lobbyists had previously worked in Congress, close to 400 of them as senators or representatives in the House.[36] Another study found that "half the senators and 42 percent of House members who left Congress between 1998 and 2004 became lobbyists."[37] All of them, of course, still retained deep connections on Capitol Hill. The reality is that members of Congress are confronted by hordes of deeply experienced people vigorously representing the interests of thousands of corporations, trade associations, labor unions, churches, charities, universities, and state and local governments—indeed virtually every distinct interest in American society.

And these interest groups are well armed in money and sophisticated techniques to pursue their goals—"so damn much money," as uber-lobbyist Robert Strauss once said.[38] In 2013, the nation's special interest groups spent $3.24 billion to lobby Congress.[39] In the 2012 elections cycle their political action committees spent about $947 million to ensure the election of members who would be responsive to their influence.[40]

Chuck Hagel, who served for twelve years in the Senate and later as Defense secretary, noted the impact that such lobbying had on the Congress: "Health care, immigration reform, environment—you name the big issues today, we have not been able to move on any of them, because of the power of the process, the power of the special interests."[41]

The post-reform Congress of the twenty-first century is especially amenable—one might better say vulnerable—to their efforts. "Greater democracy and the subcommittee government it brought did not improve Congress's capability to lead government or share leadership with the president," wrote political scientists Lance LeLoup and Steven Shull. "Power became more fragmented, and greater interest group access made the task of coalition building more difficult."[42] A legislature where power is decentralized, leadership is weak, party discipline is absent, decision making is forced into public view, and members are constantly driven by the imperatives of reelection is lobbyist heaven. And that is precisely the kind of Congress around which special interests swarm in contemporary Washington.

Especially they swarm around the veto points, the junctures where a small number of votes, even the turning of one key player, can derail a bill or a nomination. Perhaps it's a subcommittee hearing or a full committee mark-up. Maybe it's a friendly senator willing to place a hold on a bill or nomination. Perhaps it's a poison pill amendment on the floor. The knowledgeable and sophisticated representatives of special interests know exactly where the veto points lie—and how to bring the full force of their influence to bear in those places.

The legislative process is like an internal combustion engine. For success to occur, every part has to contribute. If failure occurs in one place—a spark plug or fuel pump or distributor cap—the engine won't run. So it is with legislation. A bill can be killed in a dozen different places. It has to succeed in all of them to become law.

There have always been special interests in America, of course, and they have been represented in Washington since the beginning of the Republic. Woodrow Wilson worried about the impediments these interests imposed to his own policy initiatives, "I think that the public ought to know the extraordinary exertions being made by the lobby in Washington to gain recognition for certain alterations of the tariff bill," he said in 1913. "Washington has seldom seen so numerous, so industrious, or so insidious a lobby."[43] Franklin Roosevelt never lost sight of the importance of labor unions to his New Deal coalition and, before proceeding with a new initiative, would often command his aides to "clear it with Sidney"—Sidney Hillman, the leader of the American Federation of Labor.

What is different today is the sheer scale of the special interest universe. A study of the "Washington lobby" in the late 1920s identified about 500 interests being represented in Washington; another study in the same period found only 300 effective lobby groups.[44] Today, there are thousands of such interests with more employees, larger budgets, all of the benefits of modern communication technologies, and a much broader array of sophisticated influence techniques than ever before. Every policy battle, every important appointment quickly becomes a magnet for special interests on every side of the issue.

The impact of this on the contemporary presidency has been profound. Presidents, too, must swim through this stream of special interest representatives. Some of them help in presidential efforts, supporting them and pushing them along. But many more try to force the current in the opposite direction, pouring their money, their knowledge, and their extensive connections into the task of preventing presidents from accomplishing their policy objectives.

When President Bill Clinton announced his plan for national health care in September 1993, a Washington Post/ABC poll found that 67 percent of the public supported it and 20 percent opposed.[45] That would seem to be fertile ground for policy success in a democracy. But then the opposing interests—hospital administrators, the pharmaceutical manufacturers, the insurance industry—went to work. They lobbied hard with members of Congress whose campaigns they had long supported. They did tens of thousands of pieces of direct mail urging citizens to write or call their representatives and express opposition to the plan.

And they began to run television advertisements featuring a fictional couple, Harry and Louise, who found much to lament—and fear—in the proposal. The Porter Novelli public relations firm that played a lead role in opposing the Clinton health-care initiative claimed on its website that the "Harry and Louise television ads prompted 500,000 calls to our 800 number, turned 50,000 of those callers into activists and resulted in one-quarter million contacts with members of Congress. The campaign is widely credited as being a key factor in defeating the Clinton plan."

Overall, according to a study by the Center for Public Integrity, the special interests opposing the Clinton health-care initiative spent at least $100 million in 1993 and 1994.[46] By February, public support for Clinton's plan had dropped by 23 percentage points. It never recovered from the special interest onslaught. Hillary Clinton, who had been assigned the lead in designing and securing passage of the plan later noted, "This battle was lost on paid media and paid direct mail."[47]

Similar resistance now also regularly occurs to presidential appointments, especially judicial appointments. As judges and justices have come to play a steadily increasing role in shaping public policy, special interests have become ever more alert to appointments to those positions and ever more active in trying to secure the confirmation of those whom they believe will be sympathetic to their concerns and to oppose those whose sympathy they doubt.

When Ronald Reagan nominated Robert Bork in 1987 to fill a vacancy on the Supreme Court, his administration was unprepared for the interest group opposition the nomination would incite. The Bork nomination was announced on July 1, 1987. Senate hearings would not begin until September 15. Most Reagan officials did what Washingtonians often do in August of odd-numbered years: they went on vacation. In their absence interest groups—145 of them by one count[48]—went to work. By the time the hearings began, many Democrats on the Judiciary Committee were primed to oppose Bork's confirmation. When the nomination came to the floor after nearly a month of contentious hearings, it was defeated by a vote of 58–42.

Interest group activism in Supreme Court nominations became the norm after that. But it soon came to pervade the appointments process for judges at all levels. For most of American history, the lower federal courts, especially the district courts where federal trials occur, inspired little inter-est outside the states where they reside. Presidents granted broad deference to senators from those states in the selection of nominees for those posi-tions. But district court judges now compose an important on-deck circle for nominations to the appellate courts. Interest groups are wise to that and now focus increased attention on those district court nominations. And because of the low political salience of these nominations, interest groups can play a significant role in derailing a potential nomination, even one that has the support of home state senators. "Interest group opposition is today the most influential force driving the lower court confirmation pro-cess," note political scientist Nancy Scherer and her colleagues who exam-ined a wide array of these nominations.[49]

Every recent president has had to confront the reality of a Washington pervaded by special interests and a policy-making process deeply affected by their activities. What Clinton experienced with the health-care lobby George W. Bush experienced with the American Association of Retired Persons (AARP) in his efforts to privatize a portion of Social Security and Barack Obama experienced with the National Rifle Association (NRA) in his attempt to tighten gun control laws after the massacre of schoolchildren in Newtown, Connecticut. The policy-making process in all branches is more open to outside influences than it has ever been. And the outcomes of those processes are more affected by the multitudes of special interests than they have ever been. For presidents in our time, the task of initiating policy change is greatly complicated as a result.

It has never been easy to be president; but it's never been harder than it is now. Newton's Third Law of Motion—"For every action there is an equal and opposite reaction"—might apply to politics as well. But today the reac-tion, though opposite, is often greater than equal. And it comes from many directions.

Washington has always been a city where it was easier to play defense than offense, easier to preserve the policy status quo than to foment change. The American constitutional system is an intricate set of traps and catches requiring skill and strength and persistence to overcome. Presidents have always had to confront that constitutional puzzle. But now, as the political scientist Hugh Heclo has noted, they must also penetrate many layers of institutional and political complexity: "A less manageable, more individu-alistic Congress; disappearing party hierarchy; and proliferating groups of single-minded policy activists. All of these add up to a sandy, shifting politi-cal base of support for presidents."[50]

The simple fact is that contemporary members of Congress have few incentives to follow the lead of the president, even when they are members of the same party. They have many incentives, however, to oppose him. The result is a Congress that is effectively led by no one—a Congress in gridlock. Members of that kind of Congress can survive in their own careers in spite of the collective agonies of their institution. Some thrive in spite of it. But presidents only suffer when Congress is gridlocked as nearly all recent Congresses have been. Presidential success is measured by results, by accomplishments, by lists of legislative achievements. Members of Congress, on the other hand, measure their success by reelection. Legislative accomplishments, bills enacted into law, have little to do with that. As Congress has sloughed into gridlock in recent decades and the measures of its accomplishments have steadily declined, the reelection rates for members have remained well above 90 percent.

It is a common and frequently recurring theme of political commentary in our time that presidents need to go to school on the lessons of Franklin Roosevelt and Lyndon Johnson in their relations with Congress. They need to be more "pro-active": they need to "schmooze" more with members; they need to do a better job of "selling" their initiatives on Capitol Hill. And, no doubt they would—if it mattered.

But the members of the twenty-first-century Congresses are largely immune to that kind of personalized presidential persuasion. They know who keeps them in their jobs. It's their constituents and the communications media who report their activities to those constituents. It's the special interests who applaud their votes and reward them with campaign contributions and positive ratings on their "report cards."

It's not the president. The scarce supply of presidential favors and gratitude is a commodity of very limited value in the contemporary electoral market place. Standing up to the president is often a more successful career move than standing with the president.

We should not be surprised then, in light of these prevailing dynamics, that the forces of resistance often triumph and that presidential leadership capabilities are diminished as a result.

NOTES

1 Neustadt, *Presidential Power and the Modern Presidents*, 50.

2. Louis Fisher, *The Politics of Shared Power: Congress and the Executive* (Washington, DC: CQ Press, 1993), ix.

3. Facts on File, *Encyclopedia of the American Presidency* (New York, New York: Infobase Publishing, 2009), 435.

4. Ehrenhalt, *The United States of Ambition*, 248.

5. Bill Moyers, *Moyers on America: A Journalist and his Times* (New York: New Press, 2004), 167.

6. Ira Shapiro, *The Last Great Senate: Courage and Statesmanship in Times of Crisis* (New York: Public Affairs, 2012), xv, xvii.

7. Gary Jacobson, "Party Polarization in National Politics: The Electoral Connection," in *Polarized Politics: Congress and the President in a Partisan Era*, edited by Jon R. Bond and Richard Fleisher (Washington, DC: CQ Press, 2000), 15.

8. James Sundquist in "American Presidential Democracy: Discussion," *Political Science Quarterly* 109 (1994): 424.

9. George C. Edwards III, "The Limits of the Bully Pulpit," in *Readings in Presidential Politics*, edited by George C. Edwards III (Belmont, CA: Wadsworth, 2006), 211.

10. Obama campaign remarks in Springfield, Illinois, August 23, 2008.

11. Gary Andres, "'The Contemporary Presidency': Polarization and White House/Legislative Relations: Causes and Consequences of Elite-Level Conflict," *Presidential Studies Quarterly* 35 (2005): 763.

12. Ronald Brownstein, "Reconcilable Differences," *The Atlantic Magazine*, September 2008, accessed October 15, 2015, http://www.theatlantic.com/magazine/archive/2008/09/reconcilable-differences/306942/.

13. See David Lawder, "Republican Strategy Memo Focuses on Obamacare, Not Immigration," *Reuters Edition*, April 30, 2014, accessed October 15, 2015, http://www.reuters.com/article/2014/04/30/us-usa-congress-republicans-idUSBREA3T12I20140430.

14. Rhodes Cook, "Obama and Redefinition of Presidential Coattails," *Rasmussen Reports*, April 17, 2009, accessed October 15, 2015, http://www.rasmussen-reports.com/public_content/political_commentary/commentary_by_rhodes_cook/obama_and_the_redefinition_of_presidential_coattails.

15. Gary Lee Malecha and Daniel J. Reagan, *The Public Congress: Congressional Deliberation in a New Media Age* (New York: Routledge, 2012), 137.

16. Sarah A. Binder, *Stalemate: Causes and Consequences of Legislative Gridlock* (Washington, DC: Brookings, 2003), 67.

17. Thomas E. Mann and Norman J. Ornstein, *The Broken Branch: How Congress is Failing America and How To Get It Back On Track* (New York: Oxford University Press, 2008), 146.

18. See Richard F. Fenno, Jr., *The Power of the Purse: Appropriations Politics in Congress* (Boston: Little Brown and Company, 1966), 352ff.

19. Aaron Wildavsky, *The New Politics of the Budgetary Process*, 2nd ed. (New York: HarperCollins Publishers, 1992), 26.

20. Binder, *Stalemate*, 76.

21. Fisher, *Constitutional Conflicts Between Congress and the President*, 5th ed. (Lawrence, KS: University Press of Kansas, 2007), 203.

22. Keith E. Whittington, *Constitutional Construction: Divided Powers and Constitutional Meaning* (Cambridge, MA: Harvard University Press, 1999), 172.

23. Cited in Shailagh Murray, "Storms Show a System Out of Balance: GOP Congress Has Reduced Usual Diet of Agency Oversight," *Washington Post* (October 5, 2005): A21.

24. Quoted in Joel D. Aberbach, "Improving Oversight: Congress's Endless Task," *Extensions*, Fall 2001, accessed October 15, 2015, http://www.ou.edu/special/albert-ctr/extensions/fall2001/Aberbach.html.

25. See Elaine Sciolino, "Awaiting Call, Helms Puts Foreign Policy on Hold," *New York Times*, September 24, 1995, accessed October 15, 2015, http://www.nytimes.com/1995/09/24/world/awaiting-call-helms-puts-foreign-policy-on-hold.html.

26. Gary J. Andres, "'The Contemporary Presidency': Parties, Process, and Presidential Power: Learning from Confirmation Politics in the U. S. Senate," *Presidential Studies Quarterly* 32 (2002): 150.

27. American National Election Studies, http://www.electionstudies.org/nes-guide/toptable/tab5a_1.htm.

28. Kevin P. Phillips, *The Emerging Republican Majority* (New York: Arlington House, 1969).

29. Quoted in David S. Broder, "Common Cause Prods Senate," *The Tuscaloosa News*, November 13, 1977, accessed October 15, 2015, http://news.google.com/newspapers?nid=1817&dat=19771113&id=JEggAAAAIBAJ&sjid=_50EAAAAIBAJ&pg=5506,3076968.

30. See G. Calvin Mackenzie, *The Politics of The Appointment Process* (New York: The Free Press, 1980), especially 179ff.

31. See, for example, Charlie Savage, "President Weakens Espionage Oversight," *Boston Globe*, March 14, 2008, accessed December 21, 2015, http://www.boston.com/news/nation/articles/2008/03/14/president_weakens_espionage_oversight/?page=full.

32. Daniel Patrick Moynihan, "The Iron Law of Emulation," in *Counting Our Blessings: Reflections on the Future of America* (Boston: Little Brown, 1980), 115–37.

33. Stephen Skowronek, "Shall We Cast Our Lot with the Constitution?," in *The Presidency in the Twenty-First Century*, edited by Charles W. Dunn (Lexington, KY: University Press of Kentucky, 2011), 46.

34. Jay Costa, "What is the Cost of a Seat in Congress?," *Maplight: Revealing Money's Influence on Politics*, March 10, 2013, accessed October 15, 2015, http://maplight.org/content/73190.

35. Center for Responsive Politics, "Lobbying Database," accessed October 15, 2015, https://www.opensecrets.org/lobby/.

36. T. W. Farnam, "Study Shows Revolving Door of Employment Between Congress, Lobbying Firms," *Washington Post*, September 13, 2011, accessed October 15, 2015, http://www.washingtonpost.com/study-shows-revolving-door-of-employment-between-congress-lobbying-firms/2011/09/12/gIQAxPYROK_story.html.

37. Robert G. Kaiser, *Too Damn Much Money: The Triumph of Lobbying and the Corrosion of American Government* (New York: Alfred A. Knopf, 2009), 343–44.

38. Quoted in Kaiser, *Too Damn Much Money*, 360.

39. Center for Responsive Politics, "Lobbying Database," accessed October 15, 2015, https://www.opensecrets.org/lobby/.

40. Center for Responsive Politics, "Outside Spending," accessed October 15, 2015, https://www.opensecrets.org/outsidespending/fes_summ.php?cycle=2012.

41. Quoted in Kaiser, *Too Damn Much Money*, 23.

42. Lance T. LeLoup and Steven A. Shull, *The President and Congress: Collaboration and Combat in National Policymaking* (Boston: Allyn and Bacon, 1999), 103.

43. Quoted in *New York Times*, May 27, 1913.

44. Reported by Mark P. Petracca, "The Rediscovery of Interest Group Politics," in *The Politics of Interests: Interest Groups Transformed*, edited by Mark P. Petracca (Boulder, CO: Westview Press, 1992), 3–31.

45. Darrell M. West and Richard Francis, "Electronic Advocacy: Interest Groups and Public Policy Making," *PS: Political Science and Politics* 29(1), (March 1996): 26.

46. West and Francis, "Electronic Advocacy," 25.

47. Quoted in Graham K. Wilson, "The Clinton Administration and Interest Groups," in *The Clinton Presidency: First Appraisals*, edited by Colin Campbell and Bert A. Rockman (Chatham, NJ: Chatham House, 1996), 228.

48. Thomas T. Holyoke, *Interest Groups and Lobbying: Pursuing Political Interests in America* (Boulder, CO: Westview Press, 2014), 188.

49. Nancy Scherer, Brandon L. Bartels, and Amy Steigerwalt, "Sounding the Fire Alarm: The Role of Interest Groups in the Lower Federal Court Confirmation Process," *The Journal of Politics* (2008): 1026.

50. Hugh Heclo, "Introduction: The Presidential Illusion," in *The Illusion of Presidential Government*, edited by Hugh Heclo and Lester M. Salamon (Boulder, CO: Westview Press, 1981), 9.

6

Foreign Policy

A Special Case?

When World War I ended, most of the American men who had fought the battles in Europe went home. Not just home to America, but home to their families, their work, and their private lives. There was little reason to keep them in the armed forces after the Armistice was signed in November 1918. America faced no imminent threats, maintaining armed forces was expensive, and national politics bore—as it long had—deep strands of isolationism and pacifism. "Bring the boys home" was a popular call that rang loudly in the ears of politicians. The army which had 2 million men in Europe at the end of the war was reduced to a strength of 280,000 in 1921 and 111,000 in 1924.

The peacetime army of the interwar years remained small until the late 1930s when war clouds from Europe and the Far East began to darken even American skies. A force so small had little to do and was largely out of the public eye. For obvious reasons, presidents of the period did not regard the military as much of an instrument of international relations. Even in 1939, the American Army was the seventeenth largest in the world. And moving that army to distant shores to serve American interests posed formidable logistical challenges for which it was ill prepared.

As a result, mobilization for World War II was not much more than starting from scratch. In both men and materiel, the armed forces were deficient. A genuine ability to fight successfully in theaters around the globe would not come until more than a year after war had been declared against Germany and Japan. But the relentless power of American industry and the induction and training of millions of volunteers and conscripts eventually yielded an army of 8.3 million and an overall military force of over 12 million.

The war had pervasive effects at home as well. Rationing of critical resources, price controls, mass construction of new bases and factories, the harnessing of science and higher education to the war effort: these and many other unprecedented changes in American life swept over the country—all of them the result of policies mandated by an invigorated and dramatically enlarged federal government.

At the head of that government was Franklin D. Roosevelt. When war came in December 1941, Roosevelt had been president longer than any other man. After years as Dr. New Deal, he would now become, in his words, Dr. Win-the-War. But he fully understood that this would require a new kind of presidency, a leader equipped with powers that pushed the very limits of democratic tolerance. He assumed those powers—sometimes through congressional delegation or acquiescence, sometimes by broad interpretation of the Constitution, sometimes merely by doing what he thought had to be done. This was a power grab with a purpose, but Roosevelt reassured the country that "when the war is won, the powers under which I act will automatically revert to the people of the United States—to the people to whom these powers belong."[1]

But it didn't quite turn out that way. That war was won, but it unleashed forces that lingered, sometimes dangerously, into its aftermath: weapons of unprecedented lethality, an emboldened Soviet Union with a proud Red Army, a Communist insurgency on the brink of takeover in China, devastation in Europe and elsewhere, intense pressures for an end to colonialism. And it yielded in America a superpower, both economic and military, which was the central element of a new world order—a novel reality for Americans. America at war's end produced half of the world's GDP and it alone possessed fearsome atomic weapons.

And there was more. It wasn't just America that rose to new prominence because of the war. So, too, did the American president. Roosevelt died before the war ended. Harry Truman took his place. To many Americans and probably to many others around the world, Truman seemed a man of much smaller stature than Roosevelt. But the office he inherited had accumulated such power and such visibility during the war that Truman's real or perceived stature seemed to matter little. The expanded powers, especially in matters of national security policy, were more institutional than personal. The presidency would never shrink back to its prewar status The impact of World War II demonstrated James Madison's prescience. "War," he wrote in 1795, "is in fact the true nurse of executive aggrandizement."[2]

The country demobilized after World War II, but not in the way it had after previous wars. There was no return to normality, but rather a rapid recognition that the new normal was a world full of threats, a world from which two broad oceans and impotent neighbors were insufficient protection. American troops remained in Europe and Japan. The American navy sailed on all the seas. American planes and pilots were stationed around the globe. The wartime military shrunk, but only to a new set of powerful dimensions, not to invisibility. Fascism was gone, but a new menace—communism—was spreading. The Cold War rose quickly from the dust of the World War.

In its new role as leader of the democratic countries of the world—or at least the noncommunist countries—America faced new strategic challenges and these required new institutional and policy responses. By the end of 1947, the defense establishment was significantly reorganized, enhancing the president's ability to develop and implement more coherent national security policies. The foreign aid program was initiated that year as well. When the Soviet Union threated the survival of a free West Berlin in 1948, President Truman ordered an around-the-clock airlift to supply its citizens. Two years later, in a place most Americans barely knew, Truman ordered American armed forces into war. He sought no congressional declaration of this war, claiming it was part of a United Nations response to the invasion of South Korea by North Korea. And he told the American people that "what is at stake here is nothing less than our own national security and the peace of the world."[3]

This began what became the pattern of the Cold War and even of the years that followed it. America assumed the prime and sometimes sole responsibility for protecting democracy. American military forces would play a key role in that. The president would deploy those forces, on his own initiative and timetable, whenever he alone deemed it necessary to do so. Intelligence collection and covert action moved from the periphery to the main stage of Cold War enterprise. Secrecy and classification became matters of high national importance. For the first time, America entered mutual defense treaties with scores of countries around the world.

There were other elements to this pattern as well. The Congress largely acquiesced in these actions, rarely standing up for the Constitution or its own prerogatives. The American people followed the leader, at least until their patience was spent in military endeavors that seemed endless and unproductive. Despite occasional journalistic doubters and critics, the bulk of the American communications media stood on the sidelines and sometimes on the front lines and watched the wars that presidents made.

The postwar era gave birth to a dramatically expanded set of presidential powers and institutions of presidential authority. And these challenged the ability of countervailing forces within the government and of the Constitution itself to restrain the chief executive. This chapter is the story of that expansion, the resistance it inspired, and the unbalanced outcome it has yielded.

THE PRESIDENCY IN A TIME OF DANGER

What diminished presidential power in domestic policy in the last few decades of the twentieth century often enhanced that power in some aspects of foreign policy. New initiatives in domestic policy nearly always required new legislation. But significant legislation was hard to obtain from a recalcitrant and often dysfunctional Congress mired in a gridlock fueled by competing special interest groups.

Much of foreign policy, however, is nonstatutory. It does not require legislative action. And competing interest groups have historically been fewer in number and weaker in resources on matters of foreign policy than in domestic or economic policy. The field is more open for the president in the former; the potential opposition more limited.

The Constitution bears much of the responsibility for this. There is sparse language about foreign policy in that document and even the words themselves leave ample room for debate and conflicting interpretation. The silences of the Constitution have loomed large as well in the face of complex foreign policy challenges, and presidents have rarely failed in their efforts to claim those silences for their own purposes. As political scientist Andrew Polsky has noted, "For more than two centuries, the Constitution has invested presidents with a broad warrant to act on matters of national security. . . . Situations often arise in which 'strict construction'—a literal reading of the wording—cannot fix the extent of presidential authority."[4] And in those situations, presidents have often taken aggressive action, unhindered by the constitutional constraints that loom so large in matters of domestic policy.

The character of foreign policy also lent itself to a history of presidential predominance. Managing the nation's relations with other countries often requires qualities of which the executive is well equipped and the legislature deficient. As Woodrow Wilson wrote, "When foreign affairs play a prominent part in the politics and policy of the nation, its executive must of necessity be its guide: must utter every initial judgment, take every first step of action, supply the information upon which it is to act, suggest and in large measure control its conduct."[5]

In the decades that followed World War II, the character of American foreign policy evolved in several new directions. Those seemed to demand an even greater role for the president, and the need for strong presidential leadership became an assumption of wide acceptance among the American people and often in the Congress as well. It could hardly have been otherwise. On the one hand, there were the enormous new responsibilities for leading not only the United States but all of the countries of the "free world" in a Cold War. On the other, there was the unprecedented concentration of national security institutions and capacities in the president's hands.

The postwar presidents had a Defense Department, a National Security Council, a Joint Chiefs of Staff, a Central Intelligence Agency, and a National Security Agency that no prewar president possessed. They had under their command several million well-trained soldiers, sailors, and airmen stationed all over the world and deploying the most sophisticated weapons science and industry could create. They had the atomic bomb and its thermonuclear descendants. And they had a broad and largely unfettered warrant to use them all.

As postwar experiences accumulated, it became easier and easier for presidents to act unilaterally in foreign policy and harder and harder for Congress or other potential sources of resistance to stand in their way. President Truman alone made the decision to use atomic bombs against Japan. Most members of Congress were unaware such a weapon existed. Truman alone decided to send American forces into what came to be known as the Korean War. Dwight Eisenhower single-handedly ordered the CIA to execute a coup against the government of Mohammed Mosaddegh in Iran in 1953. In a tense and potentially calamitous confrontation with the Soviet Union over nuclear weapons in Cuba, President Kennedy met secretly with a hand-picked group of advisers to determine his response.

Each of these experiences and many others like them accumulated to forge a well understood and widely accepted reality: in the dangerous postwar world, there could be no substitute for singular responsibility and singular leadership. Presidents assumed that responsibility; with few exceptions other actors deferred. "Nineteenth-century presidents had had to contend with congressional influences in foreign affairs, and particularly with the Senate Foreign Relations Committee," wrote the historian Robert Dallek. "But by the early 1960s, the president had become the undisputed architect of U.S. foreign policy."[6]

Scholars of the postwar era quickly reported the predominance of the presidency in foreign policy and just as quickly embedded that notion in the conventional wisdom. A seminal article by political scientist Aaron Wildavsky in 1966 stated the case starkly: "The United States has one president, but it has two presidencies; one presidency is for domestic affairs, and the other is concerned with defense and foreign policy. Since World War II, presidents have had much greater success in controlling the nation's defense and foreign policies than in dominating its domestic policies."[7]

The "two presidencies thesis" inspired much scholarly argument and reexamination in the years that followed, but little of that debate dislodged the perception of an enlarged presidential role in foreign policy from the popular mind nor from the *modus operandi* in Washington.

Why was it that presidents did not suffer the full range or intensity of constraints in foreign policy that often plagues them in domestic policy? The answer is not simple, for the relationship between president and

Congress in foreign policy went through cycles even in the postwar period, and it was always more nuanced than many of the descriptions would admit. In explaining the president's role it is helpful to begin by noting that "foreign policy" is, in fact, a nest of sometimes related but often quite different forms of government activity. Much of the rest of this chapter will focus on the war power, but that is hardly the sum of foreign policy. The United States conducts its relations with other countries through bilateral diplomacy; through collective security in the form of treaties, executive agreements and participation in international organizations; with foreign aid, both economic and military, to more than 184 countries; through educational and humanitarian efforts like the Peace Corps and the Fulbright program. In addition, American companies, under government supervision and regulation, engage in trade with foreign countries that now regularly exceeds $3.3 trillion in value.[8]

The Congress and the president are jointly engaged in all of these aspects of foreign policy, but the character of their engagement and the relative influence of each branch vary, often significantly, across the spectrum of components. Foreign trade, for example, has long been a matter of profound concern to members of Congress. For much of the early history of the country, tariffs were a primary source of revenue, and tariff policy played a large role in the development of the American economy. Today, every member of Congress represents constituents whose businesses are affected by the conditions that Washington imposes on international commerce. And this is an area where policy often does reside in law, so the Congress's influence over foreign trade legislation is a major constraint on the president. A good example of that occurred in 1993 when President Clinton was forced to enter complex negotiations with members of Congress to achieve congressional approval for the North Atlantic Free Trade Agreement (NAFTA). Clinton's perception of these was described in personal conversations with historian Taylor Branch. "Predicting safe passage in the Senate," Branch reported, "President Clinton said the fate of NAFTA would rest on his temporary alliance with House Republicans plus a concerted effort to pick off enough Democrats from their own united leadership. Although the partisan lines were blurred, he said, it would come down to an old-fashioned struggle for votes, district by district."[9]

Presidents serve as the country's chief diplomats and in the modern era they travel widely and often to foreign countries and engage in frequent meetings with their counterparts at the head of other governments. But most of the day-to-day business of diplomacy is conducted by presidential appointees, the most important of whom must have their appointments confirmed by the Senate. In recent decades, senators have brought the same measure of scrutiny to diplomatic appointments, as they have to those serving in domestic agencies, thus narrowing the president's freedom in choosing the country's ambassadors and other representatives abroad. At the outset of President Obama's second term, for example, his widely reported intention to appoint UN Ambassador Susan Rice as secretary of state had to be scuttled in the face of significant Senate opposition.[10]

Congress is not without tools nor interest in many matters of foreign policy, and the relationship between the two branches in those areas closely resembles their interactions on domestic and economic policy. As law professors Steven Calabresi and James Lindgren concluded from their study of the president's role in foreign policy, "there is almost nothing vital that the President can do even in this realm without some help from Congress."[11] Clearly, any description of the foreign policy relationship as one sided with the president dominant is far too broad and misleading.

But in matters of war and peace, the Congress has often assumed a more restrained posture. While there is much scholarly and political debate about the meaning of the words "commander in chief," contemporary presidents have been of one mind. To them, those words have meant that the Constitution empowers them to deploy American military forces whenever and wherever they believe it is in the country's interest to do so. This need not be in response to a direct and immediate threat to the American homeland. The safety of American citizens abroad, the protection of American economic interests, support for friendly regimes in other countries, prevention of genocide, containment of communism: all of these have been trotted out by presidents at various times to justify their deployment of American forces into combat or hostile situations.

In almost every case, in the short term at least, criticism and opposition have been swept away by the advantages that accrue to presidents when they exercise their assumed powers as commander in chief. Primary among those advantages is initiative, the ability of presidents to act first. When presidents commit American forces in advance of consultation or debate outside their immediate advisers, other actors are forced to respond to a fait accompli. It would be much easier to question a potential commitment before it occurs than after it is under way. Once troops are on the ground or missiles have been fired or bombs dropped, those who try to second guess the initiative risk being accused of giving aid and comfort to the enemy or of undermining American troops in battle. Whatever the wisdom of the initial commitment, few politicians want to face those accusations.

And, even when criticisms of the president's initiatives arise, converting those to real constraints is an arduous and rarely successful enterprise. In Congress, any challenge to the president has to survive layers of subcommittees and committees, elaborate rules of debate, and the common unwillingness of many members of Congress to take risky positions on military matters that promise little electoral payoff. The courts can't act on their own and must await the filing of lawsuits challenging the legal or constitutional validity of a president's military initiatives. The largely unsuccessful history of those is not a very inviting prospect for critics. The press and the airwaves may be hospitable to debate and criticism of the commander in chief, but they are not a foundation of authority. Korea, Vietnam, and Iraq all testify to the limited and very slow impact of even harsh criticism—when it is only words.

In exercising their commander-in-chief powers, presidents also have powerful information advantages over potential critics. They can claim they know things that made it necessary for them to order American forces into action. As Arthur Schlesinger noted in his warning about the rise of an imperial presidency, "confronted by presidential initiatives in foreign affairs, Congress and the courts, along with the press and the citizenry, often lack confidence in their own information and judgment and are likely to be intimidated by executive authority."[12]

The information on which presidents base their actions may or may not be accurate. Was an American naval vessel really attacked by North Vietnamese gunboats in the Gulf of Tonkin in 1964, as Lyndon Johnson asserted? Was the new regime in Grenada really likely to become another Soviet foothold in the Caribbean, as Ronald Reagan claimed? Did Saddam Hussein possess weapons of mass destruction, as George W. Bush argued? The proof was hardly rock solid for any of these justifications. But in the swell of patriotism and public toughness that so often surrounds the entry of American forces into combat, careful research, thoughtful analysis, and open debate are shoved aside. By taking the initiative, presidents shift the burden of proof—which ought to be very high in justifying any placement of young American women and men in harm's way—to potential critics.

To the advantages of initiative, one should add the veil of secrecy that nearly always accompanies it. Executive branch employees—spies, surveillance technicians, analysts, most with top security clearances—gather and collect information in secret. Only those who "need to know" get to see that information. Plans are formed in secret. Sometimes even the actions themselves are secret. How can other institutions and actors participate in decisions when they don't even know those decisions are in process? The obvious answer is that they cannot. Advantage president.

Then, of course, there is the spectacular numerical advantage the president possesses over any potential opponents or critics. In the federal government, the Defense Department at the outset of the Obama presidency had 718,000 civilian employees in addition to 1.4 million men and women in uniform, and over 1.1 million in reserve. Its total budget in that year—over $650 billion—exceeded the GDP of many developed countries. Best estimates are that the CIA has more than 20,000 employees and the National Security Agency another 30,000–40,000. Adding in the 240,000 people who work at the Department of Homeland Security yields a total executive branch force of approximately three and a half million people engaged in the business of national security. Left unmentioned here are the hundreds of thousands of people who work in the civilian defense industry manufacturing the weapons and conducting the studies that support the government's national security enterprise.[13]

How could a few score committee staff in Congress or the constantly shrinking foreign bureaus of newspapers and television networks match forces with that growing juggernaut of resources in the executive branch? The answer for much of the postwar period was that they could not and they did not.

Congress

What then is the role of Congress in national security policy and how does that effect presidential leadership? It's useful here as it was in our earlier discussions of Congress to try to see the world as the institution's members see it. The ways in which the Congress as a whole interacts with the president in national security policy is, in large part, the product of the individual perceptions and incentive systems of its members.

Let's begin with the obvious. Foreign policy is the primary concern of few members of Congress. In every Congress, there are a few members who, because of the long service on committees that deal with foreign policy or perhaps their experiences before entering Congress, take a special interest in foreign policy. J. William Fulbright, John McCain, Lee Hamilton, and John Kerry are examples of this small cell. But most members represent constituencies composed of citizens who have little more than peripheral interest in what happens outside of the United States. They may want their government to make national security its highest priority but the details of that undertaking do not compel their interest and have little effect on how they perceive and evaluate their elected representatives.

As of 2014, only 35 percent of the American people possessed a passport. A substantial percentage of those have never traveled further than Canada, Mexico, or a Caribbean island. In an average year, only about 5 percent of the American people travel to any foreign country. A common trend in the business of journalism over the past two decades has been a shrinkage in the number of foreign bureaus, foreign correspondents, and foreign news.[14] Study after study shows that Americans have little interest in foreign policy and little knowledge of geography, international relations, or even contemporary foreign issues or crises. One such study concluded: "In the post-Cold War era, notwithstanding their massive advantages in education, Americans continue to lag behind citizens of other industrialized democracies on measures of foreign affairs information."[15] A survey by the Pew Research Global Attitudes Project found that "in the final month of the 2012 presidential campaign, no more than 6% of those surveyed cited a foreign policy issue, including the wars in Iraq and Afghanistan, as the most important problem facing the country today."[16]

Little wonder then that their representatives in Congress do not find this fertile electoral soil. Much better in the minds of most of them to focus their work on the domestic and economic issues that matter most to their constituents and are thus most likely to contribute to reelection.

Members recognize as well the potentially high costs of challenging a president on foreign policy. Presidents have the information advantages cited earlier. They have larger and more consistent access to the public through the communications media. And they have the defense establishment standing with them. To take a public stand against all that, to vote against an initiative that the president has told the American people is necessary for national security is a very risky career move. Few members of Congress ever take the risk.

As this suggests, congressional apprehension may have contributed as much as executive aggrandizement to the contemporary presidential role in war making. After more than three decades as a member of the House of Representatives, for example, Barney Frank wrote, "When it comes to authorizing military action in anything short of an invasion of America, members of Congress would rather leave the decision to the president. That way they preserve their freedom to either attack it or endorse it depending on how things turn out. The complaint that too many decisions to go to war have been unilateral executive ones is accurate, but it is not as much an example of presidential overreach as it is of a congressional proclivity to duck."[17]

In matters of national defense another motive shapes the actions of many members. That is the widespread desire to serve and protect the interests of what President Eisenhower termed the "military-industrial complex." There are approximately 310 military installations on American soil, scattered through a majority of congressional districts and forty-eight states. The development, manufacture, and testing of weapons takes place all over the country. Pentagon spending on development and procurement of weapons has exceeded $200 billion in recent years. Defense industries have long understood the political advantage of scattering their facilities through as many congressional districts as possible. If the defense establishment in Washington is lined up with the president on a national security initiative, it's difficult for members of Congress not to join the line.

The simple facts have been these. The combination of postwar national security realities and the political incentives they yield for legislators made it very difficult for Congress to resist the president in initiating or sustaining military conflicts. Congress is not a patsy for presidents. It conducts oversight, approves appropriations for the military, and its members visit and report from war zones. It has, however, little capacity and even less will to stop a military action once one has begun.

So it has tried to strengthen its role in national security policy by focusing on the general rather than the particular, on process rather than substance. When public opposition grew to high visibility during the Vietnam War, increasing numbers of members of Congress sought to force an end to that war. But they could not muster the collective will to do so by ordering the troops home or by cutting off appropriations that supported the war. The steadily harsher antiwar statements from individual members did little to change the policies of Lyndon Johnson or Richard Nixon. A Congress that can't act collectively can't act.

But once that war was in the final stages of winding down, the Congress passed the War Powers Resolution, a statute designed to set limits on a president's ability to commit troops to combat and to establish a role for Congress in deciding upon such commitments and in ending them. Richard Nixon thought this act a violation of his constitutional prerogatives as commander in chief and vetoed it. Congress overrode the veto. Rep. Clement Zablocki (D-WI), the author of the War Powers Resolution, said that its intent was "to ensure that [Congress] is permitted to exercise the fullest constitutional responsibilities over questions of peace and war."[18]

Congress did not intend to trump the president's responsibility to decide when such commitments were necessary nor to develop plans for implementing them. It only wanted to afford itself the right to participate in the decision to go ahead with the commitment.

But the War Powers Act never accomplished this. In the more than four decades since its passage, America has engaged in two lengthy wars in Iraq and Afghanistan and a variety of other military actions around the globe. In most of these, there was little prior consultation with Congress and no effort by that body to terminate the commitment of troops. In a few, the president sought congressional authorization for the use of force before proceeding, but in circumstances that made such authorization difficult for members to oppose. In none, of course, was there a declaration of war—the primary instrument of control that the Constitution assigns to the Congress.

The reality remains today that the war power is the president's; the Congress has found no handle to hold back the initial exercise of that power. But, as we shall see, the twenty-first-century Congress has found a number of ways to constrain the management of the wars that presidents initiate.

Courts

What, then, of the courts? If the president violates the Constitution, can't he be held accountable in the courts of law? The answer for much of American history was that when the president took action in foreign policy, especially in making or managing a war, the courts tolerated very broad interpretations of the Constitution. In fact, the courts abetted presidents in three ways especially.

One was by protecting the foreign policy decisions of presidents from direct legal challenges. Court rulings on standing, on the rights of citizens to seek judicial remedies for perceived wrongs, have often closed the courtroom door to the president's critics and adversaries. When, for example, members of Congress sought an injunction to prevent continuation of the war in Southeast Asia without explicit congressional authorization, the D.C. Circuit Court declined to adjudicate.[19] Here, as often happens in disputes between the president and Congress, a court claimed that this was a "political question" that the other two branches must resolve between themselves.

The Supreme Court often followed this practice of denying standing when presidential war powers were challenged. One analysis of these cases concluded: "The review of cases presenting basic questions concerning the constitutionality of the Government's war policies reveals that the Supreme Court had many opportunities to decide these questions, but all petitions for review were refused. The Court's silence during the Vietnam War denied guidance to the lower courts and denied the American people the Court's considered judgment on the constitutionality of this divisive military conflict."[20]

A second way in which the courts have abetted presidential leadership in foreign policy is by siding with the president when relevant cases were accepted and adjudicated. From the earliest days of the republic, the courts have been willing to grant the president wide latitude in the conduct of foreign affairs. When Martin Van Buren was challenged in 1836 on his decision to recognize Argentina's claim to sovereignty over what are now called the Falkland Islands, the Supreme Court stood firmly on his side. In the opinion of the court delivered by Justice John McLean:

> And can there be any doubt, that when the executive branch of the government, which is charged with our foreign relations, shall in its correspondence with a foreign nation assume a fact in regard to the sovereignty of any island or country, it is conclusive on the judicial department? And in this view it is not material to inquire, nor is it the province of the Court to determine, whether the executive be right or wrong. It is enough to know, that in the exercise of his constitutional functions, he has decided the question. Having done this under the responsibilities which belong to him, it is obligatory on the people and government of the Union.[21]

In 1936, a Supreme Court that had been notably unfriendly to New Deal initiatives in domestic policy granted Franklin Roosevelt broad leeway in its interpretation of the treaty-making clause of the Constitution. "The federal power over external affairs in origin and essential character [is] different from that over internal affairs," the court noted, "but participation in the exercise of the power is significantly limited. In this vast external realm, with its important, complicated, delicate and manifold problems, the President alone has the power to speak or listen as a representative of the nation. He makes treaties with the advice and consent of the Senate; but he alone negotiates. Into the field of negotiation the Senate cannot intrude, and Congress itself is powerless to invade it."[22] And then, quoting John Marshall favorably, the court added, "The president is the sole organ of the nation in its external relations, and its sole representative with foreign nations."

In the 1936 case, the Supreme Court contributed to presidential prerogatives in a third way, by doing something it had done in other foreign policy cases as well. It didn't merely resolve the specific issue in the case in the president's favor; it went well beyond the details to provide a broader foundation for presidential leadership in managing the country's foreign affairs. The Congress must "often accord to the President a degree of discretion and freedom from statutory restriction which would not be admissible were domestic affairs alone involved," wrote Justice Sutherland in the majority opinion.

Political scientist Andrew Polsky concluded from his analysis of the courts' response to challenges to the president's war powers, "The Supreme Court has helped legitimize broad presidential authority in foreign affairs that exceeds any literal reading of the Constitution."[23] Before the twenty-first century, most scholarly analyses of the courts' role in foreign affairs came out in the same place. The conclusion of political scientist Michael Genovese in a 1980 book is characteristic of those: "Presidents seem to have a great deal of freedom from judicial review in the area of foreign affairs. The courts have not stood up against presidents in foreign affairs with any regularity. More often than not, the courts have added to the already bloated powers of the presidency in foreign affairs. Constitutional limitations rarely bind the hands of a resolute president."[24]

But two significant changes occurring more recently have begun to incline the courts in different directions and then to accelerate the inclination. The first of those is what some have called the "rights revolution," the expanding definition of human and civil rights that has been underway for decades in the United States and abroad, and to which the courts have been major contributors. In expanding the categories of legally and constitutionally protected rights and in granting wider access to those seeking judicial protection of their rights, the courts have begun to permit lawsuits against federal policies—including matters of foreign policy—that would not have gotten through the courtroom door in earlier generations.

Beyond this, there have been changes in the very character of foreign affairs that have created an ever-growing list of potentially justiciable issues in that area. The distinction between the foreign and the domestic has steadily eroded in recent decades, as new technologies have shrunk the distances between peoples and countries, a global economy has come to dominate the marketplace, and wars among great powers have given way to the constant danger of terrorism and a whole new set of complicated legal challenges. Foreign affairs now engage many more Americans and American companies than ever before and often affect them in ways that ensure they will have standing to bring their concerns to court.

As we shall see, this has begun to raise new constraints on the president's role in foreign policy, even in the exercise of the war power.

Scrutiny

In earlier chapters, I described the intense scrutiny that now follows the president everywhere. In domestic and economic policy matters especially, the president's actions (or inaction) are constantly described in the communications media and discussed in a wide range of venues. The explosion of social media and political blogs has only added to this. The American people, where their interests are engaged, follow these discussions. Opinions are shaped by them. And presidential freedom of action is often constrained by this scrutiny. Presidents trespass the boundaries of media reaction and public tolerance at their peril.

In foreign policy, traditionally, the scrutiny has been less pervasive and less constraining. Foreign affairs and foreign policy have been subjects of little interest to most Americans, and public opinion of such matters was, as Louis Fisher notes, "spare and spasmodic"—where it existed at all.[25] America's geographic isolation, its tradition of melting away the ethnic identities of immigrants, the distaste for entangling foreign alliances all contributed to a prevalent national attitude that was always inner directed and sometimes xenophobic. Presidential actions in foreign policy were much more likely to shape public opinion than to be shaped by it.

Even when foreign policy initiatives raised questions of power and law, the public usually stood aside. Washington can be embroiled in heated tensions over alleged violations of the Constitution. Members of Congress can sue the president for usurping their prerogatives and lambaste administration officials at their hearings. The newspapers can jump into the fray. But constitutional disputes are widely regarded as insider games, hardly of interest to most citizens. "There is a general public indifference to issues of constitutionalism and executive power," notes political scientist Hugh Heclo. "When President Bush and officials in his administration repeatedly claimed broad, inherent executive powers, Americans seemed to yawn and await the results. This entire subject was hardly discussed during the longest presidential campaign in history—a sure sign that it had not registered among citizens and focus groups."[26]

The communications media also played a smaller historical role in foreign policy development and implementation than they had in other policy areas. The major broadcast networks and a small group of newspapers and magazines maintained foreign bureaus and employed often highly competent foreign correspondents. But they were limited in number and in the scope of their attention in a vast and complex world.

Sources were harder to find and walls of secrecy and censorship harder to penetrate before there was an internet and digital access to nearly every place and every knowledgeable person. Most reports from abroad were dependent on information provided by official sources. War correspondents in World War II and Korea were subjected to heavy censorship and were often denied access to the battlefield. The daily briefings in Saigon—which we now know to have been riddled with errors, irresponsible estimates, and lies—were a primary source for many of the correspondents in the early days of the Vietnam War. The death of millions in the Holocaust was kept secret from the outside world.

The best of the communications media are introspective, constantly evaluating and seeking to improve their performance. Errors and oversights in coverage and judgment get corrected, but often only after events have occurred in which presidents take action and public support crystallizes. When the administration of George W. Bush built congressional and public support for an invasion of Iraq by claiming that Saddam Hussein possessed weapons of mass destruction, the news media lacked the interest or capacity to challenge the claim. Later, both the *Washington Post* and the *New York Times* published criticism of their own inadequate reporting on that issue.

The news media bring high levels of resources and expertise to their reporting on and analyses of domestic and economic issues. But not so to foreign policy. There are vastly more sports reporters in America than foreign correspondents. The domestic automobile industry is covered with much greater knowledge and insight than Africa, South America, or South Asia.

It should come as no surprise then that the American presidents have historically had a freer hand in making foreign policy than they have in policies that hit closer to home. But even that is now changing in significant ways, and the presidential hand is less free even in this area than it has ever been before.

International community

Until World War II and for much of the early postwar period, the international community was a minor check on the foreign policy decisions of American presidents. While events elsewhere often set the agenda for presidential decision making, the response to those events was largely shaped at home, usually in the White House.

Before World War II, isolationism was the constant strain in shaping America's role in the world. Occasional adventurism and intervention were exceptions to the rule, and the rule was that America stayed home. Congress and its members rarely found much outside American borders to compel their interest. Joseph W. Martin Jr., who served in the House of Representatives for forty-two years in the middle decades of the twentieth century and was its Speaker when the Republicans won the majority after World War II, wrote in his memoirs:

> The great difference between life in Congress a generation ago and life there now was the absence then of the immense pressures that came with the depression, World War II, Korea, and the cold war. Foreign affairs were an inconsequential problem in Congress in the 1920s. For one week the House Foreign Affairs Committee debated to the exclusion of all other matters the question of authorizing a $20,000 appropriation for an international poultry show in Tulsa. This item, which we finally approved, was about the most important issue that came before the committee in the whole session.[27]

American presidents before the war were little constrained by foreign governments or international organizations because there was little engagement with the former and no membership in the latter. When foreign policy decisions were made in Washington, American interests dominated, foreign governments were rarely consulted in advance, and it was assumed that the chips would fall where they may. When World War II brought a sudden end to the sway of isolationism, America's superpower status granted presidents freedom of action. In the popular perception, the American president was the leader of the free world. When America acted, other democracies would come along because they were so dependent on American wealth and military power.

In the heady atmosphere of postwar superpowerdom, America shed its traditional aversion to alliances and international organizations. It encouraged and happily joined the United Nations. It developed mutual defense treaties in Europe (NATO), Asia (SEATO), and the Middle East (CENTO). It changed course in this way because American leaders were confident that they could dominate—or at least not be dominated by—these organizations. The country's national interests, especially the containment of communism, would be well served by deeper American participation in the international community.

And so it was for some years after World War II. Through humanitarian efforts, foreign aid, military action, and covert activities, America became a much more dynamic force in the world. Foreign leaders and international organizations were sometimes consulted and sometimes wooed, but they rarely limited the president's freedom of action. President Truman's deployment of American forces in Korea occurred simultaneously with a UN resolution calling on member nations to provide military assistance to South Korea. This permitted Truman to claim that it was a UN police action. But the United Nations was a minor factor in his decision making.

When President Kennedy decided to order a naval blockade of Cuba and thus to threaten a nuclear confrontation with the Soviet Union, other world leaders were informed only after the decision had been made. When Richard Nixon decided to reverse a policy of several decades by visiting and reopening relations with China, he consulted in advance with few American politicians and no foreign leaders. While it was not uncommon for foreign leaders to disagree with the actions of American presidents nor to take umbrage at the short shrift they were given in the decisions that led to these actions, they had little choice but to watch and hope for the best. American power was the foundation of unilateral action even in a world of growing multilateral connections.

But here, too, history took its toll. And, as we shall see, the twenty-first century has been far less hospitable to American leadership and to the freedom of presidents to place their stamp on American foreign policy and world affairs.

TWENTY-FIRST CENTURY REALITIES

As it did in so many other things, the Vietnam War initiated profound and durable changes to the management of foreign policy in the United States. In the early years of that war, despite its distance from the home front and its rare dependence on conscription, most Americans supported the contentions of Presidents Kennedy and Johnson that America's vital national interests were at stake in Vietnam. Let the communists win there, those presidents told the American people, and soon enough all the Southeast Asian dominoes—Laos, Thailand, and Cambodia—would fall. All of Asia would become a communist stronghold.

At first it seemed simple enough. The goal was not to conquer North Vietnam, but merely to secure freedom and democracy in South Vietnam. Only limited American forces would be needed because the superior lethality of American weapons and the superior training of American soldiers would quickly overwhelm the ragtag peasants on the other side. When George Ball, a senior state department official made the unpopular prediction that Vietnam might demand up to 300,000 U.S. troops, John F. Kennedy replied, "you're crazier than hell. That will never happen."[28]

And when the task seemed somewhat more daunting than promised by those early estimates, a few thousand more Americans were sent, then a few thousand more, and then a few thousand more. When the war grew large enough that some broader justification was needed, a cooked-up or over-stated engagement in the Gulf of Tonkin was a handy rationale for Lyndon Johnson to seek broad congressional authorization for a much bigger war.

The war dragged on. Measures of success—body counts, pacified ham-lets—were no substitute for real victory. Many Americans first began to question and then to abandon support for the war. Because the president had made this war, the president became the direct target of the swelling legions of war critics. Johnson's job approval ratings began a long deep slide. Sliding alongside them were the regular pulse takings by pollsters of popular trust in the national government. In November 1964, when John-son won his landslide victory, a survey by the Pew Research Center showed that 77 percent of Americans always or usually trusted the government. This number was down to 61 percent four years later, and 53 percent four years after that.[29]

Johnson saw the handwriting on the wall and abandoned the reelec-tion effort in 1968. Richard Nixon, never a very popular or trusted figure, miraculously rose from the ashes of his own career in that most peculiar election year to succeed Johnson in the White House. But he, too, could not or would not, shed the burden of Vietnam.

The failure in Vietnam had larger consequences than merely shrinking the reputations of the presidents who managed that war. It also stimulated a series of refinements and reconsiderations of postwar thinking about the president's role and responsibility in foreign policy.

Popular opposition to the war emboldened Congress to launch several major challenges to presidential authority. Some of them took the form of more rigorous questions of administration officials at hearings and more skeptical scrutiny of defense appropriations. But others found their way into law: requirements that Congress be informed of all executive agree-ments, restrictions on the sale of weapons to foreign governments, estab-lishment of committees to review intelligence operations, the War Powers Act. The rush to refinement was accelerated by the simultaneous occurrence of the Watergate scandal that limited the president's ability to resist.

By the end of the Ford administration in early 1977, the foreign policy landscape looked much different than it had a decade earlier. President Ford, noting the concerns earlier in the decade about an imperial presi-dency, wrote in 1980 that the problem now was not an imperial presidency but an "imperiled presidency."[30]

These new constraints on presidential authority were far from perfect. Presidents disregarded the consultation provisions of the War Powers Act and Congress did little to hold them to its obligations. The intelligence committees in Congress performed diligently, but also discovered how dif-ficult it is to ride herd on necessarily secret activities. The Congress sought to use its power of the purse to direct some aspects of foreign policy, but often found it a blunt instrument for that purpose. When both houses passed the Boland Amendments between 1982 and 1984 prohibiting any funding for the purpose of overthrowing the government of Nicaragua, for example, a small group of White House aides devised an imaginative triangular scheme for circumventing the amendment. Discovery of this scheme led to what came to be known as the Iran-Contra scandal in 1986.

But if the specifics were imperfect, the trend was increasingly clear. The days when presidents dominated foreign policy, and Congress and the courts and the American people stayed out of the way, were at an end. There were many more players in the game now and, inevitably, the game changed.

At the heart of this change was public opinion. The demonstrations of it were rarely overt, but it was the driving force for much of the momentum. By significant measures, the American people had lost trust in their government. Americans were increasingly skeptical of military engagements and that attitude inspired journalists and legislators to sharpen their own skepticism. The benefit of the doubt that had long been granted to presidents when they initiated new foreign policies was narrower and more tenuous in the years that followed Vietnam and Watergate. This did not prevent presidents from engaging actively as they always had in foreign policy. But it did ensure that new initiatives had to meet a higher burden of justification and would more often be questioned and challenged.

Small and quick engagements continued to unfold much as in the past. The rescue of the crew of the freighter Mayaguez by President Ford, the invasion of the Caribbean island of Grenada by President Reagan, the army's seizure of Manuel Noriega in Panama under the first President Bush, and a number of other similar deployments of American forces by later presidents all started with no prior public warning and endured little subsequent criticism.

Larger engagements, however, were a harder sell. When Iraq invaded Kuwait in the summer of 1990 while the Congress was on recess, President Bush began to construct a large international force to respond. But he declined to order that force into action until he had secured authorization to do so from the Congress. A little more than a decade later, after terrorist attacks on New York and Washington, the later President Bush similarly sought congressional authorization for an invasion of Iraq. Both presidents claimed that they had the right under the constitution to launch the planned attacks without congressional authorization, but both also understood the political risks of doing so on the altered landscape of foreign policy.

The Congress provided both of those authorizations, but not without significant debate and no little opposition. In 1991, the Senate voted 52 to 47 and the House 250 to 183 to support the authorization. In 2002, the votes were 77 to 23 in the Senate and 296 to 133 in the House. Compare that to 1964, when the Gulf of Tonkin Resolution was approved 88–2 in the Senate and 416–0 in the House. Skepticism was much more acute in the recent examples.

Perhaps the clearest example of how things have changed came in 2013. A civil war in Syria had raged for months. President Obama had been cautious about direct intervention. "If we end up rushing to judgment without hard, effective evidence," he said at a press conference on April 30, "then we can find ourselves in a position where we can't mobilize the international community to support what we do."[31] But pressure for a response increased as news stories accumulated of the slaughter of tens of thousands of Syrian citizens.

When evidence emerged that chemical weapons had been used by the Syrian government against its own citizens, Obama was prepared to intervene militarily and claimed he could do so without congressional authorization. But strong objections from Capitol Hill forced him to invite Congress to authorize the use of force against the Syrian government. "While I believe I have the authority to carry out this military action without specific congressional authorization," he said, "I know that the country will be stronger if we take this course, and our actions will be even more effective. We should have this debate, because the issues are too big for business as usual."

But it quickly became apparent that many in Congress were reluctant to grant that authorization, in large part because there was so little apparent public support for it. A CNN Poll found that more than seven of ten Americans opposed a military strike in Syria.[32] It began to look like a moment of colossal embarrassment for a president who couldn't get Congress to support military initiatives that he thought were necessary. Just as a vote was about to occur in Congress—a vote that Obama almost surely would have lost—the president withdrew his request for support so that he could study a proposal by Russia to remove and destroy the chemical weapons. It was an ironic moment: Russia saving an American president from failure to achieve military objectives.

With public opinion much less susceptible to the rally-round-the-flag attitudes that usually characterized its reaction to presidential initiatives in the past, foreign policy making came increasingly to resemble domestic policy making as the twentieth century melded into the twenty-first. Other environmental changes contributed to this new reality.

One of those was an expansion in the number of organized interests that sought to influence foreign policy. They came from every imaginable perspective: human rights, environmental protection, weapons sales, preservation of fisheries, drug trafficking, copyright protection, foreign trade, and so on. As the international community grew more interdependent, American interests increasingly trespassed beyond the country's boundaries. The universe of interest groups that had become so large a factor in domestic and economic policy grew to similar dimensions in foreign policy as well. The creation and implementation of foreign policies could no longer be closely held by a small group of presidential advisors and elite opinion leaders. As the stakes of those policies expanded, so did the range of those seeking to influence them.

The closed circle of foreign policy makers had endured for generations. Secrecy was an important foundation of their hegemony. But secrecy, too, no longer provides the barrier to foreign policy participation that it once did. We live in a time when secrets are very hard to keep. Most Americans carry around in their pockets a little computer—called a cell phone—that allows them to record what they hear and photograph what they see. Modern digital technologies are a pure delight for spies, hackers, journalists, whistle-blowers, and angry coworkers. But they can be a nightmare for presidents.

When a Pentagon employee named Daniel Ellsberg decided in 1969 that the public needed to know the extent of official lying about the war in Vietnam, he packed his briefcase at night with purloined secret documents—hard paper copies—carried them to an office at the RAND corporation, and over many weeks painstakingly copied them on the relatively primitive photocopying technology of the time. It took him weeks of very long nights to do this. If Ellsberg had had access to today's digital technologies, he could have copied all of what came to be known as the Pentagon Papers on a single flash drive in a few minutes. The cover of secrecy would have been blown much more quickly—not just in many days' editions of the *New York Times*, but instantly on computer screens all over the world.

A diminished capacity for secrecy has made it hard to contain foreign policy decisions in a few hands and yielded ample opportunities for broader participation. Journalists have abetted this change. Whatever feasance American journalists might once have paid to the government classification system and to respect for the boundaries of official secrecy is long gone. No successful journalist these days declines to publish or broadcast something because the information is classified. Journalists have little faith in the validity of a classification system that has so often been used to provide cover for illegal, immoral, or stupid government actions. And, in the intensely competitive environment of modern journalism, what one editor declines to publish a dozen others will happily take to print or the airwaves or their blogs. New entrants in the business of foreign policy reporting—Al Jazeera and WikiLeaks, for example—observe few of the traditional standards of deferential journalism.

Contemporary government in Washington is a sieve. Leaking is part of the culture. Information, including much that is classified or otherwise intended to be private, flows through thousands of technological sluiceways. There's no stopping it. It is an enormous aggravation to presidents, even though many of the most damaging leaks come from within their own administrations.

And when leakers are ready to leak, eager receivers of their information, in the United States or abroad, are not hard to find. "WikiLeaks is a piece of a larger technologically inspired trend that is relocating the center of gravity of U.S. national security reporting outside the United States," writes law professor Jack Goldsmith. "The growing scrutiny of American military and intelligence operations by the technologically empowered global media, and its relative indifference to U.S. government pleas, are still further reasons why U.S. government secrets are harder than ever to keep." This inability to contain information only in the hands of those who "need to know" has become a major impediment to presidential leadership in matters of foreign policy.[33]

The foreign policy bureaucracy at the top of which the president sits is yet another constraint of his freedom to direct such policy. The size of the bureaucracy has grown throughout the postwar years. The National Security Council that was created in 1947 as a small staff to coordinate the advice and activities of the State and Defense Departments has become a large and independent actor in the foreign policy bureaucracy with estimates of the size of its staff rising in 2015 to 400 people.[34] There are, in fact, few agencies of the government that don't now contain a significant foreign policy shop: trade, agriculture, commerce, environmental protection, drug czars, and so on. Gathering their advice and melding their interests has become a task of unprecedented complexity. The president's freedom of action often suffers its greatest constraints within his own administration.

As international law specialist Michael J. Glennon noted in a recent article in the *Harvard National Security Journal*:

> the several hundred executive officials who sit atop the military, intelligence, diplomatic, and law enforcement departments and agencies that have as their mission the protection of America's international and internal security . . . make most of the key decisions concerning national security, removed from public view and from the constitutional restrictions that check America's dignified institutions. The United States has, in short, moved beyond a mere imperial presidency to a bifurcated system—a structure of double government—in which even the President now exercises little substantive control over the overall direction of U.S. national security policy.[35]

Adding to the burdens is the tendency of the permanent staffs in many of these agencies to develop self-interested perspectives, standard operating procedures, and relationships on Capitol Hill and with interest groups that are far more durable than their loyalties to a transient presidential administration. Not uncommonly in recent years, for example, presidents have been frustrated in their management of the national security bureaucracy and have sought ways to work around it, often by shifting much of the responsibility for foreign policy development and even for diplomacy to the National Security Council. Condoleezza Rice, who served both as National Security Adviser and Secretary of State for George W. Bush, later wrote: "There is a tendency of foreign service officers to regard the President and his political advisors as a passing phenomenon without the deep expertise that they, the professionals bring to diplomacy. . . . The national security advisor is left to sort out those tensions."[36]

But the war power seems somehow to have been protected from these impediments. Presidents still appear to have a relatively free hand to send American forces into combat. Indeed they do, but their total dominance of the war power ends almost as quickly as the first shot is fired. One of the significant trends in the early years of the twenty-first century has been the steadily growing pattern of restrictions on presidential management of the wars they start.

Much of this is the result of a congressional reaction to the bold assertions of presidential unilateralism by the administration of George W. Bush. The Bush approach, masterminded largely by Vice President Dick Cheney and a handful of lawyers on his staff and in the Justice Department, was that there are no valid restrictions on the president's exercise of his constitutional authority as commander in chief. "These provisions" wrote Deputy Assistant Attorney General John Yoo two weeks after the attacks of September 11, 2001, "vest full control of the military forces of the United States in the President. The power of the President is at its zenith under the Constitution when the President is directing military operations of the armed forces, because the power of Commander in Chief is assigned solely to the President. . . . The scope of the President's authority to commit the armed forces to combat is very broad."[37]

When Congress reacted to this approach by passing laws regulating surveillance techniques, military commissions, treatment of detainees, and the use of torture to glean evidence from alleged terrorists, Bush signed the legislation but then issued "signing statements" declaring that parts of those laws were unconstitutional and his administration would not enforce them. Overall, Bush issued 130 of these signing statements, containing more than a thousand challenges to various statutes. When Congress passed the Detainee Treatment Act of 2005, for example, which prohibited cruel, inhuman and degrading treatment of alleged terrorists in U.S. custody, Bush signed the law, but issued a signing statement that explained in typical language "The executive branch shall construe . . . the Act, relating to detainees, in a manner consistent with the constitutional authority of the President to supervise the unitary executive branch and as Commander in Chief and consistent with the constitutional limitations on the judicial power. . . ." Clearly, the Bush administration did not intend to permit Congress to invade the broad prerogatives it assumed belonged to the president as commander in chief.

But then the courts entered the fray. The Supreme Court issued a couple of decisions near the end of the twentieth century that indicated a growing comfort level with restrictions on presidential authority. In *Morrison v. Olson* in 1988, the court upheld the independent counsel provisions of the Ethics in Government Act of 1978 act that allowed the appointment of special investigators outside the normal federal channels to examine alleged wrongdoing by the president or executive branch officials.

In *Clinton v. Jones* in 1997, the court reversed a longstanding immunity for presidents from civil lawsuits during their tenure in office for acts done before they became president. This permitted a woman named Paula Jones to sue President Clinton for sexual harassment when he was governor of Arkansas. It opened the door to a wide-ranging investigation during which Clinton made false statements under oath that eventually led to his impeachment by the House of Representatives.

So it was not a surprise in the first decade of the new century when the Supreme Court issued decisions in several cases that limited the president's freedom of action even in wartime and even against presidential claims that his authority as commander-in-chief was unlimited. Most of the key cases involved the procedures used by the Bush administration in detaining individuals it alleged to be terrorists. In *Rasul v. Bush* in 2004, for example, the central question was whether the U.S. courts had jurisdiction over matters involving the treatment of detainees—especially their indefinite detention—at the U.S. Naval Base at Guantanamo, Cuba.[38] The administration argued that the courts had no jurisdiction to hear wrongful imprisonment cases from foreign nationals because Guantanamo was not technically part of the United States. The court rejected that argument and held that U.S. courts could determine whether detainees who were not U.S. citizens were wrongfully imprisoned at Guantanamo.

In *Hamdi v. Rumsfeld* in 2004, the Supreme Court upheld the authority of the government to detain what the administration called "enemy combatants," including U.S. citizens. But it also ruled that U.S. citizens had to be provided with the due process to which all citizens are entitled and must be permitted to challenge their status as enemy combatants.[39] Equally important in this case, the court rejected the administration's contention that this was a separation of powers matter that should not be adjudicated by the courts.

In 2006, in the case of *Hamdan v. Rumsfeld*, the court invalidated the military commissions that the Bush administration had been using to try alleged terrorists. It found no specific congressional authorization for such commissions in these cases and determined that their use violated both the Uniform Code of Military Justice and the Geneva Convention.[40] Again, a key aspect of the case was the finding by the court that it had jurisdiction to adjudicate cases brought by detainees including those held at Guantanamo. The administration had argued that the court should dismiss the suit by Hamdan because it lacked such jurisdiction.

Congress subsequently passed the Military Commissions Act of 2006 which authorized the kinds of commissions that had troubled the court in *Hamdan*. The operations of these were challenged in *Boumediene v. Bush* in 2008. Here, the court struck another blow against the military commissions favored by the administration. It held that detainees at Guantanamo had a right to habeas corpus and that the Military Commissions Act of 2006 violated their constitutional protections by suspending that right.[41]

The result of the new legislation and the constraints imposed by the courts is that the conduct of wars is now shaped at every level by the rule of law. Some commentators have come to call this "lawfare." It is the notion that commanders and soldiers should know before they act that their actions will not violate the law, that they will not later have to answer in court for things they did on the battlefield. Many of these same sensitivities have been applied to espionage and covert activities at the CIA and other intelligence agencies. Lawyers are consulted before every major action. Few initiatives move forward until they've been cleared by the legal staff. Army brigades and Navy ships have their own attorneys. Legal constraints have become an increasingly important element in the development and implementation of military strategies. As Jack Goldsmith concludes from an extensive analysis of these new legal impositions:

> in the last decade, in the most unusual and challenging war in American history, and at a time when the President exercises unfathomable powers, we have witnessed the rise and operation of purposeful forms of democratic (and judicial) control over the Commander in Chief, and have indeed established strong legal and constitutional constraints on the presidency. These forms of control are messy, and at the margins it is hard to know whether they go too far or not far enough. But they are deeply consequential, and they preserve the framers' original idea of a balanced constitution with an executive branch that, despite its enormous power, remains legally and politically accountable to law and to the American people.[42]

There is another twenty-first-century reality that bears mention here because it has altered the role of the American president in shaping American foreign policy. That is the end of the postwar world and America's place as its dominant superpower. During the Cold War, the Western democracies and many of the noncommunist states elsewhere looked to the United States for protection against the Soviet nuclear threat or communist insurgencies. They came to accept the American president's role as leader of the "free world." His initiatives were rarely challenged, at least openly, and he could count on their support.

When the Cold War ended, America loomed for a decade as the world's only superpower. But even then it was becoming increasingly apparent that while America might be the world's military colossus, the value of that position was declining. Nuclear weapons, aircraft carriers, and hundreds of thousands of men and women in uniform were simply less important in an age when wars among the great powers had vanished into history and non-state terrorists and asymmetrical warfare seemed to have become the predominant form of international conflict.

America's economic status in the world could no longer match its military status and, as the twenty-first century opened, the emergence of robust economies of the European Union, China, Brazil, India, and even Russia had a profound effect on world affairs. America no longer dominated the world economy as it had in the years immediately following World War II, and an important consequence of that was a shrinkage of the American president's role as a world leader.

Increasingly, America was forced to wield what influence it possesses not through statements and actions by the president but through lengthy and complex bilateral and multilateral negotiations and through international organizations like the United Nations, the G-8, the International Monetary Fund, and the World Court. In many ways, America remained *primes inter pares*, but the *primes* shrank and the *pares* expanded. And the world leadership that American presidents had enjoyed for decades after World War II no longer fell to them automatically and often not at all. The plain fact was that the American presidency was a position of lesser world importance in the twenty-first century than it had been in the second half of the twentieth century.

THE NEW FOREIGN POLICY PRESIDENCY

What has long been accepted as conventional wisdom in analyses of the American presidency—that the president is the dominant player in the country's foreign policy—remains substantially true, especially as regards the war power. Presidents not uncommonly act on foreign-policy matters in ways for which there is no specific constitutional warrant and sometimes even in ways that seem to violate the law. The excesses of authority of which presidents are sometimes guilty in foreign policy have become an inflated measure of presidential power. They are the evidence cited most prominently and sometimes exclusively by those who seek to raise fears of an imperial presidency. But those actions are often unique to foreign policy and they mask a much different reality in domestic and economic policy where presidents' abilities to act effectively are much more constrained.

That the president retains much of the initiative in foreign affairs and remains largely beyond effective limits in committing American forces to hostilities abroad is beyond doubt. But contextual, legislative, and judicial developments in this century have begun to seek and in some ways to accomplish a different balance of influence over foreign policy. The president's initiatives must now be sensitive to a much more complex array of political forces both at home and abroad. And once an initiative is taken, the implementation of it is often constrained by other actors over whom the president has little control and by a much expanded rule of law. The president can still send American forces into battle with little consultation and little restriction. But his decisions on when to do that and how to manage their actions are subjected now to many more complications and restraints than in the past.

Criticism continues to rise among scholars, journalists, and politicians about whether the presidency remains too independent and too powerful in leading the country's foreign policy, especially in exercising the war powers granted to that office by the Constitution and tradition. Louis Fisher, a long-term analyst at the Library of Congress and author of one of the paramount studies of presidential war powers, continues to argue that presidents have usurped powers in foreign policy that more appropriately belong to Congress:

> The drift of the war power from Congress to the President after World War II is unmistakable. The framers' design, deliberately placing in Congress the decision to expend the nation's blood and treasure, has been radically transformed. Presidents now regularly claim that the commander-in-chief clause empowers them to send American troops anywhere in the world, including into hostilities, without first seeking legislative approval. Congress has made repeated efforts since the 1970s to restore legislative prerogatives, with little success. Presidents continue to wield military power single-handedly, agreeing only to consult with legislators and notify them of completed actions. This is not the framers' model.[43]

Law professor Peter Irons takes an even more jaundiced view. "In a very real and very dangerous sense," he argues, "the Imperial presidency has hijacked the Constitution, to serve the interests of the American empire."[44]

Andrew Polsky, a political scientist, takes a similar position in a recent and penetrating book about war powers. "The president," he writes, "is in a strong position to assert control, perhaps even supremacy, in national security matters. . . . Simply put, by controlling the placement of American forces, the president can all but determine when and where the nation will go to war. Deployment is destiny."[45]

Those who worry about unfettered executive control of foreign policy are not without evidence to support their concerns. The twenty-first century has already seen long wars initiated and sustained by presidents in Afghanistan and Iraq, vast expansions of invasive surveillance programs, a military prison in Guantanamo that endured for more than a decade, and presidential authorization of drone strikes, some of them aimed at killing American citizens. Evading the treaty ratification process, into which no one could successfully compel him, President Obama in 2015 secured a multiparty negotiated deal on the future of the nuclear weapons program in Iran despite the opposition of majorities in both houses of Congress.

The constitutional language and directives on the conduct of foreign and national security policy are a marinade of ambiguity. That presidents have sought to take advantage of that ambiguity is no surprise. That their actions have encountered loud criticisms of extra-constitutionality, abuse, and even tyranny is also no surprise.

There is evidence of the sort offered here that a new equilibrium may be emerging in some aspects of foreign policy, that presidents are more constrained and Congress and other political actors more assertive than they have been in earlier generations. Some of the forces that have come to encumber the president in domestic and economic policy have invaded the realm of foreign policy as well.

But the requisites of foreign policy, especially national security policy, are unique. They demand degrees of decisiveness, speed, and secrecy that only executive institutions can provide, especially in the face of immediate threats. So efforts to restrain presidential war powers will always confront aggressive resistance and harsh realities.

As we are troubled by leadership inadequacies in domestic and economic policy, so will we continue to be troubled by leadership excesses in national security policy. The appropriate balance required for effective government in the former has been skewed in one direction, in the latter in the other.

But as analysts it is important that we not confuse the two. Too often in contemporary scholarship, widely cited expansions and abuses of presidential power in foreign policy have come to be a metaphor for presidential power in all areas. Presidents remain dominant in foreign policy, even in the face of expanding efforts to constrain them. But that reality should not be allowed to mask the shrinking influence and diminished leadership capabilities of the president in other areas of national policy making.

Americans should be concerned about actions that occur when presidential authority is overly expanded. But so, too, should they be concerned about actions that don't occur when it is overly constrained.

NOTES

1. Franklin D. Roosevelt, Fireside Chat, September 7, 1942, accessed October 15, 2015, http://www.presidency.ucsb.edu/ws/?pid=16303.

2. James Madison, *Letters and Other Writings of James Madison, 1769-1793* (New York: R. Worthington, 1865), 643.

3. Harry S. Truman, "Address to the Nation on Korea," July 19, 1950, accessed October 15, 2015, http://www.presidency.ucsb.edu/ws/?pid=13561.

4. Andrew J. Polsky, *Elusive Victories: The American Presidency At War* (New York: Oxford University Press, 2012), 11.

5. Wilson, *Congressional Government*, xi.

6. Robert Dallek, "Power and the Presidency, From Kennedy to Obama," *Smithsonian Magazine*, January 2011, accessed October 15, 2015, http://www.smith-sonianmag.com/history-archaeology/Power-and-the-Presidency-From-Kennedy-to-Obama.html.

7. Aaron Wildavsky, "The Two Presidencies," *Trans-Action* 4 (December 1966): 7.

8. Includes exports and imports for 2014, accessed October 15, 2015, http://www.census.gov/foreign-trade/Press-Release/current_press_release/exh6s.pdf.

9. Taylor Branch, *The Clinton Tapes: Wrestling History With The President* (New York: Simon and Schuster, 2009), 50.

10. See Karen DeYoung and Anne Gearan, "Susan Rice Withdraws as Candidate for Secretary of State," *Washington Post*, December 13, 2012.

11. Steven G. Calabresi and James Lindgren, "The President: Lightning Rod or King?" *Yale Law Journal* 115 (2006): 2614.

12. Schlesinger, *The Imperial Presidency*, ix–x.

13. I'm grateful for the suggestion of this imbalance provided in Peter Irons, *War Powers: How The Imperial Presidency Hijacked The Constitution* (New York: Metropolitan Books, 2005), 266–67. Data from U.S. government sources and the *Washington Post*, accessed October 15, 2015, http://www.washingtonpost.com/world/national-security/black-budget-summary-details-us-spy-networks-successes-failures-and-obje ctives/2013/08/29/7e57bb78-10ab-11e3-8cdd-bcdc09410972_story.html.

14. See Priya Kumar, "Shrinking Foreign Coverage," *American Journalism Review*, December/January 2011, accessed October 15, 2015, http://ajrarchive.org/article.asp?id=4998.

15. Shanto Iyengar et al., "'Dark Areas of Ignorance' Revisited," *Communication Research Online First*, March 26, 2009, accessed October 15, 2015, http://pcl.stanford.edu/research/2009/iyengar-darkareas.pdf.

16. Andrew Kohut, "American International Engagement on the Rocks," *Pew Research Global Attitudes Project*, July 11, 2013, accessed October 15, 2015, http://www.pewglobal.org/2013/07/11/american-international-engagement-on-the-rocks/.

17. Barney Frank, "U.S. Troops Won't Win Losing Battle," *Portland (Maine) Sunday Telegram* (November 23, 2014): E1.

18. Quoted in Andrew Glass, "Richard Nixon vetoes War Powers Resolution, October 24, 1973," *Politico*, October 24, 2013, accessed October 15, 2015, http://www.politico.com/story/2013/10/nixon-vetoes-war-powers-resolution-oct-24-1973-98747.html.

19. *Mitchell v. Laird*, 488 E2d 611 (D.C. Cir. 1973).

20. Rodric B. Schoen, "A Strange Silence: Vietnam and the Supreme Court," 33 *Washburn Law Journal* 33(2), (1993–1994): 277.

21. *Charles L. Williams V. Suffolk Insurance Company*, 38 U.S. 415 (13 Pet. 415, 10 L.Ed. 226).

22. *United States v. Curtiss-Wright Export Corp.*, 299 U.S. 304 (1936).

23. Polsky, *Elusive Victories*, 18.

24. Michael A. Genovese, *The Supreme Court, The Constitution, and Presidential Power* (Washington, DC: University Press of America, 1980), 208.

25. Fisher, *Constitutional Conflicts Between Congress and the President*, 220.

26. Heclo, "'The Once and Future Chief Executive: Prophecy versus Prediction' in the Twenty-first Century: Continuity and Change," in *The Presidency in the Twenty-First Century*, edited by Charles W. Dunn, 22.

27. Joseph W. Martin, Jr., *My First Fifty Years in Politics* (New York: McGraw-Hill, 1960), 49.

28. Quoted in Stanley Karnow, *Vietnam: A History* (New York: Viking, 1991), 249.

29. Pew Research Center, accessed October 15, 2015, http://www.people-press.org/2014/11/13/public-trust-in-government/.

30. Gerald R. Ford, "Imperiled, Not Imperial," *Time*, November 10, 1980.

31. Michael O'Brien, "Obama Cautions Against Rush To Action in Syria," *NBC News*, accessed October 15, 2015, http://nbcpolitics.nbcnews.com/_news/2013/04/30/17985348-obama-cautions-against-rush-to-action-in-syria?lite.

32. Paul Steinhauser and John Helton, CNN Poll: Public Against Syria Strike Resolution. *CNN Politics*, accessed October 15, 2015, http://www.cnn.com/2013/09/09/politics/syria-poll-main/.

33. Jack Goldsmith, *Power and Constraint: The Accountable Presidency After 9/11* (New York: W. W. Norton, 2012), 75.

34. Karen DeYoung, "White House Tries For a Leaner National Security Council Staff," *Washington Post*, June 22, 2015, accessed October 15, 2015, https://www.washingtonpost.com/world/national-security/white-house-tries-for-a-leaner-national-security-council/2015/06/22/22ef7e52-1909-11e5-93b7-5eddc056ad8a_story.html. Also see Shawn Brimley, Dr. Dafna H. Rand, Julianne Smith, and Jacob Stokes, "Enabling Decision: Shaping the National Security Council for the Next President," Center for New American Security, June 2015, accessed October 15, 2015, http://www.cnas.org/sites/default/files/publications-pdf/CNAS%20Report_NSC%20Reform_Final.pdf.

35. Michael J. Glennon, "National Security and Double Government," *Harvard National Security Journal* 5 (2014): 12.

36. Condoleezza Rice, *No Higher Honor: A Memoir of My Years in Washington* (New York: Crown, 2011), 16–17.

37. Memorandum from John C. Yoo, Deputy Assistant Attorney General, U.S. Department of Justice to the Deputy Counsel to the President, "The President's Constitutional Authority to Conduct Military Operations Against Terrorists and Nations Supporting Them," September 25, 2001, accessed October 15, 2015, http://www.lawfareblog.com/wp-content/uploads/2013/10/Memorandum-from-John-C-Yoo-Sept-25-2001.pdf.

38. *Rasul v. Bush*, 542 U.S. 466 (2004).

39. *Hamdi v. Rumsfeld*, 542 U.S. 507 (2004).

40. *Hamdan v. Rumsfeld*, 548 U.S. 557 (2006).

41. *Boumediene v. Bush*, 553 U.S. 723 (2008).

42. Goldsmith, *Power and Constraint*, xvi.

43. Fisher, *Presidential War Power*, 3rd ed. (Lawrence, KS: University of Kansas Press, 2013), 291.

44. Irons, *War Powers*, 2.

45. Polsky, *Elusive Victories*, 13.

7

A Presidency for the
Twenty-First Century

The American presidency is one of history's most remarkable political inventions. For all of time before 1787, only monarchs and autocrats ruled. The brave souls who drafted the American Constitution had a different vision: a singular leader chosen by and accountable to a democratic citizenry. It was, after much debate, a triumph of hope over fear. The American president would be powerful, but accountable too—a potent chief executive, but one encased in an intricate maze of checks and balances.

The model the framers created seemed to fit their time and circumstances. In a government of few responsibilities, brilliant leadership was rarely essential in addressing the country's limited agenda of public business. But industrialization at the end of the nineteenth century and the emergence of America as an international titan in the twentieth century changed those circumstances. The federal government's tasks expanded steadily and its size grew apace. In a much larger government, burdened with a much broader range of duties and expectations, leadership came to matter in ways the framers of the Constitution could barely have imagined. Their eighteenth-century Constitution became a tighter and tighter fit on the presidency as the twentieth century rounded the turn into the twenty-first century. In many ways, in fact, it became a straitjacket on presidential leadership.

But it wasn't just an old-fashioned Constitution that constrained the twenty-first-century presidents. Their predecessors had found ways to function effectively in spite of the constraints that document imposed on them. They joined forces with political parties that connected them with state and local leaders and co-partisans in Congress. They sought and often received mandates from the people in their elections. They took advantage

167

of wondrous new technologies, of communications and travel especially, to make theirs a representative office and to reach out to citizens to build support for their initiatives. And they built political networks, in Washington and the country, to forge coalitions that contributed to their efforts at policy change.

The Constitution barely changed during the twentieth century, but American presidents developed workarounds to escape many of its constraints. The prevailing view of scholars, journalists, and citizens in the decades that followed World War II was that the American presidency was "the most powerful office on earth," the "leader of the free world," perhaps even something that had grown "imperial" in character. In some ways, there was a measure of truth in all of those perceptions. But their prevalence, the conventional wisdom of the time, also masked a fundamental reality.

Things were changing in America. The character of electoral politics, the technologies of communication, the nature of the political parties, and the protocols of the legislative process were all evolving in the latter decades of the twentieth century in ways that would directly affect and ultimately severely constrain the leadership capabilities of the American presidency. The workarounds no longer worked.

The constitutional infirmities of the presidency began to reveal themselves with increasing regularity. American presidents of both parties, often men of intelligence and character, were unable to convert the limited authorities the Constitution assigned them into the sort of genuine leadership the country needed and desperately sought. These failures created a spiral of despair among the American people, a constancy of disappointment in their presidents that added to the burden that those presidents faced. Their predecessors had sometimes overcome the limitations of the office by building political coalitions sufficient to escape them. But now those political escape routes have themselves become blocked. And we are left with no choice but to confront the deficiencies in structure and authority of the institution of the American presidency, which is the task of this final chapter.

SYMPTOMS

The purpose of government is to accomplish the goals of the polity, to act on poplar consensus and, where necessary, to contribute to the creation of that consensus. The American federal government today struggles to do any of those things. Great challenges loom—an emergent global economy, a dangerously threatened environment, an outdated and ruptured infrastructure, severe income inequality, growing population diversity, and non-state terrorists with lethal intentions. And that is only the top of the list.

Because of their magnitude and complexity, only government can meet these challenges. But the national government has few plans and little capacity to do so.

Why not? There are many answers, but none is more apparent than the current deficiencies of national leadership. Contemporary presidents can identify problems, can propose solutions, and can call for action. But when it comes time to get the American people to support their initiatives and to get the rest of the government to follow their lead, they find themselves ill-equipped and often powerfully opposed.

Some would say that problem is the people whom Americans have chosen as their presidents. Get us one of the Roosevelts or a Ronald Reagan or a Lyndon Johnson, they argue, and we'll get this creaky old system humming again. But that kind of response misses the point. In fact, it misses two points. First, our recollections of those great presidents of the past tend to recall them only on their best days. All of them struggled, too, against the limitations of their office, and all of them encountered a significant portion of failure and dismay. We remember them fondly in no small part because they held office at propitious times: times of crisis that yielded unique opportunities for leadership or times when the political stars aligned in unusually favorable ways. The lesson we should draw from those recollections is not that these were examples of brilliant leadership, though occasionally they were, but rather that effective presidential leadership requires the kind of context and political situation in which those presidents made history.

Second, little, perhaps nothing, in the contemporary environment would permit or encourage the kind of presidential leadership that shines in our rose-colored memories. Times have changed. The problem is not that contemporary presidents lack skills, intelligence, or charisma. Chapter 3 suggests that our electoral process too often repels talented people from seeking the presidency. It does. But we cannot attribute many of the failures of presidential leadership simply to the personal deficiencies of its recent incumbents. The problem today is much broader and more truculent. Contemporary presidents lack the vital connections and constituencies that a truly effective political executive requires. Their leadership is often deficient because they inhabit an unleadable system.

The American federal government today is a much bigger enterprise than it has ever been and it continues to grow. That growth in size and density steadily adds to the burdens of leadership. Perhaps more important, however, is the expansion in the complexity and difficulty of the politics and political relationships a president must manage to have any hope of accomplishing policy objectives or retaining popular support.

We recall Lyndon Johnson as the preeminent legislative leader. But Johnson was able to work his will through a handful of very powerful committee chairs in Congress, men like him who had been in Washington for decades, who knew each other well, who had acquired sturdy habits of working with each other even across ideological divides. But no such powerful chairs survive in the contemporary Congress. Even a Lyndon Johnson would be bewildered by the task of building majority coalitions in today's fractious and atomized Congress. His skills were real and there might be days now when they would afford him some leverage. But no Great Society, no parade of expansive legislation is ever going to come from the kind of Congress that now convenes infrequently and uncomfortably under the Capitol dome.

Archie Brown, the Oxford historian who has long studied national executives, recently wrote in a *tour d'horizon* of contemporary leaders: "The modern American political system is one in which power is so divided—among the White House staff, the other government departments and agencies, Congress, the judiciary and the fifty states that make up the federation—that the president has far less power domestically than most prime ministers possess."[1]

There are clearly elements of this problem that are uniquely American and this chapter will focus on those. But it would be irresponsible to overlook the broader reality. We live in a time when power in all of its permutations—public and private, political, economic, and religious—is in decline. Everywhere one looks today are challenges to traditional authority. The worldwide expansion in education and literacy, the multiplication in the number of nations, from 75 at the end of World War II to 196 at this writing, the vast expansion in wealth and in hundreds of millions of new members of the world's middle class, the technology explosion that has raised the efficiency and lowered the cost of human communication. All of these developments and many more like them have notable benefits. But they all contribute as well to a contemporary context in which powerful leadership is harder to develop and sustain than ever before.

Moisés Naím, former long-time editor of *Foreign Policy* magazine, surveys what he calls the "end of power" in a recent book. He writes:

> This is not just an American phenomenon. Everywhere, the basis of political power is growing more fragile; gaining a majority of votes no longer guarantees the ability to make decisions, inasmuch as a multitude of "micropowers" can veto, delay, or water them down. Power is seeping away from autocrats and single-party systems whether they embrace reform or not. It is spreading from large and long-established political parties to small ones with narrow agendas or niche constituencies. Even within parties, party bosses who make decisions, pick candidates and hammer out platforms behind closed doors are giving way to insurgents and outsiders—to new politicians who haven't risen up in the party machine, who never bothered to kiss the ring.

. . . Whatever path they followed to get there, politicians in government are finding that their tenure is getting shorter and their power to shape policy is decaying. Politics was always the art of compromise, but now politics is downright frustrating—sometimes it feels like the art of nothing at all. Gridlock is more common at every level of decision-making in the political system, in all areas of government, and in most countries. Coalitions collapse, elections take place more often, and "mandates" prove ever more elusive.[2]

Tony Blair, the former British prime minister, shares the view that confounding contemporary challenges confront all democracies. "Democracy is not in good shape," he recently wrote. "Many systems seem dysfunctional: The U.S. Congress, the coalition government in the U.K., and many governments in Europe have had difficulty making the decisions necessary to finding a way back to economic growth." But to Blair the heart of the problem lies with leadership deficiencies:

> The disillusionment with democratic governments is really about people believing that the changes they need in their lives can't happen quickly enough. . . . They say that the government isn't listening. But often the government is listening—it is rather that the voices that reach officials are saying different things. It is effective decision-making through strong leadership that is the missing element.[3]

Compounding the problem is the lack of recognition in the popular discourse of this changing context. Some scholars have recognized the change and some have written about it with keen insight. But few who follow public affairs in the way most Americans do—peripherally, hazily, lazily—would have much conception of how different things have become from the way they were in their grandparents' time.

And no one following a contemporary American election would ever get even a slight dose of this fundamental truth. Candidates continue to promise things they can never deliver and to pretend that they can overcome the very leadership deficiencies that will soon consume them if they win. Woe be it to the candidate who tells the truth about this, who asks Americans to recognize the limits on presidential leadership and to adjust their expectations accordingly. Jimmy Carter took that approach out for a trial run in 1980, and the only thing it got him was a quick trip back to Plains, Georgia.

No, expectations remain high even as the capacity to meet them diminishes. And the effect of this on the political system as a whole is toxic. "The bad news," writes Yale law professor Peter Schuck, "is that Americans have a dismal opinion of the federal government's performance, one that is only getting darker. Significantly, this growing antipathy is not antigovernment generally. Instead, it targets only the federal government; respect for state and local governments is both high and stable. Nor is this hostility toward the federal government in Washington a partisan matter. Instead, it is expressed by a majority of Democrats as well as Republicans."[4]

The threats to presidential leadership which this book has sought to catalog are more than the mere cannon fodder of scholarly warfare. They have real and deeply troubling practical consequences. The president today, as Steven Calabresi and James Lindgren note in the *Yale Law Journal*, "is less of a king than a lightning rod. Indeed, the constitutional and practical weakness of the presidency is, if not a threat to American democracy, at least a worrisome limitation on it."[5]

In the deeply divided contemporary political climate, where every member of Congress suffers to see much beyond the boundaries of his or her own constituency, only the president stands for election before all the people and only the president can protect the national interest against all its local and parochial challenges. In America today, the parts are at war with the whole. And the parts are very strong. Only a powerful advocate for the whole can protect the national interest.

Gouverneur Morris, whose patient advocacy at the Constitutional Convention led his colleagues to establish a single, potent chief executive, recognized this characteristic of the office: "The Executive Magistrate should be the guardian of the people, even the lower classes, against Legislative tyranny, against the great and the wealthy who in the course of things will necessarily compose the Legislative body. . . . The Executive therefore ought to be so constituted as to be the great protector of the Mass of the people."[6]

President James K. Polk echoed this view in a reflection on his own duties:

> "The people, by the constitution, have commanded the President, as much as they have commanded the legislative branch of the Government, to execute their will. . . . The President represents in the executive department the whole people of the United States, as each member of the legislative department represents portions of them. . . . " The President is responsible "not only to an enlightened public opinion, but to the people of the whole Union, who elected him, as the representatives in the legislative branches . . . are responsible to the people of particular States or districts."[7]

Weakness in the presidency has this profound political effect, or at least contributes to it: the factional and discordant voices of the parts have no reliable countervoice for the whole. Without a loud trumpet, the call to national purpose is lost in the cacophony of special interest kazoos.

Even more troubling, however, is the reality of a ship of state without a sturdy hand at the helm. The complexity of the domestic and economic challenges that face all countries in the twenty-first century and the severity of the new threats to national security in a world very different from the past all cry out for strong and effective leadership.

This is the fundamental fact: leadership matters. Effective leadership can be, indeed must be, a directing force and a driving force if an institution or a country is to prosper. That is a lesson taught to us every day as we read the business section or the sports section of the newspaper. In companies, in universities, on the football sidelines, outcomes are determined in no small part by the quality of leadership. So it is in Washington.

But in America, we have allowed our principal leadership institution to slide into a state of frailty that undermines our collective purpose. James MacGregor Burns, the distinguished historian who spent the last decades of his life exploring the essentials of effective leadership, noted this in one of his last books: "Under a system that meticulously divides and fragments power and responsibility, transforming leadership has been extraordinarily difficult, except in crises such as war or economic calamity. And while the institutional stalemates remain the same, the demands facing government have accelerated."[8]

Some presidents of the past were able to achieve success in spite of the constraints the Constitution imposes on their office. More contemporary presidents occasionally got their way by seeking to translate minor authorities (executive orders, signing statements, spending deferrals, etc.) into major ones. But those achievements were rarely more than holding actions against the flood of difficult challenges the country now faces. None of the most recent presidents has found problems as tractable, opposition as constrained, and expectations as realistic as their earlier predecessors did. This is a different country in a different world, and it needs a different presidency.

DIAGNOSES

The deficiencies in the contemporary presidency are especially evident in three areas. And in each of those the status quo is the product, not of some rational design, but of years of piecemeal evolution yielding practices that often contradict and undermine national needs.

Elections

The first area is the manner in which we choose our chief executives. The framers of the Constitution, with no experience whatsoever in this matter, drew up a bare outline of a presidential selection process. It said nothing of political parties which were unknown at the time; it offered no guidance on how candidates would be nominated; it created a two-tier election process (popular and electoral votes) that couldn't endure the first contested election in 1800, and it left many decisions on the "time, place, and manner" of elections to the states. Over the centuries since 1787, the election process has been in a state of constant evolution that has left us today with a complex morass that few Americans understand and almost no one admires.

Archie Brown writes that "there are many qualities desirable in a political leader . . . integrity, intelligence, articulateness, collegiality, shrewd judgment, a questioning mind, willingness to seek disparate views, ability to absorb information, flexibility, good memory, courage, vision, empathy and boundless energy."[9] The contemporary presidential election process may test the last of those but it permits accurate assessments of few of the others. One could hardly imagine a process better designed to repel the very people who are deeply possessed of these characteristics, nor one more likely to sap the interest of the citizens who must assess the candidates who submit to their judgment.

There are too many elections in America. Their choreography is too dependent on the whims of the communications media and the need for large and constant infusions of money. Election seasons come too often and stay too long. Electoral politics envelops and often suffocates government. There may have been a time when politicians sought to win campaigns in order to govern; now they govern in order to win campaigns.

The contemporary election process rarely affords new presidents anything resembling a popular mandate. It neither ensures that their party will control the Congress nor that the members of their party in the legislature will share their goals or priorities. And even when a presidential election provides some foundation for presidential leadership, that soon erodes at a midterm election that comes in the year after a new president is inaugurated. The "permanent campaign" that is a primary characteristic of contemporary government in Washington forces every presidential initiative to survive a peculiar scrutiny, one calculated much more on its likely impact on the next election rather than on its value to the American people.

Into this process come candidates whom no one selected except themselves. Those who have demonstrated their creativity and skills at negotiation and compromise in Congress rarely seek the presidency. Successful cabinet officers are even less likely to join the fray. The most talented of the state governors tend to remain in their states. Public intellectuals, leaders of large foundations, universities, labor unions, and interest groups are rarely even mentioned as presidential candidates. Thus the American people are usually forced to choose among an eclectic array of personages, most of whom are strangers to them. It is no surprise, given these choices, that nearly half of potential voters find nothing to inspire them to vote. Nor is it a surprise that we regularly end up with presidents who are novices in federal government service and rank amateurs at managing large enterprises.

Policy making

The second area of deficiency is simply this. Modern presidents can't accomplish much change in public policy. Some students of the presidency have focused their attention on the executive actions that recent presidents have taken to impose their policy preferences. They cite such things as executive orders, secrecy, emergency powers, signing statements, and central clearance of proposed regulations as examples. Political opponents of recent presidents seem to have found some traction in calling the incumbent an "imperial president," a "king," a "dictator," or some things much worse.

A more chastened view would suggest two things. First, recent presidents have sought to expand reliance on their executive authorities because all other avenues of significant policy impact have been closed to them. These are actions less of despotism than of desperation.

Second, few of these executive actions, no matter how frequently or aggressively undertaken, can have more than peripheral impact on major public policies. Real policy change requires legislation; it cannot be accomplished without the Congress.

But therein lies the rub. The contemporary Congress operates in a parallel and very distant universe from contemporary presidents. Members of Congress have little incentive to care about or to follow presidential leadership. To members of the opposition party any support for a presidential initiative is regarded as providing aid and comfort to the enemy. Substance be damned; whatever the president is for, they are against. And members of the president's party, few of whom owe their electoral victories to his presence on the ticket, are willing listeners to the president's pleas for their support but grudging providers of that support if they sense any future electoral risk in aligning with him. And, of course, modern presidents have no capacity, no tools, to compel the support of their party members in Congress.

But even if the other party were less truculent in its opposition and the president's party more generous in its support, presidents face another confounding reality in their efforts to secure policy-changing legislation. The contemporary Congress is deeply dysfunctional. It struggles to pass any legislation and has demonstrated little capacity for confronting the challenges that most threaten the country in the years ahead.

Since the early 1970s, the Congress has gone through a process of reform that eschewed most of the practices and protocols that made it a reasonably effective legislative body in the earlier decades of the twentieth century. The regular order of legislative decision-making has been abandoned. The important role played by committees in dividing congressional labor and providing essential pockets of policy expertise has been undermined. The historic sources of legislative leadership, the party system and the committee system, are shells of their former selves. And changes in the way congressional districts are designed and the ways that congressional elections are run have brought to Washington a generation of members with few skills and fewer incentives for the kinds of compromise and negotiation that have always been critical to the creation of important legislation.

As political scientist James Q. Wilson noted in an essay published shortly before his death,

> Congress has, to a degree, been de-institutionalized and individualized: its leadership has become weaker, power within it has been dispersed, the autonomy and resources of its individual members have been enlarged. . . . The weakening of congressional voting blocs might strike some readers as a gain: vested interests can no longer easily say no to things they oppose. But such a view neglects the price that has been paid for this change: if nobody can say no and make it stick, then nobody can say yes and make it stick. If there are no vetoes, neither are there any imprimaturs.[10]

The Congresses of the 1970s created on average over 750 new public laws; the Congresses of the twenty-first century only 400. Presidents are as dependent as ever on legislation for new policy change. But rarely, if ever, in our history have the inhabitants of the White House encountered so resistant or incompetent a legislative partner.

Government Management

A new leader in almost any organization soon comes to realize that he or she has three primary levers of administrative control and direction: budgets, personnel, and organization. Determining where the money will go, who will be the lead players, and what kind of structure will best serve institutional purposes are the keys to successful management. It is remarkable then how little control American presidents, the leaders of the federal executive branch, have over any of those.

The Budget and Accounting Act of 1921 gave formal recognition to the importance of executive leadership in formulating a budget—that is, in determining the spending priorities of the federal government. And for most of the decades that followed in the twentieth century, the budget process accommodated a significant measure of presidential leadership. It was never anyone's model of perfect rationality, but each year the president sent a budget recommendation to Congress, the committees in Congress did due diligence in responding to those proposals, and government appropriations rarely wavered more than incrementally from the president's recommendation.

In the twenty-first century, however, the wheels have come off. Whatever semblance of rationality and fiscal prudence the budgetary process may once have possessed has been replaced by a kind of trench warfare in which few members of Congress pay attention to the president's recommendations and the president, therefore, no longer takes the leadership role seriously. Members of Congress treat the budget as a political document, not one realistically related to policy or management. Presidents have responded by doing the same, drafting budgets that have no hope of enactment but that please their partisan constituencies. If the president's budget is going to be dead on arrival, as all such recent budgets have been, presidents at least want their friends to grieve the lovely corpse.

The ugly national embarrassment of government shutdowns, real or narrowly avoided, is symbolic of the deterioration of the budget process. The federal budget no longer bears any resemblance to a useful tool of presidential management of the executive branch. It is a political football kicked around in a game that no one ever wins.

Personnel matters are little different. Americans have long relied on what some call the "in and outer" system for staffing the top offices of the federal government. The idea has been that new presidents should have broad latitude to fill the top positions in their administrations with their own people, people who are loyal to them, who share their policy priorities, and who have the necessary skills to manage their agencies and contribute to the accomplishment of the president's goals. Supplementing this has been the notion that a democratic government benefits from a constant infusion of new people from the outside, that people who have to live under the governments' laws and regulations will be especially sensitive in crafting them.

But then there's the reality. These appointments matter, and everyone knows it. What you get out of government is often dependent on whom you get into government. So everyone fights over personnel. Presidents have long sought to expand the number of executive branch positions over which they have control. Congress has frequently acquiesced in these expansions because its committees get to share in that control when appointees have to be confirmed before they take office. There are now thousands of presidential appointments, and one usually has to burrow down through many layers of the administrative hierarchy before finding a career civil servant. The executive branch of the federal government has steadily thickened at the top over recent decades and the new positions are most commonly filled by presidential appointees

But presidents hardly have a free hand in filling those positions. It is not simply that most of the top appointments have to be confirmed by the Senate and are thus subject to many of the same political forces with which presidents must contend in the legislative and budgetary process. There are also frequent and significant conflicts among the president's own supporters and among members of the White House staff. Brutal battles are often fought before a personnel nomination is announced. And then another round of skirmishing begins on Capitol Hill.

All of this has dire effects on the president's ability to use the appointment power as a sharp tool of executive management. To be sure that candidates for appointment will not be embarrassing to the administration or too difficult to get confirmed, a dense and complex vetting process has developed within the White House, a kind of bureaucratic molasses. It usually takes months to complete. If a candidate survives this and is nominated by the president, a similar and frequently duplicative investigation is conducted by the Senate committee with jurisdiction. In the aftermath of Watergate, the Congress enacted "ethics" regulations that may impose heavy burdens of the personal finances of potential appointees and which require more lines of inquiry and offer even more avenues of invasion into their personal lives.

Here are the consequences. It takes most of a president's first year in office to fill even half of the appointed positions in a new administration. By the second year, initial appointees have begun to leave and new vacancies occur. The average tenure of appointees now is less than three years across all recent administrations.[11]

The in-and-outer system has become a coming-and-going system, and usually there are more appointees going out than coming in. Before an administration is very old, it finds itself plagued with executive vacancies and long waits for replacements as new appointees twist slowly in the political winds of a Senate that never seems to have a sense of urgency in filling those vacancies. Talented people, even those who might otherwise be attracted to public service, often find little to like and much to dislike in the appointment process and decline to serve. In 2001, I wrote:

> The contemporary presidential appointments process is a national disgrace. It encourages bullies and emboldens demagogues. It silences the voices of responsibility and nourishes the lowest forms of partisan combat. It uses innocent citizens as pawns in politicians' petty games and stains the reputations of good people. It routinely violates fundamental democratic principles, undermines the quality and consistency of public management, and breaches simple decency. Republicans and Democrats, legislators and chief executives, journalists and special interests all share responsibility for allowing one of the rare and genuine inventions of American political creativity to fall into a state of malignancy.
>
> . . . The contemporary appointments process is slower, more cumbersome, more contentious, more repellent to talented Americans, and more distant from the purposes of good government than it has ever been. For too long, those who could stop the deterioration of the process have failed to do so, turning away from its excesses, accepting them as the inevitabilities of high-stakes, scorched-earth politics.[12]

The appointment process has only gotten steadily worse in the years since that was written.

The ability of presidents to shape the structure of the federal government is no less constrained and politicized. The current structure of the federal government follows no logical blueprint. It is little more than the accumulation of scores of independent and narrowly focused political decisions made over the centuries. Occasional reviews of government organization by blue ribbon commissions have always found much to criticize, but their recommendations rarely resulted in significant change.

When a new structure is created—an agency, a bureau, a department—it quickly develops its own clientele, its own turf-protecting congressional overseers, and its own pack of cozy special interest lobbyists. Efforts to reshape the government encounter ferocious resistance from those who have come to love the status quo, not because it fits some scheme of administrative rationality or symmetry, but because it serves their self-interests.

When Richard Nixon sought to impose a reorganization of the relationship between the president and the cabinet, sometimes called the "Super-cabinet plan," Congress demurred. Jimmy Carter came to office promising a major reorganization of the government to reduce the common redundancy of many agencies performing similar functions. Little change resulted. When Bill Clinton sought to fulfill a campaign promise by elevating the Environmental Protection Agency to a cabinet department, Congress declined to pass the proposal without amendments that the Clinton administration could not abide. No change ensued. Most presidents since the beginning of the twentieth century have attempted to reorganize the federal government. Success, even limited success, has been rare.

New presidents inherit a federal bureaucracy with a structure that is largely beyond their capacity to alter. Increasingly, as well, they inherit an EOP that has become more and more rigid in its own patterns of institutionalization. They have to live with what they inherit because their tools for structural reshaping are practically nonexistent.

For most of the time between 1932 and 1984, Congress provided the president with something called executive reorganization authority. It was a limited tool, but it did afford presidents some opportunity to reshape aspects of the executive branch and the White House. Presidents would draw up reorganization plans and then submit them to Congress. A vote to do so by either house of Congress, a so-called legislative veto, could reject the plan. But the burden was on Congress to act, and presidents used this tool more than a hundred times to reshape elements of the executive branch. Franklin Roosevelt used this authority to create the EOP in 1939; President Eisenhower used it to create the Department of Health, Education and Welfare in 1953; Richard Nixon used it to establish the Environmental Protection Agency, the Office of Management and Budget, and a domestic policy coordinating council in 1970.

But Congress never seemed very fond of these delegations and in 1984 it declined to renew executive reorganization authority. No president since then has had even this limited tool for reorganizing the executive branch. President Obama sought a renewal of executive reorganization authority in 2012, but Congress declined to act on his proposal.

What should emerge from all this is a sense of the steady accumulation of constraints on contemporary presidents. The modern election process almost invariably wounds them before they take office—and then forces them to swim upstream against the currents of another midterm election almost immediately. Their ability to develop fruitful relations with Congress is very near its historical low point. And the capacity to perform their constitutional duty to "take care that the laws be faithfully executed" is burdened by their limited controls over government personnel, budgets, and organization. In few other governments and few other institutions in America is the chief executive so restricted.

PRESCRIPTIONS

Excesses and abuses of presidential power ought to frighten friends of democracy. But so, also, should constant evidence of presidential weakness. Power has two edges. It's important to keep one sharp while effectively sheathing the other.

The central question is how to accomplish this. One way to prevent dangerous excesses of presidential power is by erecting a dense network of checks on the exercise of that power and by permitting the continuation of less formal practices—election procedures, media coverage, political party deterioration, for example—that ensure presidential weakness. That has been our recent history. We have erected a very dense network of limitations on contemporary presidents. As former senator and Defense Secretary William Cohen has written, "Our founding fathers were convinced that power had to be entrusted to someone, but that no-one could be entirely trusted with power. They devised a brilliant system of checks and balances. . . . The difficulty with this . . . in today's cyberspace age is that everyone is in check, but no-one is in charge."[13]

Only in the minds of the most imaginative conspiracy theorists (or a president's political opponents) is executive tyranny a threat to America. The real threat is not an excess of presidential power but a deficiency of it. The task that confronts us now is this: how do we restore the presidency as an effective force for national leadership yet ensure that presidents operate within the boundaries of democratic accountability?

What is missing in America now more than anything is the ability to concentrate authority. Concentrations of authority are essential in any organization that hopes to confront its challenges and move forward. When authority cannot be concentrated for collective purposes, disorder ensues. Disorder can take many forms. In America today, it takes the form of inertia, of an inability to get things done even when and where large majorities of Americans see the need for action.

In the American political system, the logical locus of concentrated authority is the president, the only official with a national constituency and the only one chosen in a national election. The task then is to find ways to permit greater and more durable concentrations of authority in the presidency while ensuring that incumbents will be accountable to the American people and adherent to democratic boundaries in the exercise of that authority.

One approach would be a near total replacement of the structure of American government with a different model of democracy. The alternative most frequently cited is the parliamentary system which prevails in most European democracies. Woodrow Wilson, for example, found much to admire in this approach:

> Under the parliamentary form of government the people's recognized leaders for the time being, that is, the leaders of the political party which for the time commands a majority in the popular house of parliament, are both heads of the executive and guides of the legislature. They both conduct government and suggest legislation. All the chief measures of a parliamentary session originate with them, and they are under the sobering necessity of putting into successful execution the laws they propose.[14]

But broad systemic change like this is the wrong answer for two reasons. One is simply that it is a bridge too far. I will offer some strong medicine here for the ailments of American democracy, but killing the patient is not the answer. The American political culture and much of American political practice are deeply embedded in American historical experience. Those roots would be much too hard to pull up.

A second reason is that even if it were possible to reject this historical and cultural legacy, there is no guarantee that a parliamentary democracy would be much of an improvement over what we now have. Contemporary parliamentary governments suffer many of the same problems described in this book. Their systemic differences have not provided an immunity against the challenges of the twenty-first century. As Moisés Naím notes, "In many countries, the fragmentation of the political system is creating a situation where gridlock and the propensity to adopt minimalist decisions at the last minute are severely eroding the quality of public policy and the ability of governments to meet voters' expectations or solve urgent problems."[15]

Nor is the answer merely hortatory. We could ask Democrats and Republicans to tone down their rhetoric, to be nicer to each other, to seek out opportunities to "work across the aisle." We could call on the communications media to keep a more respectful distance from the personal lives of public figures and to focus more on the substance of policy initiatives rather than their impacts on the next election. We could plead with citizens to take more interest in politics, to be more trusting of government, to be more rational in their expectations of political leaders. In fact, we are drowning in such exhortations. But to little effect.

What is needed instead are structural and procedural changes in the processes of American politics and the internal operations of the national government. And these will occur only when we recognize that our eighteenth-century Constitution, wise and beautiful as it has been in so many ways, no longer fits twenty-first-century realities. If we remain slavish in our devotion to that constitutional idol, we risk irrelevance—a government that simply cannot serve the interests of its people.

No one should bear any illusions about the ease in amending or replacing the American Constitution. But neither should that be a barrier to analysis of our problems nor creative efforts to address them. The proposals that follow are not the musings of a Pollyanna but the product of an inescapable recognition: if we keep doing what we've been doing, we will keep getting what we've been getting. Only fundamental change can cure the ills of contemporary American democracy.

CURES

Any effort to enhance government performance by improving the effectiveness of the American president must begin with the root of contemporary problems: elections. Elections are extremely important in a democracy both because they are the primary mechanism of leadership selection and because they are the primary instrument of accountability. But contemporary elections in America perform neither of these functions very effectively.

Elections

We need an election process that allows us to form a coherent government and to hold that government accountable for its actions. We need a much greater separation between the daily business of government and the machinations of campaign politics. And we need to find ways for elected officials to be sensitive and responsive to a much broader citizen constituency than that composed by the activists who participate in primaries and pour money into election campaigns.

A good place to start would be with the terms of office of the president and the members of Congress. In America today, we never really elect a government; we elect an executive and representatives but at different times and often for different and unrelated reasons. If all the members of Congress and the president were all elected at the same time and for terms of the same length, Americans would have a genuine opportunity to form a government, not merely to fill a few offices. Candidates would be encouraged as well to nationalize their appeal by offering coordinated programs of action. Citizens would also have richer opportunities to use their votes to hold the whole government accountable because the whole government would be standing for reelection at the same time.

Setting these terms also offers an opportunity to reconsider the founders' decisions about their proper length. They had no magic solution for this and neither do we. But almost everything that has happened in recent decades suggests that the traditional two years for House members and four years for presidents may not be long enough for the study, analysis, popular consensus building, and internal negotiation that may be necessary to develop comprehensive solutions to the largest problems we face.

If we were to set the terms of all federal elected officials at five years, a term length not uncommon in European democracies, that would seem a prudent balance between the time needed to get things done and the necessity of periodic submission of the performance of the government to citizen review. Presidents and all the members of both houses of Congress would know that they had a reasonable amount of time to set an agenda and then to develop programs in response to it. And they would also know that the distractions of reelection would not be anywhere near as intrusive on their governmental work as they are now.

In this vein, it might be helpful as well to require that citizens who vote in federal elections must vote a "straight ticket," that is for candidates of the same political party for president and both houses of Congress. While this may seem radically restrictive of voter choices, the best estimates are that roughly 90 percent of voters now vote such a straight ticket in presidential election years. And this was the common practice for much of American history before the adoption of the Australian ballot at the end of the nineteenth century and in the decades that followed. Party ballots and "big boxes" at the top of a ballot channeled voters into straight ticket voting. Such an approach would guarantee a unified government in which one party controlled both the elected branches, thus making it much easier for citizens to hold their government accountable when it stood for subsequent reelection.

But there are other important ways to rationalize the election process and to permit it to serve its primary purposes without invading and overwhelming the task of governing. To shorten election seasons, we need fundamentally to diminish the flow of money that feeds them. Election expenditures are not demand driven, they are supply driven. Campaigns spend the huge sums that they do because the money is there and not because it's needed to wage intelligent contests that engage voters. In fact, of course, the money usually has the opposite effect.

If there are any Americans (other than campaign consultants and TV station owners) who love the current election process, they have been remarkably silent in their praise. All the evidence—low voter turnout, diminishing levels of trust in government, and growing expressions of public dismay—suggest just the opposite: that Americans hate the current election system for national offices.

So Americans should take charge and restructure the entire election process. Nominating systems should be determined by parties that offer candidates, but they should be regulated so that popular participation is limited to a very short time period that closely precedes the general election. Campaigns should be financed with public funds and use of those funds should be mandatory. No candidates could hold a national elective office if their campaigns accepted or used funds from private sources, including themselves. Public funding should be available only during significantly shortened campaign seasons and use of it would only be permitted for specified purposes. Television networks and local television stations, all subject now to federal regulation, would be required to provide free air time to candidates.

Imagine a presidential election in which the parties held their nominating conventions at the beginning of September. The delegates to these conventions would be elected officials and party leaders in each state, nowhere near the numbers that now attend conventions but the people best positioned to judge the presidential qualifications of potential candidates. Each convention would select a small number of candidates for nomination, perhaps three to five in number, who would then campaign during the month of September in advance of a national primary held on a single day, perhaps the first of October. Only people registered in the party could vote in that primary, but party registration could be established at the polls or by other communication on Election Day. Voting would be by ranked-choice ballot; that is, voters would rank their preferences among the candidates. An automatic runoff would determine the party's nominee who would select a running mate. The general election campaign would then follow in the month of October leading up to the national vote early in November.

To enlarge voter turnout, some other changes would be necessary. Elections would no longer be held on Tuesdays and polls would no longer be open only for twelve hours. Instead, the polls would open at fixed times, staggered by time zone, so that they all closed at the same time. For example, polls would open 5:00 p.m. EST on Friday and remain open until 5:00 p.m. on Saturday. Early voting and voting by mail (and presumably soon electronic voting) would be permitted. All adults would be automatically registered to vote at the time they establish residence in a community.

Other incentives for voting might also be created: a fine for nonvoting as in Australia, for example, or automatic entry in a multimillion dollar lottery for those who vote. Proof of voting might be a condition for receipt of or priority for government benefits (student loans, passports, and welfare payments). Citizens who get benefits from government would come to recognize that they also have responsibilities to participate in government.

Broader citizen participation would have several benefits. It would enlarge the mandate for those who win elections. It would make many more citizens stakeholders in government because they participated in choosing it. It would bring the electorate into much closer alignment with the entire citizenry and thus ensure an election outcome more reflective of the desires of the whole population not just the unrepresentative group that now votes in national elections. And it would be a celebration of democracy. One can imagine that election weekend, occurring only once in five years and charting a course for the following half decade, would become a festival of democracy and citizenship, a kind of Super Bowl weekend of politics and government.

In the general election, the outcome would be determined by the popular vote, not the electoral vote as now because the Electoral College would be eliminated. Every vote in every state would weigh equally in the outcome. Candidates would be forced to present programs that appeal to all voters not merely to the few who happen to reside in a handful of "battleground" states. Voters would choose among the candidates by preference ballot, ranking their choices rather than merely selecting one. An automatic runoff would ensure that the new president received at least 50 percent of the vote. Elimination of the Electoral College would add emphasis to the notion that the president, whose selection would no longer depend as heavily as it now does on the votes in a few battleground states, is the tribune of the entire population.

By shortening the campaign season, establishing a vetting mechanism for parties in the selection of their candidates, and eliminating the agonies of fund-raising, the repellent characteristics of the current election process would be significantly diminished. Parties would offer to their members a list of persons with demonstrated talent and experience appropriate to the office they were seeking. The reasons such candidates now cite for declining to seek the presidency would be collapsed almost to the vanishing point. We should expect better candidates to enter this less burdensome and humiliating process; and we should expect better presidents to emerge from it.

But what about the First Amendment? Surely there will be those who will respond to these proposals by citing the many ways in which they violate the Constitution, or at least Supreme Court interpretations of that document. But that is the point: the Constitution is the problem. There can be no real solution to the election predicament we now face without fundamental constitutional change. We need an election process that is not held hostage to one interpretation of the First Amendment.

Administration

Once in office, presidents must create a national administration. To overcome the current difficulties in accomplishing that, two important changes should be made. First, the number of positions filled by presidential appointment should be substantially reduced. Almost all of the distinguished commissions that have studied the appointment process in recent years have made this recommendation. In 2012, the Congress even made a small but encouraging move in this direction by passing the Presidential Appointment Efficiency and Streamlining Act which reduced by 163 the number of appointments requiring Senate confirmation.

That was a good start, but there is much more to be done. Reduction in the number of positions filled by appointment will reduce the burden on an overloaded system of finding talented people to staff the federal government, it will speed up the transition to a new administration, and it will open up new opportunities for the most talented members of the senior civil service by giving them access to the positions now filled by presidential appointees.

Senate confirmation should be a requirement only for the top positions in the executive branch: cabinet secretaries, independent agency heads, and regulatory commissioners. It benefits everyone when these top officials begin their tenure with legislative as well as executive support. Removing the confirmation requirement from lower-level appointments will reduce the time required to fill vacancies, allow top executives to build their own teams with less political pressure to please congressional overseers in their selections, and diminish among those appointees the divided loyalties that so often now interfere with presidential leadership.

To preclude the use of delay as tactic for preventing the confirmation of the president's nominees for executive positions, the Senate should be required to hold an up-or-down vote on every nomination no later than forty-five days after it is received from the White House. There may occasionally be nominees who cannot meet the Senate standard for confirmation. That determination would be made with a clear vote and quickly enough that a more suitable replacement could soon be selected.

A new president might also find that the inherited organizational structure of the executive branch is outdated, inefficient, or otherwise an impediment to his or her concept of good management practice. To permit presidents to address these concerns, a new form of presidential reorganization authority should be established. Presidents could draw up reorganization plans at any time and submit these to Congress. Congress would then have forty-five days to consider them. The plans would take effect after forty-five days unless both houses formally voted to reject them. The vote could not be delayed, nor the plan amended. Congress could, however, suggest alterations in the plan and request that the president resubmit the plan after considering the legislature's recommendations.

Policy

Upon taking office and even while dealing with important staffing and structural issues, presidents would turn to policy making. With a longer term for them and their congressional counterparts and without a midterm election just over the horizon, there will be time to plan a policy agenda. Presidents should take the lead in this. In fact, of course, presidents have been taking the lead in formulating a policy agenda for more than century. But now, with unified government, there will be better opportunities for leaders in Congress to participate in the development of this agenda and for congressional committees and members to play an important role in determining policy details. Everything will be less rushed and less impacted by immediate electoral concerns.

The most effective way to ensure a leadership role for the president and legislative responsiveness and participation in implementing that role is by creating new, action-forcing mechanisms in the legislative process. When the president makes a recommendation to Congress, whether program initiatives or a budget, Congress would have to vote on those proposals within a fixed period of time. Failure of Congress to act in that time, to vote for or against the president's proposal, would allow it to take effect automatically. Inaction would cease to be the dominant legislative tactic it has become in the twenty-first century. The Congress would be forced to be an active partner in the policy-making process, not simply the place where policy initiatives go to die.

For example, a presidential budget proposal would be delivered to Congress on a specified date every year—let us say, February 1, which is close to the date specified in the Budget Reform Act of 1974. The Congress would then have until the beginning of the fiscal year on October 1 to enact the appropriations and revenue legislation necessary to implement the budget. As it does now, it would have opportunities to make changes in the president's proposals. But any portions of the president's budget proposals that had not been transformed and passed as legislation by October 1 would automatically go into effect on that date. Congress would have ample opportunity to participate in these important decisions, but it could not use delay as a tactic for preventing decisions on budget priorities or allocations.

Action-forcing mechanisms could play a similar role in the central area of executive-legislative relations, the development of legislation creating new programs or amending or eliminating older ones. This might take many forms. For example, the president could be authorized to introduce legislation in both houses simultaneously without the need for a House member or senator as the formal sponsor. Proposals submitted by the president under this authority would receive fast-track consideration, higher priority than bills introduced by members of Congress.

Presidential proposals or amended versions thereof would be entitled to an up-or-down vote within 120 days of their receipt. The president could request a delay in that vote in order to negotiate further with members, but a new vote would be required within a month of each such request. Inevitably, of course, these action-forcing mechanisms would abolish the Senate filibuster as a minority tactic for defeating legislation or appointments for which there is majority support. The veto power of the president and the opportunity for Congress to override a presidential veto would not be changed from current procedures.

These proposals are not intended to shrink the legislative role in policy making which is essential in a democracy. Rather they would require congressional participation—and presumably diminish the current reliance on independent executive authorities like executive orders, directives, and memoranda. The legislature would be an active participant in the formation of public policy. What would change is the clarification and formalization of the president's leadership role and an attenuation of the Congress's ability to use delaying tactics to prevent voting on legislative proposals. In fact, as well, because a Senate minority or the party leadership in either house would no longer have the power they now have over the legislative agenda and schedule there would be increased opportunities for a wider range of members to participate in the formulation of public policies and to be ensured of the opportunity to vote on any that come from the president.

Congress

One further topic commands attention: the structure of the legislature itself. In reality, the leadership capacity of the American presidents is deeply dependent on the character of the legislature with which they must work. The current structure of Congress is the product of a vital compromise at the constitutional convention of 1787. To balance the desires of small and large states and to keep them all in the newly formed union, a bicameral legislature was created with representation in one house based on population and in the other on state sovereignty.

That necessary compromise has left a daunting legacy for presidents ever since. First, there is the problem of trying to accomplish policy objectives in not one, but two legislative bodies. Twice the time, twice the effort, twice the uncertainty in seeking the support of two very different legislative bodies. Some democracies function with just a unicameral legislature. In most of those with bicameral legislatures, one house predominates and the other has very limited legislative powers. So executives need only focus the bulk of their efforts on one legislative body. Not so for American presidents.

The second difficulty lies in the unrepresentative nature of the Senate in which each state, regardless of population, is entitled to two senators. When the compromise was reached in 1787, the largest state, Virginia had twelve times the population of the smallest state, Delaware. The imbalance has steadily grown since then. Today, the largest state, California, has sixty-six times the population of the smallest state, Wyoming. Yet each has two senators. The California senators represent 38.8 million citizens, the Wyoming senators 584,000.

In a series of long-overdue decisions in the 1960s, the Supreme Court established a firm principle of legislative representation: One person, one vote. That principle now applies to all of the thousands of governing bodies in America—state legislatures, city councils, county commissions, etc.—except one: the U.S. Senate. In practical terms, this imbalance in representation means that senators representing 16 percent of the population hold a majority of votes in the Senate.

Presidents today often find themselves negotiating with senators from very small states to get the votes needed to pass legislation that has broad support among senators representing the bulk of the population. In 2009, the fate of the health care legislation introduced by President Obama seemed to rest in the hands of a "gang of six," a bipartisan group of senators trying to craft the details of a bill that could pass. These critical players represented Iowa, Maine, Montana, New Mexico, North Dakota, and Wyoming—states that held 2.7 percent of the American population.

Questions of whether America would be better served by a unicameral than a bicameral legislature are largely academic. Forty-nine of the state legislatures have bicameral legislatures, and most of them function with considerably more efficiency than the Congress. One house or two houses is not a matter of the greatest consequence.

What does matter is the representative bases of the members of those houses. In all of the state legislatures, representation in both houses is based on population. Again, only the U.S. Senate is the outlier. As long as that continues to be the case, as long as senators representing small portions of the population can work their will against the larger majority, presidents will continue to be handicapped in the efforts to produce public policies in the nation's interests.

A PRESIDENCY FOR OUR TIME

To do nothing in the face of the enormous challenges we face is to risk everything. The days when America could move forward by "muddling through" are over now. We have muddled our way into a huge national debt, an array of improperly funded future entitlement obligations, an infrastructure in growing disrepair, a tax policy that is little more than a bunch of loopholes sewn together, a climate that is warming and a sea that is rising. The recent history of government performance offers little hope of coherent policy responses to any of those challenges. The government we have now is simply not up to the task. No election outcome will change that dire conclusion.

When it comes to governmental reform, we Americans are prisoners of inertia. Our fondness for tradition and our fear of change consign us to a steady parade of same old, same old. But that parade can never find its way to a happy future. Only fundamental change can accomplish that, and fundamental change requires not just statutory band-aids, but major constitutional restructuring.

The primary goal of such reform must be to enhance the capacity of the national government to concentrate authority, so that it can act in the face of daunting challenges. The checks and balances upon which we have so long relied to prevent violations of democratic principles and individual freedom have grown to the point of sclerosis. For every potential action there are checks and traps that overwhelm and undermine even the best of intentions, even the strongest evocations of the national interest.

The argument presented here has been that the best place to concentrate the authority we will need for national progress is in the office of the presidency, the only national office filled by and obligated to the interests of all the people. But wherever power is concentrated in a democracy so must it be held to account. Historically, and especially recently, we have come to rely too heavily on procedural and institutional checks as the primary form of accountability. We need now to loosen some of those bonds so the government we choose can act. At the same time, we need to alter the way we choose that government so that elections can become—as they should be in a democracy—the primary instrument of popular accountability.

This chapter has offered proposals to do both of those things, to loosen some of the checks that prevent effective concentrations of authority within government and to rationalize the election process to strengthen its role as an instrument of accountability for government. Reasonable people can and will disagree about whether these are the exact steps to accomplish a revitalization of the national government. And no one can doubt the difficulty in enacting any of them.

But it is long past time for a national conversation that recognizes the magnitude of the challenges and threats that confront us, that understands how unlikely we are to respond effectively to those with the kind of national government we now have in place, and that puts our most creative minds to work in seeking better ways to restore a vibrant national democracy to the country that invented it.

I hope this book has offered some stimulus, and perhaps some guidance, to that conversation.

NOTES

1. Archie Brown, *The Myth of the Strong Leader* (New York: Basic Books, 2014), 347.

2. Moisés Naím, *The End of Power: From Boardrooms To Battlefields And Churches To States, Why Being In Charge Isn't What It Used To Be* (New York: Basic Books, 2013), 77.

3. Tony Blair, "Is Democracy Dead?" *New York Times*, December 4, 2014, accessed October 15, 2015, http://www.nytimes.com/2014/12/04/opinion/tony-blair-is-democracy-dead.html.

4. Peter H. Schuck, *Why Government Fails So Often And How It Can Do Better* (Princeton, NJ: Princeton University Press, 2014), 3.

5. Calabresi and Lindgren, "The President: Lightning Rod or King?" 2612.

6. James Madison, *Notes on the Debates in the Federal Convention*, July 19, 1787, accessed October 15, 2015, http://avalon.law.yale.edu/18th_century/debates_719. asp.

7. *A Compilation of the Messages and Papers of the Presidents, 1789-1897*, vol. 4 (Washington, DC: Government Printing Office, 1897), 664–65.

8. Burns, *Running Alone*, 190.

9. Brown, *The Myth of the Strong Leader*, 1–2.

10. Wilson, *American Politics, Then & Now, and Other Essays*, 10.

11. See Kelly Chang, David Lewis and Nolan McCarty, "The Tenure of Political Appointees," Paper prepared for delivery at the Annual Meetings of the Midwest Political Science Association (2001); Anne Joseph O'Connell, "Vacant Offices: Delays in Staffing Top Agency Positions," *Southern California Law Review* 82 (2009): 913–1000.

12. G. Calvin Mackenzie, "The State of the Presidential Appointments Process," in *Innocent Until Nominated: The Breakdown of the Presidential Appointments Process*, edited by G. Calvin Mackenzie (Washington, DC: Brookings, 2001), 46–47.

13. William S. Cohen, "Why I Am Leaving," *Washington Post National Weekly Edition* (January 28–February 4, 1996): 29.

14. Wilson, *Constitutional Government*, 40.

15. Naím, *The End of Power*, 80.

Bibliography

A Compilation of the Messages and Papers of the Presidents, 1789–1897, vol. 4. Washington, DC: Government Printing Office, 1897.

Aberbach, Joel D., "Improving Oversight: Congress's Endless Task," *Extensions*, Fall 2001, 11–14, accessed October 15, 2015, http://www.ou.edu/special/albertctr/extensions/fall2001/Aberbach.html.

Ackerman, Bruce, "The New Separation of Powers," *Harvard Law Review* 113 (2000), 633–729.

Adkins, Randall E., and Andrew J. Dowdle, "The Money Primary: What Influences the Outcome of Pre-Primary Presidential Nomination Fundraising?," *Presidential Studies Quarterly* 32 (2002), 256–275.

American National Election Studies, http://www.electionstudies.org/nesguide/toptable/tab5a_1.htm.

American Presidency Project, accessed October 15, 2015, http://www.presidency.ucsb.edu/data/newsconferences.php.

Andres, Gary J., "'The Contemporary Presidency': Parties, Process, and Presidential Power: Learning from Confirmation Politics in the U. S. Senate," *Presidential Studies Quarterly* 32 (2002), 147–156.

Andres, Gary J., "'The Contemporary Presidency': Polarization and White House/Legislative Relations: Causes and Consequences of Elite-Level Conflict," *Presidential Studies Quarterly* 35 (2005), 761–770.

Barnes, John A., *John F. Kennedy on Leadership*. New York: AMACOM, 2007.

Baum, Matthew A., and Samuel Kernell, "Has Cable Ended the Golden Age of Presidential Television?" *American Political Science Review* 93 (1999), 99–114.

Beckmann, Matthew N., *Pushing the Agenda: Presidential Leadership in U.S. Lawmaking, 1953–2004*. New York: Cambridge University Press, 2010.

Berry, Jeffrey M., and Sarah Sobieraj, "Understanding the Rise of Talk Radio," *PS* (2011), 762–777.

Binder, Sarah A., *Stalemate: Causes and Consequences of Legislative Gridlock*. Washington, DC: Brookings, 2003.

Blair, Tony, "Is Democracy Dead?," *New York Times*, December 4, 2014, accessed October 15, 2015, http://www.nytimes.com/2014/12/04/opinion/tony-blair-is-democracy-dead.html.

Boumediene v. Bush, 553 U.S. 723 (2008).

Boyd, Julian P., ed., *The Papers of Thomas Jefferson*, vol. 12. Princeton, NJ: Princeton University Press, 1950–.

Branch, Taylor, *The Clinton Tapes: Wrestling History With The President*. New York: Simon and Schuster, 2009.

Brands, H. W., *The Devil We Knew: Americans and the Cold War*. New York: Oxford University Press, 1993.

Brimley, Shawn, Dr. Dafna H. Rand, Julianne Smith, and Jacob Stokes, "Enabling Decision: Shaping the National Security Council for the Next President," Center for New American Security, June 2015, accessed October 15, 2015, http://www.cnas.org/sites/default/files/publications-pdf/CNAS%20Report_NSC%20Reform_Final.pdf.

Broder, David S., "Common Cause Prods Senate," *The Tuscaloosa News*, November 13, 1977, accessed October 15, 2015, http://news.google.com/newspapers?nid=1817&dat=19771113&id=JEggAAAAIBAJ&sjid=_50EAAAAIBAJ&pg=5506,3076968.

Brown, Archie, *The Myth of the Strong Leader*. New York: Basic Books, 2014.

Brownlow, Louis, "What We Expect the President to Do," in *The Presidency*, edited by Aaron Wildavsky. Boston: Little, Brown, 1969.

Brownstein, Ronald, "Reconcilable Differences," *Atlantic*, September 2008, 54–62, accessed October 3, 2015, http://www.theatlantic.com/magazine/print/2008/09/reconcilable-differences/6942/.

Bryce, James, *The American Commonwealth*, vol. II. New York: Macmillan, 1919.

Burden, Barry C., "United States Senators as Presidential Candidates," *Political Science Quarterly* 117 (2002), 81–102.

Burke, John P., *The Institutional Presidency: Organizing and Managing the White House from FDR to Clinton*, 2nd ed. Baltimore: Johns Hopkins University Press, 2000.

Burns, James MacGregor, *The Deadlock of Democracy: Four-Party Politics in America*. Englewood Cliffs, NJ: Prentice-Hall, 1963.

Burns, James MacGregor, *Running Alone: Presidential Leadership JFK to Bush II: Why It Has Failed And How We Can Fix It*. New York: Basic Books, 2006.

Bush, George H. W., "Remarks at Dedication Ceremony of the Social Sciences Complex at Princeton University in Princeton, New Jersey," May 10, 1991, accessed October 3, 2015, http://www.presidency.ucsb.edu/ws/index.php?pid=19573&st=&st1=#axzz1V0xdEujf.

Bush, George H. W., *Decision Points*. New York: Crown Publishers, 2010.

Calabresi, Steven G., and James Lindgren, "The President: Lightning Rod or King?" *Yale Law Journal* 115 (2006), 2611–2622.

Cannon, Lou, and Carl M. Cannon, *Reagan's Disciple: George W. Bush's Troubled Quest for a Presidential Legacy*. New York: Public Affairs, 2008.

Center for Media Literacy, "Video is Here to Stay," accessed October 15, 2015, www.medialit.org/reading-room/video-here-stay.

Center for Public Leadership, *National Leadership Index 2007: A National Study of Confidence in Leadership*. Cambridge, MA: Center for Public Leadership, John F. Kennedy School of Government, Harvard University, 2007, 1, 20.

Center for Responsive Politics, "2012 Presidential Race," accessed October 3, 2015, http://www.opensecrets.org/pres12/.

Center for Responsive Politics, "Lobbying Database," accessed October 15, 2015, https://www.opensecrets.org/lobby/.

Center for Responsive Politics, "Outside Spending," accessed October 15, 2015, https://www.opensecrets.org/outsidespending/fes_summ.php?cycle=2012.

Chang, Kelly, David Lewis, and Nolan McCarty, "The Tenure of Political Appointees," Paper prepared for delivery at the Annual Meetings of the Midwest Political Science Association (2001).

Charles L. Williams V. Suffolk Insurance Company, 38 U.S. 415 (13 Pet. 415, 10 L.Ed. 226).

Clinton, Bill, *My Life*. New York: Alfred A. Knopf, 2004.

Cohen, Jeffrey E., *The Presidency in the Era of 24-Hour News*. Princeton, NJ: Princeton University Press, 2008.

Cohen, Jeffrey E., *Going Local: Presidential Leadership in the Post-Broadcast Age*. New York: Cambridge University Press, 2010.

Cohen, William S., "Why I Am Leaving," *Washington Post National Weekly Edition*, January 28–February 4, 1996.

Cohen, William S., and George J. Mitchell, *Men of Zeal: The Inside Story of the Iran-Contra Hearings*. New York: Viking, 1988.

Commission on Economy and Efficiency, *The Need for a National Budget*. Washington, DC: Government Printing Office, 1912.

Cook, Rhodes, "Obama and the Redefinition of Presidential Coattails," *Rasmussen Reports*, April 17, 2009, accessed October 3, 2015, http://www.rasmussenreports.com/public_content/political_commentary/commentary_by_rhodes_cook/obama_and_the_redefinition_of_presidential_coattail.

Cook, Rhodes, "Obama and Redefinition of Presidential Coattails," *Rasmussen Reports*, April 17, 2009, accessed October 15, 2015, http://www.rasmussenreports.com/public_content/political_commentary/commentary_by_rhodes_cook/obama_and_the_redefinition_of_presidential_coattails.

Cooper, John Milton, *Woodrow Wilson: A Biography*. New York: Alfred A. Knopf, 2009.

Corwin, Edward S., *The President: Office and Powers*, 4th ed. New York: New York University Press, 1957.

Costa, Jay, "What is the Cost of a Seat in Congress?" *Maplight: Revealing Money's Influence on Politics*, March 10, 2013, accessed October 15, 2015, http://maplight.org/content/73190.

Crenson, Matthew, and Benjamin Ginsberg, *Presidential Power: Unchecked and Unbalanced*. New York: W. W. Norton, 2007.

Croly, Herbert, *The Promise of American Life*. Boston: Northeastern University Press, 1989.

Cronin, Thomas E., *Inventing the American Presidency*. Lawrence, KS: University of Kansas Press, 1989.

Cronin, Thomas E., "The Textbook and Prime-Time Presidency," in *The State of the Presidency*, edited by Thomas E. Cronin, 2nd ed. Boston: Little Brown, 1980.

Cronin, Thomas E., *On The Presidency: Teacher, Soldier, Shaman, Pol*. Boulder, CO: Paradigm Publishers, 2009.

Cronin, Thomas E., and Michael A. Genovese, *The Paradoxes of the American Presidency*. New York: Oxford University Press, 2010.

Dallek, Robert, "Power and the Presidency, From Kennedy to Obama," *Smithsonian Magazine*, January 2011, accessed October 15, 2015, http://www.smithsonianmag. com/history-archaeology/Power-and-the-Presidency-From-Kennedy-to-Obama. html.

DeYoung, Karen, "White House Tries For a Leaner National Security Council Staff," *Washington Post*, June 22, 2015, accessed October 15, 2015, https://www.wash-ingtonpost.com/world/national-security/white-house-tries-for-a-leaner-national-security-council/2015/06/22/22ef7e52–1909-11e5–93b7–5eddc056ad8a_story. html.

DeYoung, Karen, and Anne Gearan, "Susan Rice Withdraws as Candidate for Secretary of State," *Washington Post*, December 13, 2012.

Dickinson, Matthew J., and Matthew J. Lebo, "Reexamining the Growth of the Institutional Presidency, 1940–2000," *The Journal of Politics* 69 (2007), 206–219.

Doherty, Brendan J., *The Rise of the President's Permanent Campaign*. Lawrence, KS: University Press of Kansas, 2012.

Dunn, Charles W., "The Presidency in the Twenty-first Century: Continuity and Change," in *The Presidency in the Twenty-First Century*, edited by Charles W. Dunn. Lexington, KY: University Press of Kentucky, 2011.

Edwards, George C. III, *On Deaf Ears: The Limits of the Bully Pulpit*. New Haven, CT: Yale University Press, 2003, 241.

Edwards, George C. III, "The Limits of the Bully Pulpit," in *Readings in Presidential Politics*, edited by George C. Edwards. Belmont, CA: Wadsworth, 2006.

Edwards, George C. III, *The Strategic President: Persuasion and Opportunity in Presidential Leadership*. Princeton, NJ: Princeton University Press, 2009.

Ehrenhalt, Alan, *The United States of Ambition: Politicians, Power, and The Pursuit of Office*. New York: Random House, 1991.

Eisner, Marc Allen, *From Warfare State to Welfare State: World War I, Compensatory State Building, and the Limits of the Modern Order*. University Park, PA: Penn State University Press, 2000.

Ellis, Richard J., *Founding the American Presidency*. Lanham, MD: Rowman and Littlefield, 1999.

Eshbaugh-Soha, Matthew, and Jeffrey S. Peake, *Breaking Through the Noise: Presidential Leadership, Public Opinion, and the News Media*. Stanford, CA: Stanford University Press, 2011.

Farnam, T. W., "Study Shows Revolving Door of Employment Between Congress, Lobbying Firms," *Washington Post*, September 13, 2011, accessed October 15, 2015, http://www.washingtonpost.com/study-shows-revolving-door-of-employment-between-congress-lobbying-firms/2011/09/12/gIQAxPYROK_story.html.

Fenno, Richard F., Jr., *The Power of the Purse: Appropriations Politics in Congress*. Boston: Little Brown and Company, 1966.

Fiorina, Morris P., Paul E. Peterson, and D. Stephen Voss, *America's New Democracy*. New York: Longman, 2002.

Fisher, Louis, *The Politics of Shared Power: Congress and the Executive*. Washington, DC: CQ Press, 1993.

Fisher, Louis, *Constitutional Conflicts Between Congress and the President*, 5th ed. Lawrence, KS: University Press of Kansas, 2007.

Fisher, Louis, *Presidential War Power*, 3rd ed. Lawrence, KS: University of Kansas Press, 2013.

Foner, Eric, *The Story of American Freedom*. New York: W. W. Norton, 1998.

Ford, Gerald R., *A Time To Heal*. New York: Harper and Row, 1979.

Ford, Gerald R., "Imperiled, Not Imperial," *Time*, November 10, 1980.

Frank, Barney, "U.S. Troops Won't Win Losing Battle," *Portland (Maine) Sunday Telegram*, November 23, 2014.

Friendly, Fred, "Foreword," in *Presidential Television, A Twentieth Century Fund Report*, edited by Newton N. Minow, John Bartlow Martin, and Lee M. Mitchell. New York, New York: Basic Books, 1973.

Geer, John G., *In Defense of Negativity*. Chicago: University of Chicago Press, 2006.

Genovese, Michael A., *The Supreme Court, The Constitution, and Presidential Power*. Washington, DC: University Press of America, 1980.

Gergen, David, *Eyewitness to Power: From Nixon to Clinton*. New York: Simon and Schuster, 2001.

Glass, Andrew, "Richard Nixon vetoes War Powers Resolution, October 24, 1973," *Politico*, October 24, 2013, accessed October 15, 2015, http://www.politico.com/story/2013/10/nixon-vetoes-war-powers-resolution-oct-24-1973-98747.html.

Glennon, Michael J., "National Security and Double Government," *Harvard National Security Journal* 5 (2014), 1–114.

Goldsmith, Jack, *Power and Constraint: The Accountable Presidency After 9/11*. New York: W. W. Norton, 2012.

Goldwater, Barry, *Where I Stand*. New York: McGraw-Hill, 1964.

Hamdan v. Rumsfeld, 548 U.S. 557 (2006).

Hamdi v. Rumsfeld, 542 U.S. 507 (2004).

Haskell, John, "Reforming Presidential Primaries: Three Steps for Improving the Campaign Environment," *Presidential Studies Quarterly* 26 (1996), 380–390.

Healy, Gene, "The Cult of the Presidency," *Reason*, June 2008, accessed October 3, 2015, http://reason.com/archives/2008/05/12/the-cult-of-the-presidency.

Heclo, Hugh, "Introduction: The Presidential Illusion," in *The Illusion of Presidential Government*, edited by Hugh Heclo and Lester M. Salamon. Boulder, CO: Westview Press, 1981.

Heclo, Hugh, "Campaigning and Governing: A Conspectus," in *The Permanent Campaign and Its Future*, edited by Norman Ornstein and Thomas Mann. Washington, DC: Brookings and the American Enterprise Institute, 2000.

Heclo, Hugh, "'The Once and Future Chief Executive: Prophecy versus Prediction' in the Twenty-first Century: Continuity and Change," in *The Presidency in the Twenty-First Century*, edited by Charles W. Dunn. Lexington, KY: University Press of Kentucky, 2011.

Holyoke, Thomas T., *Interest Groups and Lobbying: Pursuing Political Interests in America*. Boulder, CO: Westview Press, 2014.

Hughes, Emmet John, *The Living Presidency*. New York: Penguin Books, 1972.

Irons, Peter, *War Powers: How The Imperial Presidency Hijacked The Constitution*. New York: Metropolitan Books, 2005.

Iyengar, Shanto, Kyu S. Hahn, Heinz Bonfadelli, and Mirko Marr, "'Dark Areas of Igno-rance' Revisited," *Communication Research Online First*, March 26, 2009, accessed October 15, 2015, http://pcl.stanford.edu/research/2009/iyengar-darkareas.pdf.

Jacobson, Gary, "Party Polarization in National Politics: The Electoral Connection," in *Polarized Politics: Congress and the President in a Partisan Era*, edited by Jon R. Bond and Richard Fleisher. Washington DC: CQ Press, 2000.

Johnson, Lyndon B., *The Vantage Point: Perspectives on the Presidency, 1963–1969.* New York: Holt, Rinehart and Winston, 1971.

Jones, Charles O., *The Presidency in a Separated System.* Washington, DC: Brookings, 1994.

Kahn, Jonathan, *Budgeting Democracy: State Building and Citizenship in America, 1890–1928.* Ithaca, NY: Cornell University Press, 1997.

Kaiser, Robert G., *Too Damn Much Money: The Triumph of Lobbying and the Corrosion of American Government.* New York: Alfred A. Knopf, 2009.

Karnow, Stanley, *Vietnam: A History.* New York: Viking, 1991.

Kernell, Samuel, *Going Public: New Strategies of Presidential Leadership,* 4th ed. Wash-ington, DC: CQ Press, 2007.

Kiewit, D. Roderick, and Matthew D. McCubbins, *The Logic of Delegation: Congres-sional Parties and the Appropriations Process.* Chicago, IL: University of Chicago Press, 1991.

King, Elliot, *Free for All: The Internet's Transformation of Journalism.* Evanston, IL: Northwestern University Press, 2010.

Klein, Joe, *Politics Lost: How American Democracy Was Trivialized By People Who Think You're Stupid.* New York: Doubleday, 2006.

Kohut, Andrew, "American International Engagement on the Rocks," *Pew Research Global Attitudes Project*, July 11, 2013, accessed October 15, 2015, http://www.pew-global.org/2013/07/11/american-international-engagement-on-the-rocks/.

Kovarik, Bill, *Revolutions in Communications: Media History from Gutenberg to the Digi-tal Age.* New York: Continuum, 2011.

Kravchuk, Robert S., and James W. Douglas, "The Centennial of the Taft Commis-sion: The Executive Budget as a Milestone in American Political Development," Paper presented at the Annual Meeting of the Association for Budgeting and Financial Management, Omaha, Nebraska, October 2010.

Kumar, Martha Joynt, *Managing the President's Message: The White House Communica-tions Operation.* Baltimore: Johns Hopkins University Press, 2007.

Kumar, Priya, "Shrinking Foreign Coverage," *American Journalism Review*, December/January 2011, accessed October 15, 2015, http://ajrarchive.org/article.asp?id=4998.

Ladd, Jonathan M., *Why Americans Hate the Media and How It Matters.* Princeton, NJ: Princeton University Press, 2012.

Lawder, David, "Republican Strategy Memo Focuses on Obamacare, Not Immigra-tion," *Reuters Edition*, April 30, 2014, accessed October 15, 2015, http://www.reuters.com/article/2014/04/30/us-usa-congress-republicans-idUSBREA3T12I20140430.

LeLoup, Lance T., and Steven A. Shull, *The President and Congress: Collaboration and Combat in National Policymaking.* Boston: Allyn and Bacon, 1999.

Leuchtenberg, William E., *In the Shadow of FDR: From Harry Truman to Barack Obama,* 4th ed. Ithaca, NY: Cornell University Press, 2009.

Lewis, David E., *The Politics of Presidential Appointments.* Princeton, NJ: Princeton University Press, 2008.

Mackenzie, G. Calvin, *The Politics of The Appointment Process*. New York: The Free Press, 1980.

Mackenzie, G. Calvin, ed., *Innocent Until Nominated: The Breakdown of the Presidential Appointments Process*. Washington, DC: Brookings, 2001.

Madison, James, *Letters and Other Writings of James Madison, 1769–1793*. New York: R. Worthington, 1865.

Madison, James, *Notes on the Debates in the Federal Convention of 1787*. New York: W. W. Norton, 1966.

Malecha, Gary Lee, and Daniel J. Reagan, *The Public Congress: Congressional Deliberation in a New Media Age*. New York: Routledge, 2012.

Mann, Thomas E., and Norman J. Ornstein, *The Broken Branch: How Congress is Failing America and How To Get It Back On Track*. New York: Oxford University Press, 2008.

Marples, Gareth, "The History of Cable TV--Can You Remember?" accessed October 15, 2015, www.thehistoryof.net/history-of-cable-tv.html.

Marshall, William P., "Break Up The Presidency? Governors, State Attorneys General, and Lessons From Divided Executives," *Yale Law Journal* 115 (2006), 2446–2479.

Martin, Joseph W., Jr., *My First Fifty Years in Politics*. New York: McGraw-Hill, 1960.

Martinez, Jenny S., "Inherent Executive Power: A Comparative Perspective," *Yale Law Journal* 115 (2006), 2480–2511.

Miroff, Bruce, "The Presidential Spectacle," in *The Presidency and the Political System*, 9th ed., edited by Michael Nelson, Washington, DC: CQ Press, 2010.

Mitchell v. Laird, 488 E2d 611 (D.C. Cir. 1973).

Mondale, Walter F., *The Good Fight: A Life in Liberal Politics*. New York: Scribner, 2010.

Moore, James, and Wayne Slater, *Bush's Brain: How Karl Rove Made George W. Bush Presidential*. Hoboken, NJ: John Wiley and Sons, 2003.

Morris, Dick, *Because He Could*. New York: Regan Books of HarperCollins, 2004.

Morris, Edmund, *Theodore Rex*. New York: Random House, 2001.

Moyers, Bill, "Second Thoughts: Reflections on the Great Society," *New Perspectives Quarterly* 4 (Winter 1987).

Moynihan, Daniel Patrick, *Counting Our Blessings: Reflections on the Future of America*. Boston: Little Brown, 1980.

Murray, Shailagh, "Storms Show a System Out of Balance: GOP Congress Has Reduced Usual Diet of Agency Oversight," *Washington Post*, October 5, 2005.

Naím, Moisés, *The End of Power: From Boardrooms To Battlefields And Churches To States, Why Being In Charge Isn't What It Used To Be*. New York: Basic Books, 2013.

Nelson, W. Dale, *Who Speaks for the President?: The White House Press Secretary from Cleveland to Clinton*. Syracuse, NY: Syracuse University Press, 1998.

Neustadt, Richard E., *Presidential Power and the Modern Presidents: The Politics of Leadership from Roosevelt to Reagan*. New York: The Free Press, 1991.

Neustadt, Richard E., "Memo on Presidential Transitions," *American Prospect* 3 (1992), accessed October 3, 2015, http://prospect.org/cs/articles?article=memo_on_presidential_transition.

Neustadt, Richard E., "Presidential Leadership: The Clerk Against the Preacher," in *Problems and Prospects of Presidential Leadership*, edited by James Sterling Young. Lanham, MD: University Press of America, 1982.

Nevins, Allan, ed., *Polk: The Diary of a President*. New York: Capricorn Books, 1968.

New York Times, "A Million Persons Will Hear Coolidge's Voice When He Addresses Congress This Afternoon," December 5, 1923.

Nissen, Beth, "A Presidential Sheen: Fans of West Wing say Bartlet character has right stuff," CNN.com, August 18, 2000, accessed October 3, 2015, http://b4a. healthyinterest.net/news/archives/2000/08/a_presidential.html.

Nixon, Richard M., *RN: The Memoirs of Richard Nixon.* New York: Grosset and Dunlap, 1978.

O'Connell, Anne Joseph, "Vacant Offices: Delays in Staffing Top Agency Positions," *Southern California Law Review* 82 (2009), 913–1000.

Paine, Thomas, *Common Sense,* accessed October 3, 2015, http://www.ushistory.org/paine/commonsense/sense3.htm.

Patterson, Bradley H., *To Serve the President: Continuity and Innovation in the White House Staff.* Washington, DC: Brookings, 2008.

Patterson, Thomas E., *Out of Order.* New York: Random House, 1994.

Pestritto, Ronald J., ed., *Woodrow Wilson: The Essential Political Writings.* Lanham, MD: Lexington Books, 2005.

Petracca, Mark P., "The Rediscovery of Interest Group Politics," in *The Politics of Interests: Interest Groups Transformed,* edited by Mark P. Petracca. Boulder, CO: Westview Press, 1992.

Pew Research Center for the People and the Press, "GOP Candidates Hardly Household Names," October 5, 2011, accessed October 3, 2015, http://www.people-press.org/2011/10/05/gop-candidates-hardly-household-names/?src=prc-headline.

Pew Research Center for the People and the Press, "Many Fault Media Coverage of Health Care Debate: Partisan Divide Over Coverage of," August 6, 2009, accessed October 15, 2015, http://www.people-press.org/2009/08/06/many-fault-media-coverage-of-health-care-debate/.

Pew Research Center for the People and the Press, accessed October 15, 2015, http://www.people-press.org/2014/11/13/public-trust-in-government/.

Pew Research Internet Project, "Internet Use Over Time," accessed October 15, 2015, http://www.pewinternet.org/data-trend/internet-use/internet-use-over-time/.

Phillips, Kevin P., *The Emerging Republican Majority.* New York: Arlington House, 1969.

Pious, Richard M., *Why Presidents Fail.* Lanham, MD: Rowman and Littlefield, 2008.

Polsky, Andrew J., *Elusive Victories: The American Presidency At War.* New York: Oxford University Press, 2012.

Ponder, Stephen, *Managing the Press: Origins of the Media Presidency, 1897–1933.* New York: St. Martin's, 1998.

Posner, Eric A., and Adrian Vermeule, *The Executive Unbound: After the Madisonian Republic.* New York: Oxford University Press, 2010.

Rasul v. Bush, 542 U.S. 466 (2004).

Reagan, Ronald, *An American Life.* New York: Simon and Schuster, 1990.

Relyea, Harold C., "The Executive Office of the President: An Historical Overview," *CRS Report for Congress,* March 17, 2008, Washington, DC: Order Code 98–606 GOV.

Renshon, Stanley A., *The Psychological Assessment Of Presidential Candidates.* New York: Routledge, 1998.

Rice, Condoleezza, *No Higher Honor: A Memoir of My Years in Washington*. New York: Random House, 2011.

Rich, Spencer, and David Hess, "State of the Union promises often go unfulfilled," *Congress Daily*, January 27, 2003, accessed October 3, 2015, http://www.govexec.com/dailyfed/0103/012703cdam1.htm.

Rockoff, Hugh, "By Way of Analogy: The Expansion of the Federal Government in the 1930s," in *The Defining Moment: The Great Depression and the American Economy in the Twentieth Century*, edited by Michael D. Bordo, Claudia Goldin, and Eugene N. White. Chicago: University of Chicago Press, 1998.

Rossiter, Clinton, *The American Presidency*, 2nd ed. New York: New American Library, 1960.

Rudalevige, Andrew, *The New Imperial Presidency*. Ann Arbor, MI: University of Michigan Press, 2005.

Savage, Charlie, *Takeover: The Return of the Imperial Presidency and the Subversion of American Democracy*. New York: Little Brown, 2007.

Scherer, Nancy, Brandon L. Bartels, and Amy Steigerwalt, "Sounding the Fire Alarm: The Role of Interest Groups in the Lower Federal Court Confirmation Process," *The Journal of Politics*, 70 (2008), 1026–1039.

Schlesinger, Arthur M., Jr., "On Heroic Leadership and the Dilemma of Strong Men and Weak Peoples," *Encounter* 15 (1960).

Schlesinger, Arthur M., Jr., *The Imperial Presidency*. New York: Houghton Mifflin, 2004.

Schoen, Rodric B., "A Strange Silence: Vietnam and the Supreme Court," *Washburn Law Journal* 33 (1993–1994), 275–277.

Schuck, Peter H., *Why Government Fails So Often And How It Can Do Better*. Princeton, NJ: Princeton University Press, 2014.

Sciolino, Elaine, "Awaiting Call, Helms Puts Foreign Policy on Hold," *New York Times*, September 24, 1995, accessed October 15, 2015, http://www.nytimes.com/1995/09/24/world/awaiting-call-helms-puts-foreign-policy-on-hold.html.

Shapiro, Ira, *The Last Great Senate: Courage and Statesmanship in Times of Crisis*. New York: Public Affairs, 2012.

Siegel, Fred, "Liberalism," in *The Reader's Companion to American History*, edited by Eric Foner and John A. Garraty. Boston: Houghton Mifflin, 1991.

Sigelman, Lee, *Attack Politics: Negativity in Presidential Campaigns Since 1960*, 2nd ed. Lawrence, KS: University Press of Kansas, 2009.

Silver, Nate, "A Brief History of Presidential Polling, Part II," *New York Times*, May 6, 2011, accessed October 3, 2015, http://fivethirtyeight.blogs.nytimes.com/2011/05/06/a-brief-history-of-primary-polling-part-iii/.

Skowronek, Stephen, *Presidential Leadership in Political Time*. Lawrence, KS: University of Kansas Press, 2008.

Skowronek, Stephen, "Shall We Cast Our Lot with the Constitution?," in *The Presidency in the Twenty-First Century*, edited by Charles W. Dunn. Lexington, KY: University Press of Kentucky, 2011.

Smith, Steven S., and Melanie J. Springer, *Reforming the Presidential Nominating Process*. Washington, DC: Brookings, 2009.

Sorensen, Theodore C., *Kennedy*. New York: Harper and Row, 1965.

Steinhauser, Paul, and John Helton, "CNN Poll: Public Against Syria Strike Resolu-
   tion," *CNN Politics*, accessed October 15, 2015, http://www.cnn.com/2013/09/09/
   politics/syria-poll-main/.
Sundquist, James, "American Presidential Democracy: Discussion," *Political Science
   Quarterly* 109 (1994), 415–438.
Thach, Charles C., "Creation of the Presidency," *Classics of the American Presidency*,
   edited by Harry A. Bailey, Jr. Oak Park, IL: Moore Publishing Company, 1980.
The Economist, "Only Freaks," May 9, 1987.
The Miller Center, "American President: A Reference Resource," accessed October 3,
   2015, http://millercenter.org/president/lbjohnson/essays/biography/5.
The Pew Center on the States, *2008 Primary in Review*, July 10, 2008, accessed Octo-
   ber 3, 2015, http://www.issuelab.org/resource/2008_primary_in_review.
Time, "The Underdog Underdog," November 6, 1964.
Troy, Gil, "Nasty, Brutish, and Long: The Brilliance of the Modern Campaign," *New
   York Times*, November 6, 2011, accessed October 3, 2015, http://campaignstops.
   blogs.nytimes.com/2011/11/06/nasty-brutish-and-long-the-brilliance-of-the-
   modern-campaign/.
Tulis, Jeffrey K., *The Rhetorical Presidency*. Princeton, NJ: Princeton University Press,
   1988.
U. S. Bureau of the Census, *Statistical Abstract of the United States*, various years.
   Washington, DC: Government Printing Office, 1926.
U.S. Bureau of the Census, *Historical Statistics of the United States, Colonial Times to
   1970*. Washington, DC: Government Printing Office, 1975.
U. S. President's Committee on Administrative Management, *Administrative Manage-
   ment in the Government of the United States*. Washington, DC: U.S. Government
   Printing Office, 1937.
United States v. Curtiss-Wright Export Corp., 299 U.S. 304 (1936).
University of Minnesota, *Media History Project*, accessed October 15, 2015, www.
   mediahistory.umn.edu/timeline/1960–1969.html.
Wald, Matthew, "Cyber Mouse That Roared, Implausibly," *New York Times*, Week in
   Review, October 10, 1996.
Waterman, Richard W., Hank C. Jenkins-Smith, and Carol L. Silva, "The Expecta-
   tions Gap Thesis: Public Attitudes Toward an Incumbent President," *The Journal
   of Politics* 61 (1999), 944–966.
West, Darrell M., *Air Wars: Television Advertising in Election Campaigns 1952–2008*.
   Washington, DC: Brookings, 2010.
West, Darrell M., and Richard Francis, "Electronic Advocacy: Interest Groups and
   Public Policy Making," *PS: Political Science and Politics* (March 1996), 25–29.
Whittington, Keith E., *Constitutional Construction: Divided Powers and Constitutional
   Meaning*. Cambridge, MA: Harvard University Press, 1999.
Wildavsky, Aaron, "The Two Presidencies," *Trans-Action* 4 (December 1966),
   162–173.
Wildavsky, Aaron, *The New Politics of the Budgetary Process*, 2nd ed. New York: Harp-
   erCollins Publishers, 1992.
Wills, Garry, *Lincoln at Gettysburg: The Words That Remade America*. New York: Simon
   and Schuster, 1992.

Wills, Garry, *Bomb Power: The Modern Presidency and the National Security State*. New York: Penguin Press, 2010.

Wilson, Graham K., "The Clinton Administration and Interest Groups," in *The Clinton Presidency: First Appraisals*, edited by Colin Campbell and Bert A. Rockman. Chatham, NJ: Chatham House, 1996.

Wilson, James Q., *American Politics, Then & Now, and Other Essays*. Washington, DC: AEI Press, 2010.

Wilson, Woodrow, *Congressional Government: A Study in American Politics*. Boston: Houghton Mifflin, 1885.

Wilson, Woodrow, *Constitutional Government in the United States*. New Brunswick, NJ: Transaction Publishers, 2007.

Woodward, Bob, *The Agenda: Inside the Clinton White House*. New York, NY: Simon and Schuster, 1994.

Yoo, John, "Fighting The War On Terrorism Requires Relaxing Checks On Presidential Power," in *Debating the Presidency: Conflicting Perspectives on the American Executive*, edited by Richard J. Ellis and Michael Nelson. Washington, DC: CQ Press, 2010.

Index

About the Author

 **G. Calvin Mackenzie** is Goldfarb Family Distinguished Professor of Government at Colby College where he has taught since 1978. He is a graduate of Bowdoin College and has a PhD in Government from Harvard.

Mackenzie's many publications on American politics and government include *The Politics of Presidential Appointments, The Irony of Reform: Roots of American Political Disenchantment, Scandal Proof: Can Ethics Laws Make Government Ethical?*, and more than a dozen other books. *The Liberal Hour: Washington and the Politics of Change in the 1960s*, written with historian Robert Weisbrot, was one of two finalists for the 2009 Pulitzer Prize in History.

In addition to his scholarship and teaching, Mackenzie has been a frequent consultant to presidential personnel staffs and congressional committees, and he has testified often before congressional committees. His service on many national commissions exploring problems with American governance has spanned four decades.

Mackenzie has also been the John Adams Fellow at the Institute of United States Studies at the University of London and a Fulbright Professor in Beijing, China, and Hanoi, Vietnam. In honor of his scholarly contributions to the understanding of government in America, Mackenzie was elected in 2003 as a Fellow of the National Academy of Public Administration.